# Reimagining Black Masculinities

# Communicating Gender

Series Editors: Diana Bartelli Carlin, Saint Louis University
Nichola D. Gutgold, Pennsylvania State University
Theodore F. Sheckels, Randolph-Macon College

*Communicating Gender* features original research examining the role gender plays in communication. It encompasses a wide variety of approaches and methodologies to explore theoretically relevant topics pertaining to the interrelation of gender and communication both in the United States and worldwide. This series examines gender issues broadly, ranging from masculine hegemony and gender issues in political culture to media portrayals of women and men and the work/life balance.

### Recent Titles in This Series

*Reimagining Black Masculinities: Race, Gender, and Public Space*, edited by Mark C. Hopson and Mika'il Petin
*Intersectionality: Understanding Women's Lives and Resistance*, edited by Dawn L. Hutchinson and Lori Underwood
*Misogyny and Media in the Age of Trump*, edited by Maria Marron
*The Rhetorical Arts of Women in Aviation, 1911–1970: Name It and Take It*, by Sara Hillin
*Food Blogs, Postfeminism, and the Construction of Expertise: Digital Domestics*, by Alane Presswood
*Developing Women Leaders in the Academy through Enhanced Communication Strategies*, edited by Jayne Cubbage
*Empowering Women: Global Voices of Rhetorical Influence*, by Julia Spiker
*Technofeminist Storiographies: Women, Information Technology, and Cultural Representation*, by Kristine Blair
*Women of the 2016 Election: Voices, Views, and Values*, edited by Jennifer Schenk Sacco
*Adolescence, Girlhood, and Media Migration: US Teens' Use of Social Media to Negotiate Offline Struggles*, by Aimee Rickman

# Reimagining Black Masculinities

*Race, Gender, and Public Space*

Edited by Mark C. Hopson and Mika'il Petin

LEXINGTON BOOKS
Lanham • Boulder • New York • London

Published by Lexington Books
An imprint of The Rowman & Littlefield Publishing Group, Inc.
4501 Forbes Boulevard, Suite 200, Lanham, Maryland 20706
www.rowman.com

6 Tinworth Street, London SE11 5AL, United Kingdom

Copyright © 2020 by The Rowman & Littlefield Publishing Group, Inc.

*All rights reserved.* No part of this book may be reproduced in any form or by any electronic or mechanical means, including information storage and retrieval systems, without written permission from the publisher, except by a reviewer who may quote passages in a review.

British Library Cataloguing in Publication Information Available

**Library of Congress Control Number: 2020943842**

ISBN: 978-1-7936-0703-4 (cloth)
ISBN: 978-1-7936-0705-8 (pbk)
ISBN: 978-1-7936-0704-1 (electronic)

Dedicated to my father, son, brothers, and nephews. Onward.
—Mark

Dedicated to Arthur Samuel Petin Jr., my sons, and any men finally discovering the power of their voices.
—Mika'il

# Contents

| | |
|---|---|
| Editors' Note: On Black Masculinity Studies, Yesterday and Today<br>*Mika'il Petin and Mark C. Hopson* | ix |
| Foreword: The Sheer Force of Our Reimagination—Exploring Black Masculinity and the Public<br>*Ronald L. Jackson II* | xiii |
| Introduction: On Reimagining<br>*Mark C. Hopson and Mika'il Petin* | 1 |
| 1 "Mama Knows Best": Exploring Black Men's Perceptions and Reimaginations of the Phrase "Mama's Boys"<br>*Sakile K. Camara and Carmen M. Lee* | 5 |
| 2 She's Just a Friend (with Benefits): Examining the Significance of Black American Boys' Partner Choice for Initial Sexual Intercourse<br>*Tommy J. Curry and Ebony A. Utley* | 33 |
| 3 Reverse Interest Convergence, Kaepernick, and Nike: An Educational Lobbyist Playbook for Equitable Funding by Investment in Urban Public Education<br>*Aaron J. Griffen and Derrick Robinson* | 53 |
| 4 Outkasted Black Masculinity: Shifting the Geographical and Performative Landscape of 1990s Hip-Hop<br>*Marquese McFerguson* | 67 |
| 5 The Killing of Black Boys: A Collaborative Critical Autoethnography on "the Talk"<br>*Mark C. Hopson, Gina Castle Bell, and Richard Craig* | 75 |

6  A Conversation on Black Masculinity with Principal John Hawkins Snowdy of Baltimore Collegiate School for Boys   91
*Kimberly Moffitt*

7  (Re)Educating Boys and Men of Color by Shaping Community Support   103
*Kenneth Brown*

8  "We Demand an Equal Show upon Matters Effecting Our Industrial Welfare": Black Manhood and Labor Activism in Early Jim Crow Illinois   113
*Alonzo M. Ward*

9  The Essence of the Black Man: An Exploration of Black Masculinity through Double Consciousness in *Native Son*   129
*Isaih Dale*

10  The Battle of the New Age Black, Male Hero and Hegemonic/Toxic Masculinity: An Examination of the Representations of Black Masculinity in *Black Panther*   139
*Erika M. Thomas and Malcolm D. Gamble*

11  "Me Miran Raro": Bad Bunny and the Creation of a New Discursive Space in Latin Trap Music   157
*Larissa Hernandez*

12  Dual Socialization and Black Academic Intellectuals: A Research Report   163
*Rutledge Dennis*

Afterword: The Beautiful Ones Were Born Some Time Ago   173
*Mark Anthony Neal*

Index   177

About the Contributors   187

# Editors' Note

## On Black Masculinity Studies, Yesterday and Today

## Mika'il Petin and Mark C. Hopson

The chapters in *Reimagining Black Masculinities: Race, Gender, and Public Space* are testaments to the many pathways of sorting out Black masculinities in public life. Each chapter in this anthology might not exist if it were not for controversies surrounding Donald Trump in the White House, or the chapters being firmly situated within the twenty-first century. This claim is not about a post-postmodern philosophy of gender, the intersection of race and gender in virtual reality, or a technologically infused lens for looking at maleness. The claim is not about any new academic study or fledgling academic disciplines. To the contrary, the claim suggests something way more mundane: the passing of time. Notions, attitudes, and limits of what might be imagined, understood, and associated with Black men in public life have been forever altered.

The field of Black masculinity studies has humble beginnings in the late 1970s/early 1980s—as affirmed by Robert Staples (1982) in *Black Masculinity: The Black Male's Role in American Society*. The field has had to exist as an ideology for decades, to be relevant in this day and time. Concerning the cultural impression of Black maleness, what was singularly meant to be a Black man in public life was usually narrowed to a sexual stud, athlete, and rapacious criminal. Those characterizations continue to persist because these ideas have been equally imposed, adopted, and internalized. Remarkably, while perpetuating and dispelling these ideas is central to the field, this volume reflects an evolution from a seemingly linear trajectory to a new brilliant multimodal stage. To conceptualize this book, where an assemblage of contemporary writers offer forward-looking perspectives on the characteristic meanings of Black maleness in public life, necessitates attentive consideration.

*Reimagining Black Masculinities* came about through conversations between the editors. The impetus and backdrop of these late night phone calls included the #MeToo movement, and life as a Black American man. The incredulousness of the experience paled into unimportance with the sexual misconduct and assault accusations against celebrities and public figures such as Bill Cosby, John Conyers Jr., R. Kelly, Ben Vereen, the late Michael Jackson, Donovan McNabb, Tavis Smiley, Marshall Faulk, Morgan Freeman, and Russell Simmons. What happened in hyperreal time, through the legal system and court of public opinion, involuntarily developed the makings of a unique project.

This book also developed during protests surrounding the murder of George Floyd.

On May 25, 2020, Minneapolis police officers arrested Mr. Floyd, a 46-year-old Black man, after a convenience store employee accused Mr. Floyd of purchasing cigarettes with a counterfeit $20 bill. Seventeen minutes after the first squad car arrived at the scene, Mr. Floyd was unconscious and pinned beneath three police officers, showing no signs of life. Consequently, Mr. Floyd died with his neck under Michael Chauvin's knee.

The United States has a complex history of police violence against Black people. We are angry, sad, frustrated, and disturbed by the murder of George Floyd. However, we are not entirely surprised because we have seen it before. We saw it with Breonna Taylor, Michael Brown, Freddie Gray, Eric Garner, Philando Castile, Natasha McKenna, Sandra Bland, India Kager, and 12-year-old Tamir Rice. Furthermore, we saw it with wannabe-authorities who took the lives of Trayvon Martin, Jordan Davis, and Ahmaud Arbery. Seemingly, anti-Black racism pervades every dimension of social life to the extent that Black people are struggling to breathe.

*Reimagining Black Masculinities* is an analysis of where we are currently, and potential directions for the future. The project would not have been possible without supportive networks and enormous encouragement along the way. It is especially important to thank the Petin and Hopson families. Projects like this one have the potential to impact immediate, extended, and chosen families. Eva Russo and Danielle Hopson, respectively, have been enormous towers of strength. Their tremendous assistance included listening to thoughts about the direction of this volume when it was in its infancy stage. Furthermore, an anthology is the product of its contributors, and for that, the editors would like to thank: Sakile K. Camara, Carmen M. Lee, Tommy J. Curry, Ebony A. Utley, Aaron J. Griffen, Derrick Robinson, Marquese McFerguson, Gina Castle Bell,

Richard Craig, Kimberly Moffitt, Kenneth Brown, Alonzo Ward, Isaih Dale, Erika M. Thomas, Malcolm D. Gamble, Larissa Hernandez, and Rutledge Dennis. A special thanks goes to Ronald L. Jackson II and Mark Anthony Neal for submitting chapters that serve as bookends to the volume, and establishing a high bar of prolific, productive, accessible, relevant, and honest scholarship. We also remember Maurice Hudson, Rex L. Crawley, and Gregory Tillman.

# Foreword

*The Sheer Force of Our Reimagination — Exploring Black Masculinity and the Public*

Ronald L. Jackson II

As we traverse the terrain of contemporary gender studies it is apparent there is a growing intellectual region of Black masculinity studies. Arguably we are long past the time of apologizing for studying men and masculinities. In the 1990s and 2000s a portion of men's studies entered a phase of apologia as a sign of humility or an ode to feminist studies, because feminist scholars had called out the hegemonic instinct of men's studies. Some scholars had even gone so far as to presume that being a male precludes men from being feminist, so at best the most any man could ever be is pro-feminist. Male scholars should have never been any more afraid to talk about gender than a White person should have been to talk about race. There is a unique set of experiences, histories, tendencies, politics, and predicaments that confound masculinity and manhood, in general. When we add culture to masculinity and manhood studies the composite portrait gets exponentially more complex.

Hopson and Petin's *Reimagining Black Masculinities: Race, Gender, and Public Space* is an intricate exploration of the confluence between Black masculinity, activism, and the public. This is fascinating, since the notions of race and gender are already quite public. In fact, it seems we tend to principally apprehend the meaning of these twin social registers vis-à-vis the public. That is not to say that race and gender are not complicated within private relations, but rather our initial understanding of what these terms mean and why they matter happens via public social apparatus like media, schools, government, and businesses. The public is the set of spaces and places where the grand narratives about race and gender take place and hold a firm grasp on social relations.

The sheer force of public discourses has left us with epistemological ambiguities, and therefore an unprecedented social paralysis around race and gender. If the whole notion of linguistic relativity is true then the language/terminology related to race and gender that shapes our worlds has only added complexity. Consider for a moment the linguistic singularity of gender. We have lots of names for gender, but in each case the terms we use box us into such a tight space that when we use a label we think we know what that means. We can automatically cull our experiences and understanding of that label. Try it. What comes to mind when I say, "Latina," "Lesbian," "Black," "Trans," "Gender Fluid," or "Masculine." At the very moment we seek to assign meaning to each word, we imagine a previous reference, experience (personal or vicarious), news story, fantasy, or image, and it is that exact moment where the seedlings of bias and injustice are cultivated.

Only those who are high self-monitors tend to practice mindfulness and are able to shift their impulsive cognitions and behaviors, but that takes work. There is significant labor that goes into reimagining race, gender, and the public. I was recently watching the Netflix original series *100 Humans*, a show that routinely recruits one hundred random people across the United States to participate in a battery of experiments to test human behavior. Like all science each experiment begins with a hypothesis or research question driven by a simple curiosity regarding human behavior. There was one episode on bias. They lined up six people—three males and three females. They asked one hundred people, one after another, to play matchmaker, and granted the guesser the opportunity to ask one question per person to determine who might be best suited for the other. The host even told the guessers that the six people were already couples and asked if that would influence their decision. I remember my daughter's boyfriend asking my wife, my wife's parents, and I to pause the show and provide our predictions before the couples were revealed. We all did so, and none of us instinctively guessed that two of the couples were gay. Despite the fact that we all have no stated bias against queer relationships, our reflexes were to match all six people as heterosexual couples. In fact, 99 out of 100 people in the experiment did the same thing, even one person who self-identified as queer. Why did we do it? Our language, our discourse, and our social worlds are shaped by hegemonic notions of gender, which inform us that heterosexual lives matter most and are normal, and queer lives matter less and are not normal. Hopson and Petin's book does the same work around Black masculinity.

*Reimagining Black Masculinities* informs us of an existing hegemonic social impulse to relegate blackness and therefore Black masculinities to a position of non-normativity. In the case of race, we as social beings are taught distinct lessons about Black masculinity and the public. We are taught

Black masculinity is bereft of intelligence, honor, dignity, productivity, safety, concern for others, responsibility, and civility. As a result, Black masculine persons are to be feared in public, no matter whether he is confronted via a routine traffic stop or is seen at a retail store, park, school, business, and so forth. He is dangerous, ignorant, lazy, irresponsible, and altogether inferior no matter where he is seen. So, the presumption is that he must be handled like an animal, or treated like a hopeless individual bound for the prison system. We are taught he is not to be treated equitably. This interferes with our imagination. It interferes with the public's ability to see him as a normal, law-abiding, intelligent, loving, caring, talented, capable, responsible, and normal human being, deserving of mutual respect, dignity, honor, equity, and love.

The extant literature on Black masculinity is varied. Some of it reshapes the conversation by addressing progressive perspectives on gender such as Morgan Mann Willis's *Outside the XY: Black and Brown Queer Masculinity* (2017), Steven Cureton's *The Social Construction of Black Masculinity: An Ethnographic Study* (2019), Mark Anthony Neal's *New Black Man* (2015) and *Looking for Leroy* (2013), as well as Anthony Mutua's *Progressive Black Masculinities* (2006). Others have problematized existing social relations and pinpointed limitations and inconsistencies such as Wesley Muhammad's *Understanding the Assault on the Black Man, Black Manhood, and Black Masculinity* (2016), Jared Sexton's *Black Masculinity and the Cinema of Policing*, and Ron Jackson's *Scripting the Black Masculine Body in Popular Media* (2006). Still other volumes have historicized the social conundrum of Black masculinity in America in such books as Rashad Shabazz's *Spatializing Blackness: Architectures of Confinement and Black Masculinity in Chicago* (2015) and Riche Richardson's *Black Masculinity and the U.S. South: From Uncle Tom to Gangsta* (2007). In either case, each book demonstrates the now apparent understanding that Black masculinity is not okay as is. Something must be done with it. It must be managed, negotiated, politicized, or deconstructed to decipher its meaning or to reconcile how it can be made normal, if indeed that is even possible given the current sociopolitical machinery at work.

That is why we need *Reimagining Black Masculinities* at this time. We are desperately in need of fresh voices and perspectives that can guide us out of this entangled web of debilitating social discourses and public pedagogies that have left us socially paralyzed for what is now over four centuries that Black people have been in the United States. I would encourage readers to think of each chapter as a glimpse into the epistemic violence that has been transferred onto Black masculine lives, and simultaneously as an invitation and opportunity to reimagine the radical progressive work we must all do to make our world better.

# Introduction

## *On Reimagining*

## Mark C. Hopson and Mika'il Petin

In 1965, Malcolm X argued that you can't separate peace from freedom because no one can be at peace without freedom. These words are especially relevant to a book that examines the communication of race, gender, and social identity. More specifically, the edited volume brings together contemporary discourses to interrogate how Black masculinities inform, and are informed by, social and political contexts. We focus on when, where, and how these identities occur in public spaces.

The book begins with imagination. Imagination is the process whereby we stimulate new knowledge. It is the power to create entities not yet created. It is the integration of the past and present. To imagine is to form a mental picture of what the world can be, yet imagination does not necessarily exclude reality. We acknowledge a rich tradition of Black imagination. W. E. B. Du Bois drew from Black imagination to conceptualize double consciousness felt by Black Americans of the twentieth century. In 1925, Alain Locke drew from Black imagination to edit a special issue of *Survey Graphic*, titled "Harlem, Mecca of the New Negro." Later, Locke's *The New Negro* became a cornerstone for the Harlem Renaissance, and a potent philosophy among Black people. Bayard Rustin also combined creativity and consciousness to organize for human rights alongside A. Philip Randolph, Ella Baker, and Martin Luther King Jr. Certainly, Dr. King's "I See the Promised Land" conjured a rhetorical location and historical covenant for God's people.

To reimagine is to reexamine the ontology of the Black experience. Over a decade ago Jackson and Hopson (2011) situated Black masculinity within a panoptic lens. Today's observations include new cultural, social and political standpoints. Within this book, authors call attention to racialized masculinities living, thinking and performing in public space. We also present multiple strategies for liberation. Plurality is intentional. Masculinities are not static; they are dynamic and alive with meaning. Masculinities are not fixed; they are active. Indeed, there are multiple ways to be Black and masculine, and sometimes race and gender collide at the intersections of power.

This book also extends Brent Staples's seminal essay "Black Men and Public Space" (*Harper's Magazine*, 1986). Staples spoke to domestic terrorism "where fear and weapons meet, and they often do in the United States, there is always the possibility of death." Staples's prescient observation became more visible with the deaths of George Floyd, Darius Tarver, Ariane McCray, Botham Shem Jean, Antwon Rose, Stephon Clark, and Terrance Franklin. The tragedies continue. Black people are disproportionately victimized by police violence, incarceration, voter suppression, and other public health crises. We saw it with Hurricane Katrina. We saw it with contaminated water in Flint, MI. We saw it with the coronavirus pandemic.

*Reimagining Black Masculinities: Race, Gender, and Public Space* serves as a method and means to understand critical issues. These chapters frame the essence of lived experience. Jackson's foreword "The Sheer Force of Our Reimagination" situates canonical studies in Black masculinities. The scholar reminds us that social identity is a dynamic and ongoing phenomenon.

This book begins with a focus on private and public interactions. In chapter 1, "Mama Knows Best," Camara and Lee assess relationships, attachment, and perceptions of Mama's boys. The authors provide empirical insight to how masculinity is reimagined by Black men. In chapter 2, Curry and Utley foreground friendship and sex. Their study "She's Just a Friend (with Benefits)" also calls attention to anti-Black misandry and oppressive academic assertions. In chapter 3, "Reverse Interest Convergence, Kaepernick, and Nike," Griffen and Robinson illustrate how race and economics inform public education for Black and Brown children.

This book also focuses on mediated images. Chapter 4, "Outkasted Black Masculinity" centers hip-hop to explore racialized and gendered scripts within popular culture. McFerguson begins with personal experience to describe how Outkast expanded a spectrum of performative possibilities. In chapter 5, Hopson, Castle Bell, and Craig's "The Killing of Black Boys" is a collaborative critical auto-ethnography about racial talk emanating from the murder of Trayvon Martin, and the acquittal of George Zimmerman. Here, the talk includes communication strategies to manage and survive historic conflict, construct race in the mass media, and contribute to dialogue.

We also focus on education and occupation. In chapter 6, "A Conversation on Black Masculinity with Principal John Hawkins Snowdy of Baltimore Collegiate School for Boys," Moffitt demonstrates the imaginative vision to create a safe and academically rigorous learning space for young Black boys. Chapter 7, "(Re)Educating Boys and Men of Color by Shaping

Community Support" addresses the value of mentoring programs. Brown's themes include resiliency, the potential of mentoring relationships, and the role of education for boys and men. In chapter 8, Ward explores Black manhood and labor activism in Jim Crow Illinois. The chapter, "We Demand an Equal Show upon Matters Effecting Our Industrial Welfare" recalls African American working-class activism in an era when Black manliness and patriotism is repetitively called into question.

The latter part of the book focuses on theoretical perspectives. In chapter 9, "The Essence of the Black Man," Dale theorizes masculinity and double consciousness within predominantly White structures. The author builds on historic views of agency and societal (dis)connection. In chapter 10, "The Battle of the New Age Black, Male Hero and Hegemonic/Toxic Masculinity," Thomas and Gamble apply critical discourse analysis to the film *Black Panther* to explore shifting assumptions about hegemonic masculinity and hypermasculinity. In chapter 11, Hernandez's "Me Miran Raro" foregrounds the intricate dynamics of Latin trap-rap including conflicting notions of gender, ethnicity, and sexual identity. In chapter 12, Dennis's "Dual Socialization and Black Academic Intellectuals" examines the formation of Black intellectualism. Finally, the afterword "The Beautiful Ones Were Born Some Time Ago" is Neal's imagism on how Black creatives come to represent promise, possibility, and strategies for survival in U.S. spaces.

As you read *Reimagining Black Masculinities*, be encouraged to reimagine social identities under current contexts. Consider the following discussion questions: How do you deconstruct and reconstruct the politics of race, gender, and space? How are social identities produced, negotiated, and contested in public spheres? Where does theory meet praxis when mobilizing for social change? Surely, your responses will inform your actions, and your actions will impact possibilities for peace and freedom in the world around you.

*Chapter One*

# "Mama Knows Best"

*Exploring Black Men's Perceptions and Reimaginations of the Phrase "Mama's Boys"*

Sakile K. Camara and Carmen M. Lee

Through the lens of adult attachment theory (Hazan & Shaver, 1987) and Freud's (1965) Oedipal complex, this chapter takes an enhanced look at "Mama's boys" (MBs) in the African American/Black community. Using a mixed methods approach, data were first obtained from forty in-depth interviews with African American/Black males who self-identified as "non-mama's boys" (n = 19) and "mama's boys (n = 21). Qualitative results reveal four essential themes about MBs: (a) extending adolescence; (b) approval and validation; (c) Mama knows best; and (d) Power of the First Love. And three types of roles that MBs enact: (1) the great communicator; (2) the caregiver; and (3) the beneficiary. The second data collection set included 357 Black males, self-identifying as "non-mama's boys" (n = 205) and "mama's boys" (n = 152), who completed a self-report questionnaire comprised of measures of attachment, interpersonal closeness, and masculine behavior. Quantitative results indicate several significant differences where mama's boys, compared to non-mama's boys, reported greater feelings of closeness and intimacy with their mothers. Although there were no differences in masculine behavior, masculine behaviors were associated with different attachment styles. Based on these findings, this chapter considers implications relevant to mother-son relationships, the antagonism toward Black MBs, and the reimagination of Black masculinity.

## MOTHERS LOVE THEIR SONS AND RAISE THEIR DAUGHTERS (A BLACK SAYING)

The commonly known saying that "Mothers love their sons and raise their daughters," not only aligns with research indicating that Black mothers socialize boy and girl siblings differently (Mandara, Varner, & Richman, 2010), but also displays the origins of the term "Mama's boy" (MB). Mothers "loving" their sons and "raising" their daughters highlights the idea that there is a higher expectation of girls to achieve full independence financially, socially, and relationally, while less responsibility is expected of the boy child to achieve this same independence (Cauce, Hiraga, Graves, Gonzales, Ryan-Finn, & Grove, 1996; Epstein, Blake, & González, 2017). This lack of responsibility leads to several negative assumptions associated with a MB—immature, passive, poor achievers, and socially deficient. The phrase "Mama's boy" is not only an expression of a man's closeness to his mom, but a colloquialism that is considered a gendered verbal insult often associated with an unhealthy Oedipal themed mother-son relationship. This trope not only facilitates an expression of dependence (excessive attachment), and control between mother and son, but the perceived MB's masculinity/manhood is rejected or questioned because masculinity is directly linked to the MB's autonomy from his mother and to a female substitute (Kimmel, 1996; Rotundo, 1993). Thus, an MB is defined as an adult male "who has never [or rarely] left the sphere of influence of his mother" (J. Malinak & S. Malinak, 2008, p. 7) to learn what it means to be a responsible and accountable man.

Masculinity is defined in terms of being independent, self-reliant or tough, while the phrase "Mama's boy" often evokes images of effeminacy and challenges notions of machismo and bravado (Brod & Kaufman, 1994; O'Reilly, 2001). Thus, the phrase "Mama's boy" is considered a tangible problem for constructing a male gendered identity because MBs fail to embody, in perceptions of other men or non-MBs, the role of caregiver and protector and are often emasculated by others. Yet, Black MBs occupy a peculiar position in our society.

The primary focus on Black male bodies tends to illuminate the existence of the macho Black male and his relational detachment, and on the other side—the effeminate Black male body and his relational attachment. Popular culture cherishes a host of Black male images generally and MB images specifically. For example, self-help books, films, songs, and reality TV shows have surged in the past ten years providing advice about how to date MBs, how not to raise MBs, to sounds and images depicting MBs; but how these tropes are socially constructed and understood have received little to no scholarly attention. Far less is known about how Black males perceive the phrase "Mama's boy," or whether Black men perceive themselves as "Mama's boys." Even less is known about Black male attitudes about their relational attachment to their mothers, which is often shaped by a familial structure not of their own choosing or doing. Conceptions of MBs have everything to do with masculinity and attachment and therefore deserve careful consideration and analysis.

Our task in this chapter is to investigate some perceptions of MBs and relational attachment styles from Black men who perceive others and reimagine themselves as "Mama's boys." Perceptions are themselves an effort to understand the trope of MBs within and across various relationships and the images that come along with it. Therefore, how Black men react, respond to, and negotiate complex meanings of the phrase "Mama's boy" is essential to understanding Black men's relational attachment to others. Through this chapter, we hope to capture the plurality of Black male relational attachment using a mixed methods approach. As Black males respond to their relational attachment to others, we explore the varied attachment styles to relational partners and masculine behavior. As Black men also construct and react to the phrase "Mama's boy" through their stories, we are better able to understand the state of unity with Black men and their mothers and how they perceive masculinity and manhood. We also acknowledge that there is a tendency for individuals to talk about MBs as a monolithic group with little variance. Therefore, it is important to consider that MBs may navigate and conceptualize their relationships with their mothers differently, but under the same colloquial rubric.

## CONTEXTUALIZATIONS OF MAMA'S BOYS

The phrase "Mama's boy" is a universal phrase that cuts across race, class, and cultural contexts and is depicted as a male who clings to his mother as a crutch. The celebration of maleness and manhood is thought to be interrupted by the conception of MBs. A man's attachment to his mother is a symbiotic relationship that is dangerous and parasitic. The phrase "Mama's boy" as it relates to Black males, lies in historical and social conceptions of slavery and what it means for Black men to be men. For example, the inferior manhood of the slave implied that he was unfit to be part of manhood. So, the term ascribed to him was "boy"—meaning less of a man than White males. Black men, when referred to as boy, also meant that Black males could not be perceived as a man if his social status was that of a slave.

Today the notion of calling a Black man a boy places him in an inferior status and is part of the social hierarchy where the Black male body and masculinity is couched in oppression and oppressiveness (Alexander, 2000). Alexander (2000) suggests that societal standards of the past were the primary reasons why Black mothers kept their sons close and protected—which may have escalated the attachment between mother and son.

However, in the medical field during the early 1970s, MBs were diagnosable and considered a problem that needed to be resolved in counseling and therapy (Hann-Morrison, 2012; Khan, 1971) for fear that a boy's closeness to his mother would lead to sexual problems, addictions, indecisiveness, and unhealthy mother-son interactions (Adams & Morgan, 2007; Hann-Morrison, 2012; Underwood, 2000). While conducting an experimental study with 15-year-old boys with attachment issues, Khan (1971) suggested that boys hospitalized for a short period of time, while going through counseling, had some progression in diagnoses and became less attached to their mothers. However, boys in outpatient care reverted to attachment behavior. These studies presume that distance can be a key factor in preventing the mama's boy syndrome and is evidence that men enmeshed with their mothers (MEM) have a host of commitment issues because their mothers keep them too close (Adams & Morgan, 2007).

Perhaps the most influential and controversial psychiatric work on MBs is that of Sigmund Freud (1965). Freud coined the phrase the Oedipal complex and in its simplest form postulates this: A young boy has an unconscious desire and sexual attraction to his mother through early relationship attachment. The father or male figure is pivotal in his transition. Thus, there is contention with his father or other male figure due to forced repression of attraction toward the mother as he [the son] is socialized by his father or father figure to divide his affection for the women in his life. The boy is distanced from his mother and is pressured to walk in the world that men walk in. Lombardi refers to this as a "model of separation" (2012, p. 17) that sustains conventional wisdom surrounding masculine identities and healthy boundaries (i.e., independence, boundaries, and clear guidelines and rules of appropriate affection) among and between family subsystems (Hann-Morrison, 2012).

Therefore, MBs are reflected in contemporary accounts of the Oedipus complex in that he is in adoration and reverence of his mother, which affects his milestone toward independence and maturity. However, when the father or male figure is immediately absent, whether physically or emotionally (Gurian, 1994), there is no competition and the boy's attachment to his mother is not redirected or adjusted (Burleson, 2015). Additionally, the father's absence forces a shift in energy toward the mother. As a result, the mother is blamed for condoning and encouraging her son's codependence. This subversive style of parenting, which interferes with male growth toward maturity and pulls him into his mother's world, is referred to as "momism" (Wylie, 1942).

## "MAMA'S BOY," "MOMISM," AND THE VILIFICATION OF MOTHERS

The view that MBs is a product of "momism" was put forth by Phillip Wylie who first coined the term "momism" in the 1940s. Lombardi (2012) suggests that mothers generally endure the responsibility (i.e., blame) of the dysfunction of the children, in general, and MBs more specifically. The practice is best characterized as the "blame-the-mother ethos" (p. 81). Wylie's position on "momism" was that mothers were too overprotective of their sons. This protection softened his steps toward maturity; therefore infantilizing him and preventing his ability to hold healthy relationships with other women. Van Den Oeuvre (2012) further advances our understanding or "momism" and MBs through his postmodern interpretation of four cultural representations (*The Grotto* by Grace Zaring Stone, *Suddenly Last Summer* by Tennessee Williams, Alfred Hitchcock's *Psycho*, and *Portnoy's Complaint* by Philip Roth). He notes that moms were first blamed for their son's defects and arrested social development, especially in Alfred Hitchcock films. The mom was either detached, dominating the son, or over affectionate, which led to the son's psychotic and schizophrenic existence. In most cases, you saw the darker side of motherhood.

Another important reiteration of "momism," and the creation of MBs is Levy's (1943) categorization of overprotective mothers and Love's (1990) maternal enmeshment. Again, the defects of the male children were blamed on the mom because males, who were perceived to be too close to their mothers, generally had personality difficulties and behavioral problems, leaving him powerless over the relationship. Levy's categories included: (1) prolonged infantile care; (2) maternal control; and (3) self-preservation of independent behavior. The problem was that if the mother continued fixing meals for the son, using aggressive methods to maintain submission, or substituting the son's love because of loneliness and isolation (Lawrence, 1997), these relational connections would suppress his maturity as an adult male and affect his ability to develop mature relationships with other women as well as friends and peers (Love, 1990).

Because of the social status of Blacks in post slavery, the term "momism" was not even applied to Black women until the 1960s when the Moynihan Report (1965) blamed Black women and their nonmarital status on the heightened Black male incarceration rates, increased school dropouts, and disciplinary behavior that made Black males unfit for social civic duty. Moynihan's premise was that the missing father influences the developmental outcome of the Black male child. Moynihan presumed that an absent male father figure leads Black males to more likely drop out of school, commit crimes, become addicted to drugs, and engage in delinquent behavior. All of this was due to Black female headed households. His report ignored how

Black women participate in the development of their son's manhood (Bush, 1998a, 1999b, 2004).

## THE NEW "MOMISM" AND "MAMA'S BOYS": BREAKING TRADITION

Van Den Oeuvre (2012) advises that discrediting "momism" removes blame from the mom and puts responsibility back on the one with agency and choice—the son. When the blame is removed from the mother, the male is now responsible for regulating his own growth and constructing his own manhood and masculine identity. "Momism" is now transformed and a new and improved "Momism" emerges that bears no resemblance to that of Wylie's 1940s conceptualization and extends Douglas and Michaels' (2004) role of mother. Instead, the new "Momism" suggests that mothers and their sons can remain close without the danger of dysfunction (Douglas & Michaels, 2004; Lombardi, 2012). The son makes a conscious choice to engage with his mother in ways that change the models of masculinity. In other words, he breaks what Pollack (1998) calls the "boy code" and is no longer expected to be disengaged or detached from mom.

For Lombardi (2012) the new "Momism" brings the feminist movement to full circle by rejecting traditional wisdom of men being engaged in non-emotional pursuits. The new "Momism" creates a "new narrative" (p. 20) that reflects a positive interaction between mothers and their sons. The fact that mothers are nurturing close bonds with their sons and aiding them in developing traits that are considered the domain of women (i.e., sensitivity, tenderness, emotional awareness, and the ability to articulate feelings), questions traditional notions of masculinity and lessens the divide between men and women's worlds. Lombardi defends the bond between mothers and sons, arguing that their level of closeness is not about feminizing or infantilizing, but making sons aware of the male emotional self. Lombardi also notes that even with a high level of bonding, she is not his best friend, but his mother. Setting boundaries suggests that there is a clear dichotomy between mother and son.

To support this new narrative, there are only a few studies that document the benefits of a mother-son close relationship. Trentacosta, Criss, Shaw, Lacourse, Hyde, and Dishion's (2011) study 285 mother-son dyads and concluded that sons who had close relationships with their moms had fewer problems like those associated with bad behavior or addiction. Santos's (2010) study also debunks the MBs myth. In his study on gender type behavior, Santos found that boys with strong relationships with their mothers tend not to accept traditional roles about masculinity and his relational closeness is a predictor of emotional availability, and better mental health. Dooley and

Fedele (2001) suggest that the MBs relational closeness only comes through the mother-son relationship and enhances his emotional development. The mother's ability to teach her son how to put certain skills into action (i.e., empathy, respect, and listening) is called parenting-in-connection model (p. 201). Although there is support that MBs lead healthier lives there is still stigma attached to their manhood. Thus, the conceptualization of MBs opens space for understanding and even redefining Black masculinity.

## THE EMERGENCE OF BLACK MASCULINITY

A considerable amount of research has been conducted on masculinity (Akbar, 1991; Connell, 1994; Kimmel & Messner, 1989) from dimensions of power and domination to what manhood is and is not. Historical roots of manhood scholarship suggests two things: (1) we can understand men from the prism of gender where studies were often about gender and race (Kimmel & Messner, 1989); and (2) there is a split between masculinity and femininity, where masculinity is the entry into a new phase for understanding the lives of men. Therefore, a man's orientation to manhood includes his ability to distinguish himself as a man from woman or that which is embodied as woman and his ability to have power over woman, which validates his heterosexual success.

According to Kimmel and Messner (1989), men must be inducted into a social nonbiological process in which they participate from infant to boyhood to manhood. Levinson's (1977) Life Span Development Model demonstrates this socialized process. The model demonstrates man's task of distancing himself psychologically from his immediate family to developing a clear self-concept. When entrance into adulthood takes place, he moves into a career by the age of 30 to settle down with family to stabilize his adult lifestyle, which is affirmed by society. Thus, man's participation in becoming a gendered being ensures that there is agency in his becoming a man socially and historically. However, to speak of masculinity as some identifiable commodity is to assume that there is only one version of masculinity and that experiences are universal when they vary. Black masculinity is one of those variations.

## BLACK MASCULINITY AS HARD AND MANLINESS

The Black body is produced with complex social mechanisms (West & Lay, 2000) which makes Black men endure what bell hooks suggest is the "worse imposition of gendered masculinity" (p. 16). Because the models of masculinity have been historically steeped in White male culture, ethnic variations of masculinity accounts for oppression (Alexander, 2000; West, 2000). Thus, reconstructing Black masculinity posits Black men in very specific arenas in which he is to be publicly encountered (i.e., gangsta culture, militant group, athletic, musical). As a result of understanding Black masculinity, a method of strategy is enacted (lawful and unlawful; Klein, Spears, & Reicher, 2007) to survive the arenas, while struggling to overcome worldwide stereotypes steeped in mediated distorted images that frame how Black men are fictionally described and nonfictionally defined (Anderson, 1990; hooks, 2004; Jackson & Hopson, 2011). These stereotypes further sustain the arenas that block opportunities for success (Hurwitz, Peffley, & Sniderman, 1997; Madhubuti, 1990).

A more comprehensive study by Billson (1996) confirms that Black masculinity is consumed under the rubric of oppression/blocked opportunities, criminal behavior, and antisocial personalities. This longitudinal study followed five Black males in Roxbury, Massachusetts. The study attempts to understand the struggle of Black males living in the inner city where environment and its associated behavior are disregarded as markers of identity. Results indicate that regardless of context all men constructed an identity of manliness (i.e., tough guy, conformist, the actor, the cool guy, and the retreater) compatible to existing expectations and values. Yet, the pathways and journey to understanding one's own identity as a Black man was varied. The one consistent factor was that the coping strategies used to synthesize their social and environmental existence often lead to illegal and unlawful behavior.

## BLACK MASCULINITY AS SOFT AND FEMININE

Masculinity is grounded in one's ability to provide and protect, which demands a certain level of assertiveness and mobility. This characterization indicates that not all forms of masculinity are equally considered (Hondagneu-Sotelo & Messner, 1994). Thus, the idea of soft masculinity was a response to sexual politics and the meanings associated with masculinity (Rutherford, 1997; Chapman & Rutherford, 1988). The new image of MBs is an example of soft masculinity that challenges us to understand what it means to be a man whose identity is not fixed in traditional notions of manhood. Therefore, what is appropriately male changes with MBs because the leading discourses surrounding MBs paints a contradictory picture of manhood. MBs is a complex relationship that must be negotiated and renegotiated in ways that does not look like aggression, competition, and anxiety prone behavior (Kimmel, 1994), but manifests itself as both masculine and feminine.

Moreover, MBs is not a marker that is paraded in the conversations on gender because it is often linked with gender role conflict (i.e., effeminacy, sexual orientation, and homosocial enactment; Kimmel, 1994). Because gay men are categorically expected to play the role of sissy (Eguchi, 2011; Yep, 2003), the fear of being perceived as gay, feminine, or a sissy is highly stigmatized in gay and heterosexual culture and may propel Black men to deny or mask being an MB. Thus, as Black men navigate Black masculinity within the context of MBs there is another dilemma that creates conflict. The issue of encouraging homophobia is at play, which can be painful and threatening. Men are pitted against and criticize other men's behavior (i.e., gay against straight; masculine against feminine), which further displays how power is exercised over one other.

When men enter the realm of soft masculinity, they not only subvert masculinity, but challenge traditional gender expectations. MBs research helps to explore the political as well as the personal implications of men having close relationships with their mothers. The concept of MBs further opens the dialogue to address diverse lines of inquiry in the area of masculinity. MBs are a revolutionary point of inquiry both in how men perceive the phrase "Mama's boys" and how men display closeness to their mothers. Thus, the following research questions are proffered:

Research Question 1: How do Black men perceive the phrase "Mama's boys"?

Research Question 2: How do Black MBs enact MB behavior?

## ATTACHMENT THEORY AS THEORETICAL FRAMEWORK

Attachment Theory (Ainsworth, Blehar, Waters, & Wall, 1978; Bowlby, 1982, 1980, 1973) is a theory about the nature and quality of relationships. Originally developed to examine the bond that develops between a child and their primary caretaker, the theory has been extended to explain how the bond between a parent and child during childhood affects that child's relationships in adulthood (e.g., friendship, romantic, etc.). Ainsworth et al. (1978), through their observations of infants and caretakers, identified three patterns of attachment: secure, anxious/avoidant, and anxious/ambivalent. Later, Hazan and Shaver (1987), translated the three infant attachment styles into adult relationships indicating that individuals can develop into adults who are secure (e.g., find it easy to be close to someone and comfortable depending on them), avoidant (e.g., are uncomfortable being close to others and find it difficult to trust them), and anxious/ambivalent (e.g., worry that their partner doesn't really love them and has a desire to merge completely with another).

In early work, attachment styles were anchored to masculinity (see Blazina & Watkins, 2000; DeFranc & Mahalik, 2002). Specifically, it has been found that masculine gender role conflict is linked to low parental attachment and fear of intimacy. One way of assessing the relationship between masculine gender roles and attachment is by examining masculine behavior. Masculine behavior is suggested to involve four areas of emphasis: success dedication, restrictive emotionality, inhibited affection, and exaggerated self-reliance and control (Snell Jr., 1989). Success dedication is defined as an excessive concern for attaining success. Restrictive emotionality is characterized by public restrictions of privately felt emotions. Inhibited affection refers to an inhabitation of feelings of affection for loved ones. Exaggerated self-reliance and control refer to an exaggerated concern with self-reliance and personal control. Research indicates that restrictive emotionality is strongly correlated to low attachment to parents (Blazina & Watkins, 2000; Fischer & Good, 1998). In contrast, secure attachment to mothers is associated with increased gender role conflict with success dedication. Schwartz, Waldo, and A. J. Higgins (2004), in a study investigating adult attachment styles and gender role conflict in college men found that those with a secure attachment style were lower on restrictive emotionality. Moreover, those with an anxious attachment style were lower on reliance on others. Thus, we proffer the following research questions:

Research Question 3: What attachment differences exist between MBs and non-MBs?

Research Question 4: Is there an association between masculinity and parental attachment?

## Study 1: Method

This inquiry into MBs and relational attachment was conducted in two studies: a qualitative study based on the perceptions of thirty-nine Black males and a quantitative study that surveyed 357 Black males. Both studies aimed to understand how Black men perceive MBs and their relationships with significant others.

### Qualitative Participants

Qualitative data were collected from twenty-eight Black self-identified MBs and eleven Black self-identified non-MBs for a sum of thirty-nine participants. The mean age of the Black MBs was 25 with a range from 19 to 64 and non-MBs average age was 36 years with a range of 21 to 58. Most participants had some college or college degree (n = 35), employment status ranged from full-time employment (n = 18) to being a student (n = 14). The marital status of the Black males was now married (n = 8; 22%), divorced (n = 4; .05%), and never married (n = 27; 77%). In general, all participants self-identified as Black (n = 34) with others indicating that they were biracial (n = 5).

*Qualitative Data Collection Procedures and Measures*

For the qualitative portion of the research, 39 personal interviews were conducted with Black males using a snowball technique. All interviews were recorded. Participants were solicited based on acquaintance, and additional men were produced via researcher solicitations and participant suggestions. The qualitative study was designed in accordance with a thematic analysis, which is ideal for identifying patterns and themes because it allows the researcher to transcribe conversations in which patterns can be listed (Spradley, 1979). Thematic analysis is sometimes referred to as thematic interpretation and looks for "recognizable reoccurring topics, ideas, or patterns (themes) occurring within the data that provide insight into communication" (Allen, 2017).

Themes are identified based on three criteria: recurrence, repetition, and forcefulness. Recurrence is evident when at least two parts of a communication episode have the same thread of salient meaning, whereas repetition is the explicit reiteration of key words, phrases, or ideas. Finally, forcefulness is present when the data reveal changes in vocal quality that stress or subordinate some utterances from others (Keyton, 2011). This study followed the recommendations outlined by Keyton (2011), which permitted the themes to emerge inductively. Extensive notes were taken during the recorded interviews to keep track of emerging themes and patterns. Comparison across transcripts identified themes by using a repetitive process. The analysis of themes in one transcript was applied to another to validate the theme. Comparison occurred throughout data analysis and across respondent talk and incidents, and interpretations were constantly scrutinized and refined. Six themes were identified and collapsed into four themes. Themes were then grouped to form conceptual categories that were used to explain the quantitative findings, along with investigating research questions one and two.

*Relevant Themes*

Emerging themes from the participants' narratives included: (a) extending adolescence; (b) approval and validation; (c) Mama knows best; (d) power of the First Love and three MB roles that are enacted by MBs; (e) the great communicator; (f) the caregiver; and (g) the beneficiary. To address research question one, the first three themes are discussed from non-MBs and MBs. The first two themes are related to perceptions from non-MBs and the third and fourth themes are perceptions of MBs from MBs. The last theme is related to the second research question related to how MBs enact their closeness with their MB behavior.

*Extending adolescence.* The idea of extending adolescence references the lack of accountability attributed to Black males who rely on their mothers. The mother is assumed to fix things to benefit the son. This emerging theme for non-mama's boys, assumes that "Mama's boys" are "coddled and carried" by their mothers. Additionally, he is immature, weak, overly or excessively attached, and effeminate acting in his behavior. Non-mama's boys tended to point out negative traits than did mama's boys. The phrase was often associated with one's parental attachment and conceptions of embodied manhood. Many non-MBs described MBs as childlike and can never "say no to their mom." If they had been called an MB, being labeled an MB was perceived as an insult, especially if they considered themselves "very independent." One 46-year old, non-mama's boy who has been married for twenty-five years had this to say about MBs and non-MBs as he references his 33-year-old friend:

> [An MB is] Somebody who can't take care of themselves. They may have a great relationship with their mother, but they have to call her on every issue that comes up. They want to get her input on every life decision on everything that they do in life and can't make a decision for themselves. He is someone who is very dependent on their mother almost like a fetal kind of position person. A non-MB looks like me, someone who is going to make decisions for himself, is going to take the bumps and the bruises and come up swinging. Someone who is going to take what their mother taught them as a kid and go on in life and use those principles and not go back. I don't mean don't have a relationship with her, but not get her validation on everything that you do. A non-MB is a provider whether it is for a wife, kids or just for yourself.

Another 26-year-old single personal trainer describes his 38-year-old cousin as someone who "fully depends on his mother and looks to her to solve all of his problems. The mother has to fix everything that is going wrong with his life." A similar sentiment was presented by another 26-year-old single graphics coordinator who had this to say about a MB as he makes declarations about his adult brother:

> A mama's boy is someone who leans on his mother for everything; basically as a fall back and like a security blanket. They are someone who is kind of babied by their mother. . . . He kind of takes advantage of everything a mother would do for a child for longer than a normal person would.

*Approval and validation.* Madhubuti (1990) argues that Black communities dominated by Black women further fragments Black life because the interactions between men and women in those communities are unstable and insecure. He suggests that being without land, finances, and power renders the manhood of Black men unmeasurable, because Black men must provide the guidance and protection he seeks out. Many "non-Mama's boys" supported this statement by acknowledging that "Mama's boys" can't stand on their own two feet and must go through some approval or validation process from his mother to stand in his manhood experience. One 47-year-old single male who is unable to work, but lives with his mother had this to say:

> Guys who are like "Mama's boys" need to be validated by their mother. When we are talking about dating someone, they are looking for someone just like their mother and there's nothing wrong with that, but when you continue to live your day in and day out to be validated by your mother ... I have an uncle who is like that to this day. He needs to be helped by his mother now that my grandmother just passed away. He is lost without her, so he grabs hold of his sisters to hold on to that which he lost. He is looking to be validated. ... It is not helping him. My aunts and my mother have a life of their own and their brother is lost, and I don't like it because I feel that they are enabling my uncle. I feel it is time for my uncle to grow up to be a man and take responsibility for himself. If he is looking for his lost mama, go out there and find yourself a woman who's going to take care of you.

Non-MBs tend to perceive attributes about MBs as not completely detached from his mother and appear not fully a man, and in some cases a wimp. He is rendered dependent on a woman and is therefore emasculated. As noted by one MB, who stressed dominance and conquest, for his uncle, the fabrication of manhood is about being independent, which requires detachment from or the renouncing identification with one's mother. Yet attaching to another female who can provide or perform the same duties, does not give the appearance of being completely detached, thus, MBs can be read from an open Oedipal identity (Connell, 1994; Kimmel, 1996; Krimmer, 2000) where man becomes fully effeminized inwardly because of his relationship with his mom.

There are certainly deeper issues of equity and equality that are dismissed. The idea that women are to be conquered and controlled is reinforced when detachment becomes a redirected practice of pursuing a substitute in a qualified significant other. For the participants in this study there were key differences in how non-MBs and MBs perceived forms of masculinity. Contrasting these perspectives is where we see the beliefs about MBs collide with two diametrically opposed responses. There is a new reimagined masculinity that owns the mother-son closeness. The harbor of mom is a safe space where men can be vulnerable and are likely to defer to their moms, which exceeds the 1960s models of manhood and masculinity to something more innate.

*Mama knows best.* For MBs, there is great value in being an MB. The mother is an omnipresent figure in Black communities, therefore in the life of Black men. Although this theme is an antithesis of the 1950s TV series *Father Knows Best*, where the kids in the family could always count on the dad for advice, it is indicative of how MBs perceive their mothers. Non-MBs and MBs similarly highlight the role that a mother plays in the MBs life;

however, MBs clearly saw their mother-son relationship much more positively and viewed the term as an endearment and not as an insult. One 23-year-old single, library shelfer stated the following:

> It [the phrase MBs] comes off as sounding negative. Whenever I hear about it on TV or people talking about it, they always make it like it's a negative thing being that you are attached to your mother or like that being the woman in your life. To me, it means having a relationship or connection with your mother, but like more than normal. Obviously, you are going to love your mother, care for her, but at the same time, I don't think that everyone has to have such a close connection with their mother; especially boys.

Other MBs saw their mother-son relationship as reciprocal, but one where acquiescing to the advice of the mom was critical to relational success. A 19-year-old single student suggested the following about MBs:

> I think of a guy that is just always around his mother and does what she wants him to do regardless of how he feels. . . . I really try to do everything that my mom asks me to do regardless of how I feel. I just want to make sure to make her proud . . . when I do bring a girl around the house and my mom is not feeling her, I do tend to separate myself. That's a big one for me. I want someone that both my parents can get along with her. I don't want just my dad to like her and my mom doesn't because they are just going to argue about that. If my mom doesn't like her that probably isn't the best girl for me because Mama does know best.

The practices associated with MBs are signified practices of "behaving," "listening," and "respecting" one's mom because "you trust her, and you don't want to let her down." A 22-year-old single student who has been called an MB and a 54-year-old entertainment industry official who is married and considers himself a mama's boy articulated the following:

> I don't see it [MBs] as a negative connotation. It is just a word like, just what people call people, like a category. When I was younger, I felt like it was negative but as I got older, like, I love my mom as well and I respect her. She was a single mom and all that good stuff but, I don't depend on her for everything financially or emotionally or anything like that. I take care of her and when it's all said and done, I make sure I contribute as much as I can to her life, but I don't consider myself a momma's boy for that. If my grandmother called to me while I was in the field to come home, I knew I'd better come, or she was going to get a switch. Being a Black kid in rural Oklahoma, if you were a kid who didn't take chances or doing things you weren't supposed to be doing with other boys, then you were a mama's boy. Mama's boy means a number of things to me. I love my mother, I always listen to my mother, I didn't act out, I never cursed my mother, and I never yelled at my mother. I think Mama's boys are boys that behaved.

Another 21-year-old single student articulates his respect for his mom by not introducing women to her if they didn't meet a certain standard. He stated:

> If you were like my girlfriend, you had to be like an awesome person. My mom is like on a pedestal for me, so I feel like if you are not an awesome person, you weren't going to meet my mom at all. There have been very few. It was never something I ever rushed into, because there are always phases and steps to a relationship . . . you know some people are shallow and they go for looks and things like that. For me it's just a feeling you get that makes you comfortable with that person. It is reciprocated back and forth. It's like a great sense of trust and being there for each other like when you really need it. When you see it, you come to the conclusion like ok, this person is pretty awesome.

To contrast generations on the issue, a 22-year-old single male who had been called an MB and the previous 54-year-old entertainment industry worker both note that there is fear around being called an MB, because it hinges on effeminacy and questions one's sexuality. Nonetheless, there are environmental influences that further emasculate MBs even when the father is present in the home. They state the following about MBs being called an MB and observing other MBs:

> I kind of think of the last time I was talking to one of my friends and she asked me like am I going home? Because I live in northern California because that's where my mom lives. And then I told her I don't really want to go back this was for Thanksgiving or Christmas or one of them. And then I told her I really just want to see my mom and probably my sister or something. And she's like "Yeah you're a momma's boy" and I tried to cover it up. I'm like "I want to see my cousins and my dad too." They dare not. When I was younger or when you are older, the term when I was coming up, if you were called a mama's boy you were considered a sissy. You were considered a sissy if you didn't break windows with a sling shot to abandoned homes. I lived in a rural area and there were a lot of abandoned homes. I didn't get a kick out of that. I can hear my grandmother saying Malcom [alias] those boys don't have good home training and you don't need to be hanging out.

*Power of the first love.* Love is a profound emotion. Freud (1965) suggested that a boy will bestow much of his love on his mother, until he finds a substitute. According to Freud, the mother is often replaced with the father, if the father is present. However, Gurian (1994) notes that 80–90 percent of fathers are absent, abusive, distant, or passive. The father's presence seems to be vitally important to this study in that more than half of the MBs in the qualitative portion of the study had fathers living in the home. Thus, emotional and social attentiveness was key to perceptions of how "the mother was the strong one in the family" and the father's passive role in the household was responsible for the "son's dependence on the mother" in some narratives and "the mother's dependence on her son" in others. However, several MBs recognized that mom was first and, in some cases, "She [the mom] is the first woman you fall in love with when you are lucky enough to have a great and wonderful mother." A 36-year-old non-MB said this:

> I used to really adore my mom. . . . See at birth, she is the first woman you are ever gonna love. . . . I guess that's where my dad came into play. He kept that balance there. Because if he would have never been there, I probably would still be living with my mom right now, still in love with her, on all levels.

For this non-MB, there is much clarity that the father stepped in to separate this metaphorical umbilical cord. Although there is recognition from both that mom is a first love, there is much difference in the meanings of mother-son relationships. MBs appreciate the role that moms play in their lives. They see her as a wealth of knowledge and information that plays a critical role in how decisions will be made regarding life choices. Although non-MBs believe the mom is enabling irresponsibility and are hyper-involved, MBs seem to delight in the fact that they are free to negotiate mother-son interactions, anchor an MB identity that is not attached to old models of protector/caregiver and possess the power to change societies, expectations of male-female behavior and masculinity.

However, when MBs describe their mother as their first love, this expression is grounded in scholarship that asserts there is a certain level of danger and something taboo about the mother-son relationship (Wylie, 1942). If MB mothers provide a standard that MBs cannot get unaccustomed to, he essentially attempts, if at all, to find a substitute just like his mother, while he [the MB] becomes the moms substitute for a male companion, even if the father is in the home. Non-MB discourses usually echo moms as overly affectionate, having little to no boundaries and enabling an unhealthy dependency (Lundberg & Farnham, 1947; Van den Oeuvre, 2012). She is essentially converting her son into a sissy and the blame resides with the mother unless agency is given to the son (Levy 1943).

*Enacting the mama's boy role.* Enacting any behavior may be thought of as a rite of passage or modern-day ritual, but in the case of MBs, it is simply doing the things that make you an MB. In addressing research question two, non-MBs and MBs identified specific behaviors associated with MBs. There is no formal passage into how men who ascribe to the role of MB enact the role. What non-MBs and MBs do provide are clear behaviors that they have observed or acted out publicly or privately; verbally or nonverbally that indicates an MB status. Some narratives restrict the MB in a childhood state where the MB never metaphorically leaves the placenta of his mother's womb. He may "throw temper tantrums" and sabotage her desire to see other men or she may sabotage his attempts to date others. There are three of the most common roles that are performed by MBs: the great communicator, the caregiver, and the beneficiary.

*Great communicator.* The most reported MB role was the great communicator. Being a great communicator involves three kinds of acts unrelated to the ability to communicate well: talking with the mom every day, interacting with her often and talking about topics generally reserved for the boys or kept in secret. The great communicator role is based on the frequency with which one communicates and conversational topics. MBs and non-MBs recall that MBs talk with their moms about everything (i.e., problems with friends, girlfriends, sex etc.). As one 23-year-old stated, "I talk to my mom more than I talk to my dad. With my dad, we may talk like once every month or two months. I talk to my mom like every other day if not every day."

These narratives are often professed as a "strong relationship" between a MB and his mother, regardless of identification. Keeping the lines of communication open clearly creates an emotional bonding between a mother and her son and forges friendship that empowers him to confide in her about his most important thoughts and deepest secrets. Being able to talk to mom about anything creates a sense of trust between Black men and their mothers. In a sense, the role of great communicator contradicts the idea that Black men "have difficulty expressing their deepest feelings to those they are expected to be close to" (Majors & Billson, 1992, p. 41). Thus, Black MBs contribute to masculinity that includes expressiveness and the display of love and affection.

*Caregiver.* MBs enact the caregiver role through provider-ship. Enacting the caregiver role is about what the MB does for his mother, whether he "wants to or not." Doing for one's mom, under any circumstance, is a sacrifice. As one MB states, "There are times when I have pampered her a little bit, like I've given her a manicure and pedicure and I do it on my own, but that's nothing extreme." A 25-year-old single graduate student who found out about his father's infidelity and a 21-year-old undergraduate student who no longer considers himself an MB had this to say about their experiences respectively:

> I send her peanuts games and wood stocks. I am always there for her and when she is down, I will go and buy her flowers. If anything, I let her know that I am here for her when I talk to her. The games get her through her day. She laughs and she smiles and that's what makes me happy. I had older brothers, so I was always the one who stayed at home with mom. They were protecting me to make sure that I didn't get in any trouble.

> I was always looking out for her [mom] in such as sense and not go off and do whatever I wanted to do. It was like second nature to me. I was like, let me make sure mom is alright before I go off. For me the interesting thing was when I was growing up, I didn't live in the best neighborhood, so if everybody wasn't home, I wouldn't go to sleep yet. I would wait up until everybody got

home before I could go to sleep. Even if my mom told me to go to bed, I would still wait up.

MBs proclaim they are doing something for their moms' happiness and safety. Enacting the caregiver role is voluntary, but simultaneously constraining. The motivation for engaging in the caregiver role is often because of the emotional or physical absence of the father. However, the primary reason for enacting the role is because of the MB's love for his mother.

*Beneficiary.* The beneficiary role is the opposite of the caregiver role. MBs enact the beneficiary role when they are not in a financial position to take care of self or when believed to be the favored child. The MB as beneficiary would be remiss to pass up the spoils of a mother's internal war. Often, the beneficiary charms his way through his mother's life so that he may receive an unlimited spring of resources to improve his current status. One 20-year-old single student remembers being called an MB by three ex-girlfriends and stated this:

> I am basically spoiled, and I get anything I want. I can charm myself out of things like I can get myself out of trouble. If I want something and do something bad then she might punish me and tell me to go straight to my room and then she will come in and ask me if I want some shoes or something and I will get the shoes but I won't get grounded . . . but I go to her [his mom] about everything. If I am mad about something one of my girlfriends did, then she will baby me and take up for me and tell me "you don't have to worry about them."

For non-MBs and MBs alike, there are many terms used to describe the MB as a beneficiary who receives resources from his mother, including "manipulator," "codependent," and "charmer." For non-MBs, the beneficiary is manipulating situations and seeking out or receiving resources that he [the MB] should be providing for himself. The constant acceptance of favors from his mother develops into an unhealthy dependency and a mutually parasitic relationship between mother and son. As one 46-year-old married man stated about his 33-year-old MB friend:

> I saw him in the mall walking behind his mom like he was fifteen years old and she was footing the bill to pay for things for him whether it's a shirt or pants. Those are some of the things that go on that says to me he is a mama's boy. He owns his own house, was married for a while, and has three kids. He pays his mother back for the taxes [on his house] . . . they [his parents] let him pay the rent and they pay his child support. I feel like she [his mother] is the benefactor for him. She pays the bills, his insurance, and his cell phone bill. She pays everything. She even comes once a month and take him grocery shopping. . . . I think that's weak and that he can do better. I don't think you should go back to your mom to do these kinds of things because you need to

take on a second job. That's what it is. I know men who have two and three jobs who are trying to take care of themselves and pay child support. You have to do what you have to do.

The MB performs the beneficiary role by actively seeking a partner that reminds him of his mother so that he continues to receive his benefits. One non-MB described it this way:

> I know a lot of men really love the fact that they are mama's boy so they kind of look for their mom in the people that they date . . . you know I think that man may look for their mother like her traits and mannerisms and then things in which she does in the people that they date whether it's male or female. You look for your mom's presence and you look for the way in which she handles things you look for the way she takes care of you she nurtures you; she feeds you. She wakes you up . . . she kisses you good night, you kind of look for those things to certain degree.

MB behavior is performed with positive and negative characteristics. On one hand, MBs protect and look after their mothers; on another hand the mother is regarded as one who is protecting and looking after him. As one of the non-MBs suggested, men should be accountable for their behavior. However, ascribing to an MB status or enacting the role is a paradox. The same behaviors that afford Black men a semblance of status in one arena (i.e., with their mothers and sometimes other women) is discredited in other arenas with men and women who discredit and devalue the help that MBs receive or the over reliance on mother's milk (i.e., her advice) as an adult male.

## Study 2: Methods

*Quantitative Participants*

A volunteer sample (N = 357) of Black men participated in the present study. The sample consisted of individuals across the United States, with most of the sample residing in California and thirty participants located in other places (e.g., Texas, Missouri, Maryland, Hawaii, etc.). The men ranged in age from 18 to 73 ($M = 28.73$, $SD = 10.71$). Although all participants can be classified as being Black, they were asked to self-identify (i.e., write-in) their ethnicity/race. Most self-identified as Black (n = 144), African American (n = 111), and African American/Black (n = 61); the remaining participants indicating that they were mixed (n = 36; e.g., Black/Latino, Black/White, etc.), African (n = 3), Jamaican (n = 1), or Moor (n = 1).

Most of the participants indicated that they grew up in a home where their father was present (n = 214, 59.9%), and 30 percent (n = 108) indicated that they currently resided with their parent(s). The majority of participants were currently employed (n = 219) or retired (n = 73), indicated that they were single/never married (n = 281), and over 85 percent had some college education with 37 percent having a bachelor's degree or higher (e.g., MA, PhD, or MD). Most of the sample identified as heterosexual (80.7%). Almost half of the participants were currently in a romantic relationship (47.6%), which ranged in length from one month to forty-two years (M = 29.82, SD = 66.03; in months).

*Quantitative Procedures*

Participants were recruited through college courses, peers, friends, and the internet. Recruited participants who met the study requirements (i.e., a Black male) were first presented with a statement of informed consent. After agreeing to the study parameters, they completed a web-based survey housed on the Qualtrics survey website.

*Quantitative Measures*

*Masculine behavior.* The Masculine Behavior Scale (MBS; Snell Jr., 1989) is a twenty-item scale that assesses four dimensions of masculine behavior: success dedication, restrictive emotionality, inhibited affection, and exaggerated self-reliance and control. Participants were asked to indicate on a Likert scale from 1 (strongly disagree) to 5 (strongly agree) the extent to which each statement accurately reflected their attitudes and behavior. Success dedication (5-items) is defined as excessive concern with attaining success (e.g., I spend a great deal of my time pursuing a highly successful career). Restrictive emotionality (5-items) is characterized by public restrictions of privately felt emotions (e.g., I don't usually discuss my feelings and emotions with others). Inhibited affection (5-items) refers to an inhabitation of feelings of affection for loved ones (e.g., I don't devote much time to intimate relationships). Exaggerated self-reliance and control (5-items) refers to an exaggerated concern with self-reliance and personal control (e.g., I try to be in control of everything in my life). All subscales were reliable: success dedication ($\alpha$ = .85); restrictive emotionality ($\alpha$ = .87); inhibited affection ($\alpha$ = .83); exaggerated self-reliance and control ($\alpha$ = .70).

*Interpersonal closeness.* The Inclusion of Other in the Self scale (IOS; Aron, Aron, & Smollan, 1992) is considered a valid single-item measurement of closeness. Consisting of a series of Venn diagrams, each consisting of two circles where one circle represents the self and the other circle represents another person, participants indicate the extent to which the overlap between the two circles represent the perceived closeness with another person. In the present study, participants were presented with two IOS scales; the scales asked them to indicate the picture which best described their relationship with their: (a) father, and (b) mother.

*Adult attachment.* The Adult Attachment Scale (AAS; Collins & Read, 1990) is an eighteen-item Likert-type that measures the extent to which a person is comfortable with closeness and intimacy, the extent to which a person feels he or she can depend on others to be available when needed, and the extent to which a person is worried about being abandoned or unloved. Participants report the extent to which statements are "not at all characteristic of me" (1) to "very characteristic of me" (5). In the present study, all participants completed the AAS in reference to their mother, and father.

Although the closeness, dependable, and anxious subscales are established reliable scales, in the present study many of the subscales had marginally acceptable reliabilities. In terms of attachment to one's mother, reliability coefficients yielded the following for: closeness ($\alpha = .67$), dependable ($\alpha = .75$), and anxious ($\alpha = .52$). In terms of attachment to one's father, reliability coefficients yielded the following for: closeness ($\alpha = .70$), dependable ($\alpha = .84$), and anxious ($\alpha = .59$). Finally, in terms of one's romantic partner, the following reliabilities were found: closeness ($\alpha = .52$), dependable ($\alpha = .69$), and anxious ($\alpha = .56$).

*Mama's boy experience.* In order to assess the extent to which the participants were considered mama's boys, a series of dichotomous questions were posed. Specifically, they were asked: Were you ever called a mama's boy as a child? Were you ever called a mama's boy as an adult?; Do you consider yourself to be a mama's boy?

*Demographics.* All participants answered a series of demographic items, which include age, sex, race/ethnicity, education level, sexual orientation, current romantic relationship status, and length of the current relationship.

*Results*

Roughly half of the sample had been called a "Mama's boy" as a child (n = 203, 56.9%); however, fewer indicated that they had been called a "Mama's boy" as an adult (n = 102, 28.6%). When asked whether they self-identified as a "Mama's boy," 42.6 percent (n = 152) said yes, and 57.4 percent (n = 205) said no. To address research question three, a series of independent samples t-test were run and revealed few differences in attachment between those who identified as a "Mama's boy" compared to those who did not (see table 1).

Research question four addressed the relationship between masculinity and attachment. Irrespective of identification as a mama's boy, correlational analyses revealed significant relationships between masculine behaviors and attachment. Success dedication, as a masculine behavior, was positively associated with secure attachment within relationships with both mothers ($r = .21$, $p < .001$) and fathers ($r = .14$, $p < .05$), and success dedication was negatively associated with anxious attachment with both mothers ($r = -.14$, $p$

**Table 1.1. Differences in Self-Perception as a Mama's Boy**

|  | Not a "Mama's Boy" | | Identifies as a "Mama's Boy" | | t-value |
|---|---|---|---|---|---|
|  | M | SD | M | SD |  |
| Interpersonal Closeness w/Mother | 4.09 | 1.83 | 4.98 | 1.71 | 4.57*** |
| Interpersonal Closeness w/Father | 3.20 | 1.92 | 3.16 | 1.70 | -.20 |
| Success Dedication | 4.06 | .88 | 4.12 | .87 | .60 |
| Restrictive Emotionality | 3.26 | 1.09 | 3.26 | 1.06 | -.00 |
| Inhibited Affection | 2.57 | 1.05 | 2.46 | .97 | -1.07 |
| Exaggerated Self-Reliance/Control | 3.53 | .84 | 3.57 | .77 | .40 |
| Closeness Attachment (Mother) | 3.88 | .85 | 4.02 | .79 | 5.90*** |
| Dependable Attachment (Mother) | 3.65 | 1.00 | 4.22 | .75 | 1.59 |
| Anxious Attachment (Mother) | 1.99 | .69 | 2.11 | .70 | 1.65 |
| Closeness Attachment (Father) | 3.63 | .92 | 3.65 | .90 | .17 |
| Dependable Attachment (Father) | 3.25 | 1.25 | 3.39 | 1.21 | 1.03 |
| Anxious Attachment (Father) | 2.17 | .81 | 2.35 | .83 | 1.97 |

NOTE: * $p < .05$, ** $p < .01$, *** $p < .001$

< .05) and fathers ($r = -.12, p < .05$). Restrictive emotionality was positively associated with anxious attachment with both mothers ($r = .13, p < .05$) and fathers ($r = .19, p < .001$), but negatively associated with avoidant attachment with mothers ($r = -.19, p < .01$) and fathers ($r = -.17, p < .01$).

Correlational analyses also revealed that inhibited affection was positively associated with anxious attachment with both mothers ($r = .26, p < .001$) and fathers ($r = .34, p < .001$); but negatively related to secure attachment (mothers, $r = -.19, p < .001$) and (fathers, $r = -.21, p < .001$); and avoidant attachment (mothers, $r = -.34, p < .001$) and (fathers, $r = -.29, p < .001$). Finally, it was revealed that exaggerated self-restriction and control was positively related to anxious attachment with only fathers ($r = .12, p < .05$).

*Discussion*

We found that Black males who are securely attached to both parents tend to be excessively concerned with attaining success (i.e., success dedication). While securely attached individuals are often credited with engaging in prosocial behaviors (e.g., compassion, generosity, gratitude, and forgiveness; Mikulincer & Shaver, 2015), research indicates that success dedication is also linked to antisocial behaviors in the work environment (e.g., sexual harassment, Berdahl, 2007; physical aggression, Bosson, Vandello, Burnaford, Weaver, & Wasti, 2009). This suggests that not all relationships are affected in the same way by masculinity.

We also found relationships between anxious and avoidant attachment styles and masculine behavior. Specifically, those attachment styles tend to be associated with restrictive emotionality, and exaggerated self-reliance and control. The existence of these masculine behaviors has been found to be detrimental to males. To illustrate, Garcia, Finley, Lorber, and Jakupcak (2011) found restrictive emotionality and exaggerated self-reliance and control are associated with PTSD avoidance symptoms in Veterans. Consistent with Diamond (2004), we contend that the gender identity which is formed with our parental units must be integrated into our identities that are part of our relationships with others (e.g., coworkers, relational partners, etc.).

*Limitations and Future Directions*

No study is without its limitations. First, there are limitations with the sample. Both studies employed a volunteer sampling technique. Consequently, the individuals who volunteered to participate in this study may not be representative of all Black males. Second, in the quantitative study the adult attachment scale reliabilities were quite low. Therefore, the lack of a reliable measurement of attachment may also indicate that the scale is not valid. Third, because these studies only focus on Black males there is no basis for understanding if all males would respond in a similar fashion or whether Black males are different from males of different ethnic groups. Perhaps examining a sample of White males and assessing the degree to which hegemonic masculinity is associated with parental attachment would lead to interesting results.

Despite these limitations, the findings of the study provide directions for future research. Future studies should include conversations with mothers and fathers about raising Black males and how they raise their sons to be "men." Moreover, comparing how single parent and dual-parent households differ from each other, or even birth order, would provide a deeper understanding of how parents and children navigate their roles. The lead author believes that mothers can set forth the moral code for their son(s) and teach them how to care, while fathers might tell their son(s) to "suck it up and deal with it."

## GENERAL CONCLUSION

While several studies have explored MBs and their relationships to their mothers and masculine behavior few investigations have been conducted on perceptions of adult "Mama's boys." This chapter addresses a gap in the literature by assessing the relationship between adult attachment and masculinity, reimaginations and perceptions of MBs. We believe that this research helps to explain the closeness that Black males have to their mothers. We also understand that this closeness could debilitate other relationships in terms of credibility with other men or in lasting relationships with a significant romantic partner. The idea of being an MB provides both negative and positive consequences regarding subversive masculinity. Even in its paradox it brings accountability and lack of accountability simultaneously. On the one hand, MBs contribute to masculinity research that includes expressiveness and displays of love, affection, and emotion toward others. On the other hand, it can inject strain on relationships with romantic others as the MBs perceived lack of responsibility by non-MBs reinforces lack of accountability and control in and over the MBs own life. Most importantly, not being socialized into the norms of hegemonic masculinity and being too close to one's mothers may be perceived as unmanly or feminine.

Discourses on Black masculinity question the early models of masculinity and how the mainstream narrative influenced Black masculinity. However, the emergence of MBs causes Black men to rethink and reimagine their own gender practices in a patriarchal society as non-polarized. Although the MBs masculinity no longer conceals femininity (Krimmer, 2000), the phrase can still be emasculating. Several ways in which MBs are thought to be emasculated include: raised by matriarchs in the family, being jobless, having no land or participation in the power game (Fanon, 1970; hooks, 2004; Staples, 1982). This idea echoes tension between men and masculinity marked by power and dominance over women and other men.

There is a widely held perception that identification as a male and being masculine is at the cost of "dis-identifying" from one's mother (Greenson, 1968). Black men are often socialized in viewing themselves in a way that perpetuates these beliefs. However, our research indicates that Black males can have strong attachment relationships with their mothers while still engaging in masculine behaviors. What is needed is not a renaissance of Black masculinity but a reimagination of the relationship Black males have with masculinity.

## REFERENCES

Adams, K., & Morgan, A. P. (2007). *When he's married to mom: How to help mother enmeshed men open their hearts to true love and commitment.* New York: Fireside.

Ainsworth, M. D., Blehar, M. C., Waters, E., & Wall, S. (1978). *Patterns of attachment: A psychological study of the strange situation.* Hillsdale, NJ: Erlbaum.

Akbar, N. (1991). *Visions for Black men.* Tallahassee, FL: Mind Productions and Associates.

Alexander, C. (2000). Black masculinity. In K. Ousu (Ed.), *Black British culture and society: A text reader* (pp. 323–84). London, England: Routledge.

Allen, M. (2017). *The Sage encyclopedia of communication research methods (Vol. 4).* Thousand Oaks, CA: Sage.

Anderson, E. (1990). *Streetwise: Race, class and change in an urban community*. Chicago, IL: The University of Chicago Press.
Aron, A., Aron, E. N., & Smollan, D. (1992). Inclusion of other in the self scale and the structure of interpersonal closeness. *Journal of Personality and Social Psychology, 63*, 596–612.
Berdahl, J. L. (2007). Harassment based on sex: Predicting social status in the context of gender hierarchy. *Academy of Management Review, 32*, 641–58.
Billson, J. M. (1996). *Pathways to manhood: Young black males struggle for identity*. New Brunswick, NJ: Transaction.
Blazina, C., Jr. Watkins, C. E. (2000). Separation/individuation, parental attachment, and male gender role conflict: Attitudes toward the feminine and the fragile masculine self. *Psychology of Men & Masculinity, 1*(2), 126–32.
Bosson, J. K., Vandello, J. A., Burnaford, R. M., Weaver, J. R., & Wasti, S. A. (2009). Precarious manhood and physical aggression. *Personal and Social Psychology Bulletin, 35*, 623–34.
Bowlby, J. (1973). *Attachment and loss: Separation, anxiety, and anger* (Vol. 2). New York: Basic Books.
Bowlby, J. (1980). *Attachment and loss: Loss* (Vol. 3). New York: Basic Books.
Bowlby, J. (1982). *Attachment and loss: Attachment*, (Vol. 1) (2nd ed.). New York: Basic Books.
Brod, H., & Kaufman, M. (Eds.). (1994). *Theorizing masculinities: Research on men and masculinities*. New York: Sage.
Burleson, C. (2015, November). *Media representations and perceptions of Black "Mama's boys": A creative ethnography*. Paper presented at the National Communication Association Conference, Las Vegas, NV.
Bush, V. L. (1998). *Manhood, masculinity, and Black men: Toward an understanding of how Black mothers raise their sons to become men* (Unpublished doctoral dissertation). Claremont Graduate University, Claremont, CA.
Bush, V. L. (1999a). Am I a man? A literature review engaging the sociohistorical dynamics of Black manhood in the United States. *Western Journal of Black Studies, 23*, 49–47.
Bush, V. L. (1999b). *Can Black mothers raise our sons?* Chicago, IL: Black Images.
Bush, V. L. (2004). How black mothers participate in the development of manhood and masculinity: What do we know about black mothers and their sons? *Journal of Negro Education, 73*(4), 381–91.
Cauce, A. M., Hiraga, Y., Graves, D., Gonzales, N., Ryan-Finn, K., & Grove, K. (1996). African American mothers and their adolescent daughters: Closeness, conflict, and control. In B. J. Ross Leadbeater, & N. Way (Eds.), *Urban girls: Resisting stereotypes, creating identities* (pp. 100–116). New York: New York University Press.
Chapman, R., & Rutherford, J. (1988). *Male order: Unwrapping masculinity*. London, England: Lawrence & Wishart.
Collins, N. L., & Read, S. J. (1990). Adult attachment, working models, and relationship quality in dating couples. *Journal of Personality and Social Psychology, 58*(4), 644–63.
Connell, R. W. (1994). Psychoanalysis on masculinity. In H. Broad & M. Kaufman's (Eds.), *Theorizing masculinities: Research on men and masculinities* (pp. 11–38). Thousand Oaks, CA: Sage.
DeFranc, W., & Mahalik, J. R. (2002). Masculine gender role conflict and stress in relation to parental attachment and separation. *Psychology of Men & Masculinity, 3*(1), 51–60.
Diamond, M. J. (2004). The shaping of masculinity: Revisioning boys turning away from their mothers to construct male gender identity. *International Journal of Psychoanalysis, 85*, 359–80.
Dooley, C., & Fedele, N. (2001). Raising relational boys. In A. O'Reilley (Ed.), *Mothers and sons: Feminism, masculinity, and the struggle to raise our sons* (pp. 185–216). New York: Routledge.
Douglas, S., & Michaels, M. (2004). *The mommy myth: The idealization of motherhood and how it has undermined women*. New York: The Free Press.

Eguchi, S. (2011). Cross-national identity transformation: Becoming a gay Asian-American man. *Sexuality and Culture, 15*(1), 19–40.
Epstein, R., Blake, J., & González, T. (2017). *Girlhood interrupted: The erasure of Black girls' childhood*. Retrieved from SSRN: http://dx.doi.org/10.2139/ssrn.3000695
Fanon, F. (1970). *Black Skin, White Masks*. New York: Paladin Press.
Fischer, A. R. , & Good, G. E. (1998). Perceptions of parent-child relationships and masculine role conflicts of college men. *Journal of Counseling Psychology, 45*(3), 346–52.
Freud, S. (1965). *The interpretation of dreams*. New York: Avon.
Garcia, H. A., Finley, E. P., Lorber, W., & Jakupcak, M. (2011). A preliminary study of the association between masculine behavior norms and PTSD symptoms in Iraq and Afghanistan. *Psychology of Men & Masculinity, 12*(1), 55–63.
Greenson, R. R. (1968). Dis-identifying from mother: Its special importance for the boy. *International Journal of Psychoanalysis, 49*(2–3), 370–74.
Gurian, M. (1994). *Mothers, sons and lovers: How a man's relationship with his mother affects the rest of his life*. Boston, MA: Shambala Publications.
Hann-Morrison, D. (2012). Maternal enmeshment: The chosen child. *SAGE Open*, 1–9. doi: 10.1177/2158244012470115
Hazan, C., & Shaver, P. R. (1987). Romantic love conceptualized as an attachment process. *Journal of Personality and Social Psychology, 52*, 511–24.
Hondagneu-Sotelo, P., & Messner, M. A. (1994). Gender displays and men's power: The "new man" and the Mexican immigrant man. In H. Brod & M. Kaufman (Eds.), *Theorizing masculinities* (pp. 200–218). Thousand Oaks, CA: Sage.
hooks, b. (2004). *We real cool: Black men and masculinity*. New York: Routledge.
Hurwitz, J., Peffley, M., & Sniderman, P. (1997). Racial stereotypes and whites' political views of blacks in the context of welfare and crime. *American Journal of Political Science, 41*, 30–60.
Jackson, R. L., & Hopson, M. (2011). *Masculinity in the black imagination: Politics of communicating race and manhood*. New York: Peter Lang.
Keyton, J. (2011). *Communication research: Asking questions, finding answers*. New York: McGraw Hill.
Khan, A. (1971). Mama's boy syndrome. *American Journal of Psychiatrics, 126*(6), 712–17.
Kimmel, M. S. (1994). Masculinity as homophobia: Fear, shame and silence in the construction of gender identity. In H. Brod and M. Kaufman (Eds.), *Theorizing masculinities: Research on men and masculinities* (pp. 119–41). Thousand Oaks, CA: Sage.
Kimmel, M. S. (1996). *Manhood in America: A cultural history*. New York: Free Press.
Kimmel, M. S., & Messner, M. A. (1989). *Men's lives*. New York: Macmillan.
Klein, O., Spears, R., & Reicher, S. (2007). Social identity performance: Extending the strategic side of SIDE. *Personality and Social Psychology Review, 11*(1), 28–45.
Krimmer, E. (2000). Nobody wants to be a man anymore? Cross dressing in American Movies of the 90s. In R. West and F. Lay (Eds.), *Subverting masculinity: Hegemonic and alternative versions of masculinity in contemporary culture* (pp. 29–48). Atlanta, GA: Brill-Rodopi.
Lawrence, D. H. (1997). *Sons and lovers*. London, England: Gerald Duckworth.
Levinson, D. J. (1977). The mid-life transition. *Psychiatry, 40*, 99–112.
Levy, D. (1943). *Maternal overprotection*. New York: Norton.
Lombardi, K. S. (2012). *The mama's boy myth: Why keeping out sons close makes them stronger*. New York: Penguin Group.
Love, P. (1990). *The emotional incest syndrome: What to do when a parent's love rules your life*. New York: Bantam Books.
Lundberg, F., & Farnham, M. (1947). *Modern woman: The lost sex*. New York: Grosset and Dunlap.
Madhubuti, H. R. (1990). *Black men: Obsolete, single, dangerous?* Chicago, IL: Third World Press.
Majors, R., & Billson, J. M. (1992). *Cool pose: The dilemmas of black manhood in America*. New York: Lexington Books.
Malinak, J., & Malinak, S. (2008). *Getting back to love: When the pushing and pulling threaten to tear you apart*. Austin, TX: Bridgeway Books.

Mandara, J., Varner, F., & Richman, S. (2010). Do Black mothers really "love" their sons and "raise" their daughters? *Journal of Family Psychology, 24*(1), 41–50.

Mikulincer, M., & Shaver, P. R. (2015). An attachment perspective on prosocial attitudes and behavior. In D. A. Schroeder & W. G. Graziano (Eds.), *The Oxford handbook of prosocial behavior* (pp. 209–30). New York: Oxford University Press.

Moynihan, D. (1965). *The Negro family: A case for national action.* Santa Barbara, CA: Greenwood Press.

O'Reilly, A. (Ed.). (2001). *Mothers and sons: Feminism, masculinity, and the struggle to raise our sons.* New York: Routledge.

Pollack, W. (1998). *Real boys: Rescuing our sons from the myths of boyhood.* New York: Holt Paperbacks.

Powell, K. (2008). *The Black Male Handbook.* New York: Atria Clothing Books.

Rotundo, E. A. (1993). *American manhood: Transformations in masculinity from the revolution to the modern era.* New York: Basic.

Rutherford, J. (1997). *Forever England: Reflections on race, masculinity and empire.* London, England: Lawrence & Wishart.

Santos, C. E. (2010). *The missing story: Resistance to norms of masculinity in the friendships of adolescent boys.* Available from ProQuest Dissertations database. (UMI No. 3426967).

Schwartz, J. P., Waldo, M., & Higgins, A. J. (2004). Attachment styles: Relationship to masculine gender role conflict in college men. *Psychology of Men & Masculinity, 5*(2), 143–46.

Snell, W. E., Jr. (1989). Development and validation of the Masculine Behavior Scale: A measure of behaviors stereotypically attributed to males vs. females. *Sex Roles, 21*(11), 749–67.

Spradley, J. (1979). *The ethnographic interview.* Fort Worth, TX: Harcourt Brace Jovanovich College.

Staples, R. (1982). *Black masculinity: The black male's role in American society.* San Francisco, CA: Black Scholar.

Trentacosta, C., Criss, M., Shaw, D., Lacourse, E., Hyde, L., & Dishion, T. (2011). Antecedents and outcomes of joint trajectories of mother-son conflict and warmth during middle childhood and adolescence. *Child Development, 82*(5), 1676–90.

Underwood, E. (2000). From son to mother: Intellectualizing the personal. In M. Brown & J. Davis (Eds.), *Black sons to mothers: Compliments, critiques, and challenges for cultural workers in education* (pp. 71–91). New York: Peter Lang.

Van Den Oeuvre, R. (2012). *Mama's boy: "Momism" and homophobia in postwar American culture.* New York: Palgrave MacMillan.

West, R. (2000). Men, the market, and models of masculinity in contemporary culture: Introduction. In R. West & F. Lay (Eds.), *Subverting masculinity: Hegemonic and alternative version of masculinity in contemporary culture* (pp. 7–26). Atlanta, GA: Brill-Rodopi.

West, R., & Lay, F. (2000). *Subverting masculinity: Hegemonic and alternative version of masculinity in contemporary culture.* Atlanta, GA: Brill-Rodopi.

Wylie, P. (1942). *A generation of vipers.* New York: Rinehart.

Yep, G. (2003). The violence and heteronormativity in communication studies: Notes on inquiry, healing, and queer world making. *Journal of Homosexuality, 45*(2), 11–59.

*Chapter Two*

# She's Just a Friend (with Benefits)

*Examining the Significance of Black American Boys' Partner Choice for Initial Sexual Intercourse*

Tommy J. Curry and Ebony A. Utley

The sexuality of Black males continues to be theorized as hypermasculine and hypersexual, as well as aggressive, immoral, and dangerous (Pass, Benoit, & Dunlop 2014). Once freed from the shackles of slavery, Black men were described within most ethnological texts as animals unable to control their sexual instincts. The renowned nineteenth-century physician, George Frank Lydston, once wrote that he failed to "see any difference from a physical standpoint between the sexual furor of the negro and that which prevails among the lower animals . . . the furor sexualis in the negro resembles similar sexual attacks in the bull and elephant, and the running amuck of the Malay race" (McGuire & Lydston 1893, p. 17). Throughout the late nineteenth and early twentieth century, Black male sexuality was thought to be predetermined. Whereas white men and women pursued sexual intercourse as a matter of intimacy, Black males were described as newly freed beasts who pursued sexual intercourse as a matter of their brutish instinct. Black males' sexuality and sexual choices would come to not only be matters of scientific inquiry, but the justification for legal sanction and racial segregation (Curry 2018; Stein 2015). The Negro male was simply thought to be too dangerous to white society, since his proclivities toward rape could not be ameliorated by education or socialization. As the sexologist William Lee Howard (1903) explained,

> With the advent of puberty the Negro shows his genesic instincts to be the controlling factor of his life. These take hold of his religion, control his thoughts, and govern his actions. In the increase of rape on white women we

see the explosion of a long train of antecedent preparation. The attacks on defenseless white women are evidences of racial instincts that are about as amenable to ethical culture as is the inherent odor of the race. When education will reduce the large size of the Negro's penis . . . then will it also be able to prevent the African's birthright to sexual madness and excess. (p. 424)

The inability to consider how Black boys make choices and reflectively engage in sexual intercourse has been a common conceptualization of Black males from ethnology to contemporary gender theory.

Throughout the mid-twentieth century, Black boys' early age of first intercourse was used as evidence of their hypersexuality and savagery. In Abram Kardiner and Lionel Ovesey's book *The Mark of Oppression* (1951) they argued that unlike their white middle class counterparts who learn about sex from their mothers and fathers in stable nuclear families, Black boys "learn about sex in the streets" (p. 68). In middle-class white families, young boys and girls are slowly socialized into full sexual intercourse through dating and masturbation. For middle-class white boys, "masturbation generally begins early six to eight. On the whole, masturbation does not play much of a role in the growing lower-class boy. This is due to the early opportunities for relations with women. First, intercourse at seven or nine is not uncommon, and very frequent in early adolescence usually with girls much older" (Kardiner & Ovesey 1951, p. 68). Kardiner and Ovesey introduced the idea that lower-class Black boys never actually matured sexually as whites did. The lower-class Black boy simply *has sex*.

This emergent framework viewing lower-class Black masculinity as a subculture that glorified hypersexuality, violence, aggression, and rape, would come to be the dominant interpretive schema of Black male sexuality for decades to come (Amir 1971; Brownmiller 1975; Wolfgang & Ferracutti 1967). In fact, it is Susan Brownmiller's theorization of the relationship between Wolfgang and Ferracutti's idea of the subculture and Menachem Amir's analysis of rape that undergirds much of our present thinking about Black masculinity. Brownmiller (1975) argues that a subculture of violence theory assumes "within the dominant value system of our culture there exists a subculture formed of those from the lower classes, the poor, the disenfranchised, the Black, whose values often run counter to those of the dominant culture. . . . The subculture, thwarted, inarticulate and angry, is quick to resort to violence; indeed, violence and physical aggression become a common way of life. Particularly for young males" (p. 180–81). Feminist theories suggesting that Black males used rape to establish dominance over Black women and participate in white patriarchal culture became more common explanations of intra-racial violence in the 1970s. Lynn Curtis's *Violence, Race, and Culture* (1975) was extremely influential on feminist theories of sexual assault because it claimed that Black on Black patterns of rape were

Black men's attempts to use violence to lay claim to white patriarchal norms. Following Curtis's work, Joyce Williams and Karen Holmes (1981) argued that Black males imitate white men through the use of rape against Black women. These authors suggested that Black male sexual violence not only mirrored white male patterns of patriarchal aggression but was a means through which Black men and boys could gain power over Black women and girls through intra-racial rape.

Black feminist authors such as bell hooks (2004) utilized these ideas to not only describe a subculture of lower class Black males who engage in violence and gain pleasure from making others fear them (pp. 45, 50, 52) but also as a means to explain why many Black males are obsessed with sex. Rather than expressing a desire for intimacy and interpersonal connection as a way to resist the racist and sexual dehumanization the world places at the feet of Black men and boys, hooks describes Black male sexuality as obsessive, addictive, and compulsive. The author hooks (2004) writes: "In the iconography of Black male sexuality, compulsive obsessive fucking is represented as a form of power when in actuality it is an indication of extreme powerlessness" (p. 68). The Black male does not make amorous or affectionate choices to have sex with women according to hooks, he fucks to ease his pain of not being a man. This soothing, but nonetheless fleeting moment, is what creates addiction. "Sex has been all the more addictive for Black males because sexuality is the primary place where they are told they will find fulfillment. No matter the daily assaults on their manhood that wound and cripple, the Black male is encouraged to believe that sex and sexual healing will assuage his pain" (hooks 2004, p. 69).

For the last four decades the (Black) feminist theories being used to understand sexual violence in the Black community presupposed that Black men were pathologically fixated on using aggression and sexual assault as the basis of developing masculinity. Consequently, Black feminist analyses influenced by the work of bell hooks reproduce racist theories that describe Black male ontogeny as maturation toward the capacity and will to rape. A position eerily similar to the perspective of William Lee Howard in 1903. Unlike many contemporary gender analyses that pathologize the sexual choices Black men and boys use as attempts to dominate others or compensate for their lack, this article explores the circumstances under which Black boys' initial sexual intercourse occurred with girls who were friends, but not their girlfriends. According to Manning, Giordano, and Longmore (2006), "although most teenagers initiate sex with dating partners, many eventually have sex outside of a dating relationship. We find that 61% of sexually active teens report having had sex outside the context of a dating relationship" (p. 468). The same authors also found "that many teenagers [74%] who have sex outside of a dating relationship reported doing so with a friend" (p. 468).

Subsequent research by Giordano, Longmore, and Manning (2006) found, contrary to previous research reporting boys as less emotionally invested in romantic relationships than girls, that adolescent boys are "relatively less confident and yet more emotionally engaged in romantic relationships than previous characterizations would lead us to expect" (p. 2, 82). Previous research by Harper, Gannon, Watson, Catania, and Dolcini (2004) remarked on the importance that friendships and friendship approval have to the dating process and mate selection among Black Americans. However, no current research investigates Black boys first intercourse with friends.

Youth alternatives to compulsory coupling, especially friends with benefits (FWB), are common in the sexual development literature. Contrary to the previous theorizations of Black male sexuality as emotionally distant and primarily driven by obsession and conquest of another's body, our research suggests that Black boys reflectively engage in sex with friends emphasizing comfort with the selected partner, a desire for intimacy, and of course, trust. Despite the growing interest in "friends with benefits" relationships, there is no current literature investigating Black boys' choice of first sexual intercourse with friends. Friends with benefits is a term that combines "the psychological intimacy of a friendship with the sexual intimacy of a romantic relationship while avoiding the 'romantic' label" (Bisson & Levine 2009, p. 67). FWB definitions vary greatly based on the intensity of sexual contact, ratio of nonsexual to sexual interaction, frequency of sex, partner intimacy and familiarity levels, as well as desired outcomes (Mongeau, Knight, Williams, Eden, & Shaw 2013; Furman & Shaffer 2011; Leemiller, VanderDrift, & Kelly 2011). There are a plethora of FWB convenience sample studies of undergraduates and even a few on high school students' FWB but both approaches minimally represent African Americans (Afifi & Faulkner 2000; Bisson & Levine 2009; Furman & Shaffer 2011; Manning et al. 2006; Mongeau et al. 2013; Wentland & Reissing 2014; Williams & Adams 2013).

To our knowledge, there are no friends with benefits studies that focus solely on African American adolescents' experiences with initial sexual intercourse. Manning et al. (2006) claim that studies of adolescent sexuality problematize non-dating sexual relationships by "assuming that sexual liaisons that occur outside the context of conventional dating relationships are not as meaningful to adolescents and may be detrimental relative to those that occur within dating relationships" (p. 463). This problem is even greater in the predominantly pathology literature on the sexual development of Black Americans generally, and Black boys in particular. For example, in the one article investigating friends with benefits among Black Americans, the emphasis was on concurrent sexual relationships and number of sexual partners Black males had while having a girlfriend (Reed et al. 2012). Our article is the first to analyze Black males and what influences their decision to have their first sexual intercourse with girls who are friends but not their girlfriends.

Black Americans tend to have greater sexual permissiveness attitudes compared to whites often due to racial differences in religious and Puritanical attitudes toward women (Staples 2006, 1982). While this is occasionally interpreted as a positive aspect of sexual development, it often devolves into racial stereotypes concerning all Black Americans and feeds historical tropes of hypersexuality ignoring the complexity and nuance of Black sexuality (Landor & Simon 2019). For example, Black children often have earlier sexual debuts (or first sexual intercourse) than white Americans (Upchurch et al. 1998).

The earlier sexual debut also carries certain risks wherein Black boys are more vulnerable to adult sexual violations than children of other races (Cavazos-Rehg et al. 2009; Curry & Utley 2018). Because Black males lose their virginity earlier than every other racial and gender group, there have been increased efforts to explain the relationship between this group's early sexual debut and negative health consequences as well as risky sexual behaviors such as unprotected sex, sexually transmitted infections, and pregnancy (Crosby et al. 2015). Black males struggle with a prison pipeline and sundry longevity compromises that result in an imbalanced sex ratio (Curry 2017), a later first marriage age, a higher divorce rate, and greater marital instability (Dixon 2009). The consistent trend across disciplines describes Black male sexual activity and choices as being related to, if not wholly determining, the poor sexual health, marital and relationship problems, and hypersexuality of the Black community. However, none of these approaches consider the origins of Black boys' (commendable or risky) sexual behavior by querying the circumstances under which Black adolescents' experience their initial sexual intercourse. This article fills that lacuna.

## METHODOLOGY

Via an IRB-approved study, the second author interviewed twenty-seven Black men over 18 who described their sexual experiences at 18 or younger.[1] Interviews were approximately one hour and took place over the phone. Participants were recruited via snowball sampling. The men were asked to define a sexual experience, describe their early sexual experiences, and discuss how those sexual experiences impacted them as adults. Initially, we were interested in how early experiences of sexual trauma impacted Black men's adult sexual relationships. However, when we found seven men who described positive initial intercourse experiences with girls who were not girlfriends but good friends, we thought further analysis would productively contribute to understanding African American boys' sexual development.

All seven relationships were heterosexual although DaVonte self-identified as 90 percent gay and 10 percent straight. The experiences of initial intercourse took place when the boys were on average 14.86-years-old with ages ranging from 12 to 18 during the years between 1977 and 2007. On average, the men were 41-years-old at the time of the interview. None of the boys received sexual education prior to their first intercourse experience. This small (yet broad with respect to years covered) sample size is significant because it offers a positive perspective on Black adolescent initial intercourse within two generations. Our approach challenges the pathology orientation and current gender theories that focus on what is wrong with Black male sexuality by asking Black men to simply tell us what happened. In contrast to the literature which would interpret FWB behavior as the origins of promiscuity, we interpret it as a progressive stage of sexual development.

In an attempt to preserve the integrity of the interviews, we include the transcripts as opposed to arranging the data via themes. Aligning ourselves with Packer (2011), we support transparent data collection and presentation. We acknowledge that the interviews were cocreated by interviewees and the second author whose presence should not be abstracted. An interpretive description methodology allows us to present snapshots of experiences, not with the intent of developing theory but to highlight commonalities among lived experiences that may broaden knowledge about an understudied phenomenon (Thorne 2008).

Originating from nursing, interpretive description offers detailed descriptions of specific cases to enhance clinical understanding. Thorne, Kirkham, and O'Flynn-Magee (2004) define interpretive description as "a coherent conceptual description that taps thematic patterns and commonalities believed to characterize the phenomenon that is being studied and also accounts for the inevitable individual variations within them" (p. 4). Because transcripts are lengthy, non-pertinent conversations within the transcripts have been edited. We minimally imposed the following organizational structure in order to present the narratives by circumstance—mutual exploration, attraction, and peer pressure.

## MUTUAL EXPLORATION

### Tom

One day in the summer after 8th grade, Tom and his ex–first girlfriend had sex for the first time.

> **Interviewer:** Were you nervous?
> **Tom:** Yeah.
> **Interviewer:** Do you think that she could tell?

> **Tom:** No—well, probably because she was nervous too. We had already established that. We just didn't want to get her pregnant or anything so we just had to figure out what we were doing.
> **Interviewer:** Did you practice safe sex that first time?
> **Tom:** Yeah, I wore a condom that first time.
> **Interviewer:** And you said you weren't together anymore when you first had sex, how did that . . . ?
> **Tom:** We had just broke up. I guess just for the summer. Just you know when you're young and just don't really care too much for all that.
> **Interviewer:** So you broke up but then you decided that you still wanted to have sex together?
> **Tom:** Yeah we both lost our virginities. It was both our first time.

Relational status was less important to Tom who didn't "really care too much for all that" than mutual acceptance—being with someone with whom he felt comfortable discussing his nervousness and concerns about preventing pregnancy. Perhaps, their familiarity as former partners increased their mutual acceptance and made their initial sexual exchange less daunting.

## Richie

Richie was 16 when he had sex for the first time with his 14-year-old neighbor. They neither planned nor had a conversation about having sex together before it spontaneously happened.

> **Interviewer:** So the first time you had sex, the little girl, did she seem to enjoy it too?
> **Richie:** Yeah.
> **Interviewer:** And did the two of you have sex again?
> **Richie:** Yes. She was my—well, she wasn't my girlfriend but she was my sex friend.
> **Interviewer:** Did you two have a conversation about that or was she just cool?
> **Richie:** We never talked. I'm telling you.
> **Interviewer:** Okay and this neighbor girl was down to be your sex friend?
> **Richie:** Yes.
> **Interviewer:** For about how long would you guess?
> **Richie:** 17 to about maybe 28, 30.
> **Interviewer:** From 17 to 30?
> **Richie:** Mmm-huh.
> **Interviewer:** And you never had to have an "us" talk?
> **Richie:** Nope.
> **Interviewer:** That is an impressive woman.
> **Richie:** Nope. Never happened.
> **Interviewer:** Okay. Are you still friends?
> **Richie:** Yeah. She's married. I know her husband and the whole shebang.

Initially they neither used condoms nor worried about pregnancy or STIs. In Tom's relationship, we suggested that their familiarity as former partners spurred their sexual communication, specifically about preventing pregnancy. In Richie's case, a thirteen-year history of never initiating sexual communication may also (albeit ironically) suggest a familiarity, mutual acceptance, and extreme comfort level between two individuals that is further proven in their continued friendship post a FWB relationship.

## ATTRACTION

### Xavier

Xavier was attracted to maturity. At 15, he pursued a slightly older woman with whom he shared a common interest for his first sexual experience.

> **Xavier**: She was 18. She ran track. I ran track so we had a little thing in common. She was from Texas, spent the summer with her grandfather who was a track coach, so we spent a little time on the track. We had an attraction that led to intercourse.
> **Interviewer**: Would you say the two of you were in a relationship?
> **Xavier**: No, we were not.
> **Interviewer**: So how often did you have sex, was it more than once?
> **Xavier**: Three times that summer.... She went back to Texas and that was the end of it. I never saw her again.
> **Interviewer**: Tell me a little bit more about the very first time. Were you nervous, were you scared, were you confident?
> **Xavier**: I was faking confidence, but yes, I was nervous. She couldn't tell.
> **Interviewer**: Did she know it was your first time?
> **Xavier**: No, she didn't know, but she didn't not know. That was never really discussed. But you know I was confident and I felt like I was doing ... making the right moves, but on the inside I was nervous as hell. All right here we go, fake it till you make it kind of thing.
> **Interviewer**: And did you use a condom?
> **Xavier**: Yes.
> **Interviewer**: Each of those three times?
> **Xavier**: Yes.
> **Interviewer**: And was that your idea or hers or was it mutual?
> **Xavier**: Pretty sure it was mutual, but it was certainly my idea.
> **Interviewer**: And then was it a pleasurable experience for both of you?
> **Xavier**: It was. I'm proud to say that it was, yeah. But I mean after there were times after where she wanted it to happen but I didn't, so yeah. I would say it was pleasurable for her for sure.
> **Interviewer**: Can you tell me more about that, why you didn't want it to happen?
> **Xavier**: I was busy, it was track season, so in the summer that's our big track season. You travel a lot every weekend and practice, so I wasn't around as much.

Xavier's summer fling is noteworthy because the woman he chose contributed to his personal growth. Their sexual relationship was less of a distraction and more of an attraction based on their common affinity for track. Having sex with another track athlete allowed him to mingle his passions while eschewing a romantic relationship with her allowed him to prioritize his athletic passion.

## Bodhi

Bodhi was pretending to be a sexually experienced 16-year-old by memorizing passages from the letters portion of *Penthouse Magazine* and reciting them to a girl he was attracted to. One day she challenged him to perform.

> **Bodhi**: So I was talking on the phone with her one day and she says "Really? You know how to do all that, really?" I was like yeah, yeah, yeah, yeah. She said, "Okay, well tomorrow, my mom is going to work. She works at night, and I'm going to come over to your house and then we'll go back to my house and we can do it." And I was like oh, okay and my mind was just like jumping out of my skin. I was like, "Oh fuck, this is really going to happen!"
> We get to her house and, of course, I had made all these descriptions about what I was going to do. I had read all this shit and so I was trying to reenact what I had read while we were in the bed together. I was going to perform cunnilingus on her. I didn't know where her clitoris was so I was actually sticking my tongue inside of her vagina and around her vulva thinking I was really doing something. Then I sucked her breasts. And then we tongue kissed and then finally I got to penetrate a woman with my penis for the first time, and I might have ejaculated maybe a second or two and then I was just blown away because I had finally lost my virginity and she just kind of looked at me with this smirk like "Oh yeah, Mr. Experience" but at that point I couldn't even be embarrassed because I was just elated to not be a virgin anymore. So yeah, that was my first sexual experience.
> **Interviewer**: And then what happened after? Were you and the girl still in communication? Did you have sex again?
> **Bodhi**: Yeah, yeah. We didn't have sex again because I was so awful at it. She was just like yeah whatever dude. Years later she was working at a place in the mall and I was walking through the mall, and I saw her, and we greeted each other, and I said, "You know what? You took my virginity." She just blushed and we just kind of looked at each other and we started laughing, and she said, "Yeah I could tell you were a virgin but really?" She was very cool, very, very cool girl, very cool.
> **Interviewer**: So you two were able to stay friends?
> **Bodhi**: Yes, yes absolutely.

Bodhi and his friend did not use condoms, worry about pregnancy or STIs, or have sex again. His underwhelming performance may have been more forgivable because they knew each other. Their attraction had developed over a couple months beginning at the end of the school year and extending through the summer. Like Richie, Bodhi's experience lacked sexual communication but it also lacked shame and embarrassment which signals mutual respect between the sexual partners.

## PEER PRESSURE

### Frank

Frank's first sexual experience was a result of teenage peer pressure. His virginity was impediment to his social status.

> **Frank**: I didn't know what I was doing—pressure. Seventh grade I didn't know what I was doing. Me and the young lady got off the bus together at my mom's house and [I] didn't really know what I was doing but kissing and playing and touching and trying to make penetration but by the time you make penetration it's ejaculation.
> **Interviewer**: Was she also in the 7th grade?
> **Frank**: She was in 8th grade.
> **Interviewer**: And at the time would have considered her your girlfriend?
> **Frank**: No. Friends, you know, good close friends and not a girlfriend.
> **Interviewer:** Had you talked about sex before you actually had it or did it just happen?
> **Frank**: Well that was in I guess the early 80s, late 70s, back then you was getting teased a lot as far as being a virgin and this and that and one thing lead to another. It was pretty much—how can I say it, calling a bluff. She said I'm a virgin, I'm telling her I'm not and we both were, but kind of like pretended we weren't and one thing lead to another.

Frank and his friend did not use condoms, worry about pregnancy or STIs. Similar to the other boys, Frank was inexperienced and uninformed about sex. He described his partner as "a good close friend." There was no prior romantic relationship like Tom and no extended relationship like Richie but they were able to explore sex and remain friends because of the friendship that was in place prior to any sexual activity. Furthermore, like Bodhi when "penetration is ejaculation" there was no teasing or messages of disapproval from her that created shame or embarrassment.

### Thaddeaus

Thaddeaus was 18-years-old in the navy when he met a college girl named D_____ on the bus with whom he exchanged numbers. When he told his navy peers about her, they teased him.

> **Thaddeaus:** So the white boy was like "You're going to get you some poon, huh" and another white boy was like "You're going to eat that pussy?" and

another Black dude is like "You're going to eat that pussy?" I was like, "Hell nah, I'm not about to do that. You're all crazy." Now remember, I'm 18, I've never had that type of experience before.

Thaddeaus and D\_\_\_\_ hung out "a little kissing and touching but nothing sexual," but the next time D\_\_\_\_ called, a friend offered Thaddeaus his car so he could finally "eat that pussy." Thaddeaus described the evening.

> **Thaddeaus:** I get over there and she's on one. She got the house all laid out, candles and everything smelling good, she was looking good. She was like "I want you to give me a bath." I was like okay. So I end up bathing her and everything, and she bathed me. It was cool. We start making out, and she started kissing me and stuff, and she gave me some head. I was like oh snap, I'm in the game now. I already had experience with that so I was cool with that. So she was like "You're going to do me?" I was like, "What do you mean do you?" She was like "I gave you some head; you're going to give me some too." I was like, "Uh okay I don't know what to do." She was like "For real?" I was like, "Nah, I've never done that before." She was like "I'll teach you." I said okay. So she told me exactly what to do. I was like hmm and then I saw her reaction to the things she was telling me to do and so I kind of responded the way she responded. I was stimulated by what she was stimulated by. I kind of figured it out and she was like yes. She was like "We cool. We good." So she was all good and that was my first experience in oral sex at least giving it, and it's been downhill ever since.
> **Interviewer:** So you liked it?
> **Thaddeaus:** I did. I didn't mind it at all. I didn't think it was nasty. I didn't think it was gross because one she was clean and two I guess because she took the care and tenderness to—she didn't clown me, she didn't make me feel bad, and here she is exposed as well as me telling me what to do to make her feel good so it was a good experience.
> **Interviewer:** And then did you go back to the base and tell the boys you ate the pussy?
> **Thaddeaus:** I didn't tell them anything. They figured it out on their own because I had this big grin on my face because I got more than—that lead to actual intercourse.
> **Interviewer:** That same night?
> **Thaddeaus:** Yes. It was a good weekend.
> **Interviewer:** And did you have sex with her again?
> **Thaddeaus:** Several times.
> **Interviewer:** Would you have considered yourselves in a relationship?
> **Thaddeaus:** Yes and no. So one, she was a college girl. I knew she was doing whatever she wanted to do on the college campus and there was a time I'd spent the night over there, like I said, we had this extended on and off and some dude kept calling her, kept calling her, and I was like, "That's your other dude?" She was like, "Well used to be" so I kind of knew she did whatever she wanted to do when I wasn't there. I was like okay it's cool. I wasn't tripping. It was what it was. So, that's how that happened, so relationship . . . not really. I wouldn't have said oh that's my girl, that's D\_\_\_\_\_; that's what she was.

D_____ was a safe space for Thaddeaus. They were vulnerable together. She did not make him feel badly about his inexperience. Although eating pussy was not in his repertoire, a little push from his peers and a little care from D_____ contributed to his sexual growth. Like everyone except Tom, at first Thaddeaus and D_____ did not use condoms either. It was not until her other dude called that Thaddeaus realized it would be a good idea. Once Thaddeaus had confirmation of her other relationship and continued to see her, they entered into a "don't ask, don't tell" arrangement which is one of many manifestations of a FWB relationship.

## DaVonte

DaVonte's first sexual experience at 13 was at the behest of his 19-year-old brother.

> **DaVonte:** He's about to graduate or graduated from high school or whatever still living with us before he went to the Air Force. I've always been like an artist and a sensitive dude and we got into an argument about something and basically he was like you need to get out and go get some pussy, but he was yelling it, "You got to go get some pussy" like "Get out. Get the fuck out of here. You need some pussy." And I think maybe he got whiff that I was gay or I don't know what made him so mad but he kicked me out of the house that day and locked the door behind me and told me don't come back until I got some pussy. So I was in junior high at the time and I went to go get some pussy, and I went and I fucked this girl inside of her closet. I was attracted to her. That's why I say 10% straight because actually around 13 I started feeling kind of attracted to women but I honestly don't know if it's because I was supposed to be or because I was actually feeling it, but nonetheless, with her she was a good friend. She was somebody I found fun to be around, and safe and I knew I could experiment with her. I felt that way. I knew she was attracted to me and I knew that she accepted me for who I am. I know she would still to this day. And we were safe—it was a safe place. I could be myself with her, and I wanted to have sex with her.
> **Interviewer:** Were her parents home? This is what it sounds like not knowing the story: your brother kicked you out, told you to go get some pussy, you run up on this white girl's house, you have sex with her in the closet, and you go home.
> **DaVonte:** No, no, no we had a relationship. We were very, very close friends.
> **Interviewer:** So you just stopped by her house like you normally would?
> **DaVonte:** Yeah we kicked it. I would go over there every once in a while.
> **Interviewer:** But this time it was different. Did you have a conversation about it?
> **DaVonte:** We had talked about sex before. We were friends. We were very, very close kid friends. We had talked about sex a lot of times and even let her know that I was attracted—she knew that I was attracted to her and she was attracted to me; we just never crossed that line. I got the push I needed to go forward with it. I honestly don't think I ever would have went that far but I had to. I didn't have a choice, and I knew she would be the person that I could do it with because we were really friends. She wanted to too, but I don't know if we

would've crossed that line had I not been pushed to do it. Her dad worked like 16 hour days so I don't think he was—I know he wasn't there. He was never there when I visited. It was always just her and her brother.
**Interviewer:** Did you use a condom?
**DaVonte:** No.
**Interviewer:** At that age were you concerned about pregnancy or STIs?
**DaVonte:** No, not at all. I heard about stuff but as a kid you don't fucking think about it. I was 13; I was getting some pussy. That's what I was doing. I wasn't thinking about if it was going to be good. I wasn't thinking about making love. I wasn't thinking about being safe. I was thinking about getting some pussy because that's what I was told to do.
**Interviewer:** Did you enjoy it?
**DaVonte:** Yeah I did, I did.
**Interviewer:** Were you surprised that you enjoyed it?
**DaVonte:** I think I was because I got a little high from it. I was surprised that I had sex with a girl that I liked it, and I got a little high from it.

DaVonte said she enjoyed their sex as much as he did. They had sex several more times until racial tensions ended their friendship. DaVonte explained,

> We were friends for a long time but I think there was a lot of shit separating us too. It seems weird because when we were 13—what year was that? That was like 1993–4 something like that. Anyway, you wouldn't think that there was separate sides of the tracks but it still was especially in that area so we had a lot of stuff working against us to be friends anyway. We weren't able to continue being friends after a certain point because she was white and I was Black, we had different paths, just different things were getting in the way. But she was my homey; I wish I could see her now. She was the homey.

Perhaps, more than the others, DaVonte spoke incredibly affirmatively about his friend. Despite his brother's insensitive decree, his first sexual experience was emotionally (although not sexually) safe—a word he used three times. For DaVonte, his first sexual experience with a friend was not only safe, but comfortable, mutually accepting, and esteem building—themes that circulate throughout all of the aforementioned narratives.

## DISCUSSION

Mutual exploration, attraction, and peer pressure are universal reasons for sexual experimentation. In that sense, these boys' experiences are not unique. Variations in the boys' levels of familiarity with their friends are acknowledged in FWB research (Mongeau et al. 2013). Sexual partner choice driven by proximity, opportunity, and familiarity is also the norm (Bisson & Levine 2009). When the boys' chose a friend as their sexual partner because of trust, safety, and positive emotions, their rationales aligned with the advantages identified in FWB research with undergraduates (Bisson & Levine 2009). This data, however, differ from traditional FWB research in four unique ways. First, most FWB are for recurring recreational sex without commitment (Bisson & Levine 2009; Mongeau et al. 2013). Because we focused on initial intercourse, our boys' primary goal was sexual exploration. Commitment is not a concern, and recurring sex is an additional benefit, not a fundamental goal in the participant's stories.

Second, as mentioned previously, none of these boys received sexual education from their parents prior to their first sexual experience, although two of them received parental sexual messages. Richie remembered his father telling him when he was about five or six, "Boy, you stick your little peanut in everything you can." Frank's parents told him "to stay safe and mainly not to have sex" and that he "better not bring no kids up in here." DaVonte's quip, "It is no such things as the birds and the bees in the motherfuckinghood" is universal in this data set. Even the two boys who received messages from their parents about sex received no sexual education. As noted previously, the early age of Black male sexual debut makes sexual education necessary (Curry & Utley 2018).

Third, this is made even more complicated as several of the stories show that many of the young women were not only willing, but initiated sexual contact and intercourse by arranging times and meeting places alone for the purpose of sexual activity. Ott et al.'s (2012) study of adolescent boys first experience of sex noted that the "narratives from young men reveal that young women were also engaging in pre-planning by defining where and when the first sex would take place and making sure that parents were absent when intercourse happened. In most of our narratives, it was the female partner who initiated the sexual act through non-verbal and verbal cues" (p. 789). In sharp contrast to the idea of the sexually passive female who accepts or declines male sexual advances, the narratives of Black males' sexual experimentation shows the women and girls as active and agentic sexual beings who had expectations of the young Black boys with whom they engaged in sex.

Fourth, sexual peer pressure is unique in the Black community because it is both personal and social. All of the peer pressure examples sent young boys searching for sex without any sexual education or preparation. According to Fletcher et al. (2015), "perceiving higher levels of sexual experience and risk taking among one's peers is associated with greater sexual risk taking by Black youth" (p. 200). While these common pressure instances are personal—friends, military mates, and family—two types of social pressure must also be considered. On one hand, there is a social expectation that Black boy children are hypersexual beings. Because Black males are stereotyped as sexually experienced (and often insatiable), Black boys must figure out how to acquire that sexual sophistication. This data suggest that girl friends are a welcoming, positive, and safe space to begin the sexual exploration, sexual maturation, and the ethnic identity development process either in alignment with or contrary to the stereotype of Black males as hypersexual (predators). The esteem building done by an accepting girl friend helps these boys feel interpersonally valuable in a society that devalues them daily.

On the other hand, seeking out the convenience of a girl who is a close friend can help Black boys mediate the social pressures of racial discrimination perceived as threats to their masculinity. In their study of rural African American male adolescents, Kogan, Yu, Allen, Pocock, and Brody (2015) conclude "to the extent that racial discrimination posts a threat to a young man's sense of masculinity and status, sexual conquest may become an avenue for affirming his right to esteem and status" (p. 223). Although their study investigates boys with multiple sexual partners, their conclusion applies to an initial intercourse partner. This "esteem and status" acquisition is akin to the "little high" that DaVonte described when he affirmed his masculinity and his racial status by having sex with a white girl on the separate side of the track.

Absent abstinence and messages that sex should occur within the confines of a committed relationship, perhaps Black children, when left to their own devices, are disinclined to couple but inclined to choose safe sexual spaces. Future research must ask, how do Black children come to understand that positive sexual experiences can (and perhaps should) occur outside of normative coupled relationships? How might the first experience with a friend shape subsequent sexual relationships? Does a first experience with a friend increase the acceptance of non-monogamous relationships? What are the positive implications of sex not just outside of marriage but also outside of a recognized coupled relationship that still provides sexual comfort and esteem building? Perhaps, the pathology data about unmarried Black parents overlooks the mutual acceptance and personal growth that can still be found in non-coupled Black co-parents.

Many Black boys do not get to choose their first sexual partners. Previous findings have shown that young Black boys are especially vulnerable to sexual violation by older women and girls. Hernandez, Lodico, and DiClemente (1993) have noted that Black males are especially vulnerable to physical and sexual child abuse. The exploratory study conducted by Curry and Utley (2018) also found that both the numbers of Black boys who are sexually violated by adults is woefully underreported and "adult sexual violations of Black male children may not always be seen as sexual violations by young boys because no one is instructing them about sex or male sexual victimization" (p.232). For boys who are urged to have group sex by and with older men as a rite of passage, are made to penetrate, are sexually coerced and violated by women babysitters, or have their choice revoked by other adults that they trusted, choosing a friend who they actually can trust is indeed a revolutionary act of sexual agency for Black boys who are forced to live with stereotypes about their sexuality or forced into having sex against their will.

While instructive in helping to explore how FWB relationships are unique for Black boys' first sexual experiences, the study has its limitations. It only considers the boys' perspective which includes no FWB disadvantages (Bisson & Levine 2009; Williams & Adams 2013). Perhaps, the girls would have considered themselves in relationships or would have wanted to be in relationships. The girls are invisible here to the point of being nameless. We have no evidence of their motivations or agency. Second, the sample is restricted to first heterosexual experiences. Third, this is an incredibly small sample accidentally discovered within larger data asking completely different questions. Future research must not only speak to male and female (preferably both same and opposite-sex sexual partners), but should be designed specifically around first sexual experiences and perhaps pay specific attention to class and geography while comparing if and how experiences change over time.

While we conclude that girl friends may be emotionally safe when it comes to learning about sex, with the exception of Tom, all of the experiences were sexually unsafe. DaVonte said, "I wasn't thinking about being safe. I was thinking about getting some pussy because that's what I was told to do." According to Mathews (2013), "Individuals who are friends may be less likely to use condoms because of a lack of communication regarding the specifics of the sexual negotiation and because there is the perception of trust" (p.13). Tom and his ex-girlfriend were likely the exception because their former status as boyfriend and girlfriend necessitated relational conversations about pregnancy that are less likely to occur between friends (Manning, Longmore, & Giordano 2000). More research should investigate how sexual health ignorance, the absence of sexual communication, and the perception of trust impact condom use for initial intercourse among friends. If DaVonte's reflection is applicable to not only a majority of these narratives, but also to a majority of Black adolescent sexual experiences, then more research must be done about how to construct applicable sexual education programs for the hood.

## CONCLUSION

Our research demonstrates that Black males are reflective and create positive conceptualizations of intimacy through friendship and sexual intercourse. Unlike current Black masculinity literature that often denies the sexual vulnerability and reflexivity of Black males in the United States, our research expands upon the foundational themes of Black male studies by introducing theories about Black men and boys informed by empirically verified claims about their social lives, their actual behaviors, and their worldview (Curry 2017, 2018, 2019). In this sense, Black males are adaptive social and sexual beings. Stereotypes concerning the violence of Black males often extend into how various aspects of their lives interpreted within the literature on Black boys. The stereotype that Black males are sexually aggressive often dictates how scholars write about the socialization of young Black boys into rape culture and misogyny. Some Black feminist and social scientists have both perpetuated the idea that young, urban Black males define their masculinity through the rape of women, violence, or sexual promiscuity (hooks 1990; Lewis 2007). The presumption that female objectification is part of Black male socialization, without any research into the actual socialization forces at play in the lives of young Black boys, preemptively categorizes Black male sexual development as pathological and exploitative. The inability to recognize Black male sexual vulnerability on the one hand which includes questions of sexual trauma and statutory rape (Curry & Utley 2018), and the anxiety and pensiveness Black boys have regarding their first sexual intercourse on the other, produces a rigid deviant subject—the always already rapist—in gender theory. As the narratives of these Black men show, Black boys think about and actively contemplate how they imagine their first intercourse. In sharp contrast to contemporary theories concerning Black male sexuality, Black boys demonstrate an investment into their sexual innocence and first experience beyond eliminating the stigma of virginity. This evidence shows that previous works by Black feminists (hooks 1990, 2004; Garfield 2010) linking manhood to sexual conquest and domination need to be questioned and reconsidered using the phenomenological weight Black males attach to their sexual debut.

These men retrospectively describe the girls and their first sexual experiences extremely positively. Within their narratives are expressions of sexual comfort, safety, mutual acceptance, personal growth, and esteem building. Although we cannot make any definitive arguments from this small sample of Black boy's first intercourse experiences, we can highlight how these surprise preliminary findings point to the need for nuanced research questions for scholars of race, early sexual development, FWB, and possibly non-monogamy. The racist underpinnings of Black sexuality pathology literature must no longer narrow the scope of questions scholars ask about early Black sexual development.

Previous literature on Black masculinity has failed to answer questions about Black male sexuality with empirical evidence or any ethnographic explorations into Black boys' sexual choices. Because Black male sexuality is almost exclusively interpreted through hypermasculinity tropes, the literature investigating the sexual vulnerability of Black men and boys (Curry 2017, 2019), and the choices they make regarding their sexual debut is not only woefully behind the research on other groups, but practically nonexistent. Hypermasculinity, hypersexuality, and other paradigms insisting that Black males are driven toward their first sexual intercourse to compensate for their lack of masculinity and powerlessness is far too narrow and limiting of a perspective to discuss how Black males actually participate in their first sexual experience. The stories of these Black men recollecting about their youth show indecisiveness, naivety, and nervousness. Contrary to the articulation of Black boys as being obsessed with sex and dedicated to the objectification of women and girls, these narratives show hesitancy, fantasy, and curiosity during their first sexual experiences. Like other sexually inexperienced groups, Black boys had fond memories of their first sexual partners. They were embarrassed by their inexperience and used friendship to comfort their nervousness and establish safety during their sexual debut. In short, conversations concerning Black males must be informed by an actual knowledge of Black males gained from the experiences of Black men and boys as they express them.

Black boys have historically been thought of as beasts driven toward sex by primal urges. The trope of Black males as misogynists who aim to harm women and girls through sex and violence is rarely interrupted by actual investigations that provide context and evidence of how Black males think about their own actions and intimate events in their own lives. For young Black boys the choice to have sex with a friend offers a freedom to positively construct aspects of their lives that remain negated by anti-Black misandry (Curry 2018; Staples 1978), and academic theory alike (Curry 2017). Gender theories that continue to frame Black males as pathological should be challenged and reoriented based on the ever-expanding knowledge scholars gain from the careful and attentive studies of Black men and boys. Intersectional theories overlooking the sexual vulnerability of Black males erroneously suggest Black males experience privilege rather than precarity over their life course (Johnson 2018; Oluwayomi 2020). The findings of this study emphasize the need to heavily scrutinize, if not outright reject, theories about Black males that do not have some basis in their lived experience or the specific sociocultural location they occupy. Given the salience of long disproven myths viewing Black males as sexual predators, it is necessary to view any theories of Black masculinity (be they feminist or otherwise) that continue historical sexual stereotypes against Black males without proper cultural contextualization and experiential inquiry with moral indignation, if not outright condemnation.

## NOTE

1. Pseudonyms were used to protect the identity of the interviewees.

# REFERENCES

Afifi, W., & Faulkner, S. L. (2000). On being 'just friend': The frequency and impact of sexual activity in cross sex friendships. *Journal of Social and Personal Relationships, 17*, 205–22.
Amir, M. (1971). *Patterns in forcible rape.* Chicago: University of Chicago Press.
Bisson, M., & Levine, T. R. (2009). Negotiating a friends with benefits relationship. *Archives of Sexual Behavior, 38*, 66–73.
Brownmiller, S. (1975). *Against our will: Men, women, and rape.* New York: Fawcett Columbine.
Cavazos-Rehg, P., Krauss, M. J., Spitznagel, E. L., & et al. (2009). Age of sexual debut among U.S. adolescents. *Contraception, 80*, 158–62.
Crosby, R., Geter, A., Ricks, J., Jones, J., & Salazar, L. F. (2015). Developmental investigation of age at sexual debut and subsequent sexual risk behaviours: A study of high-risk young Black males. *Sexual Health, 12*, 390–96.
Curry, T. J. (2017). *The man-not: Race, class, genre and the dilemmas of Black manhood.* Philadelphia: Temple University Press.
Curry, T. J. (2018). Killing boogeymen: Phallicism and the misandric mischaracterizations of Black males in theory. *Res Philosophica, 95*(2), 235–72.
Curry, T. J. (2019). Expendables for whom: Terry Crews and the erasure of Black male victims of sexual assault and rape. *Women Studies in Communication, 42*(3), 287–307.
Curry, T. J., & Utley, E. A. (2018). She touched me: Five snapshots of adult sexual. *Kennedy Institute of Ethics Journal, 28*(2), 205–41.
Curtis, L. A. (1975). *Violence, race, and culture.* MN: Lexington Books.
Dixon, P. (2009). Marriage among African Americans: What does the research reveal? *Journal of African American Studies*, 29–46.
Fletcher, K., Ward, L. M., Thomas, K., Foust, M., Levin, D., & Trinh, S. (2015). Will it help? Identifying socialization discourses that promote sexual risk and sexual health among African American youth. *Journal of Sex Research, 52*(2), 199–212.
Furman, W., & Shaffer, L. (2011). Romantic partners, friends, friends with benefits, and casual acquaintances as sexual partners. *Journal of Sex Research, 48*(6), 554–64.
Garfield, G. (2010). *Through our eyes: African American men's experiences of race, gender, and violence.* New Brunswick, NJ: Rutgers University Press.
Giordano, P. C., Longmore, M., & Manning, W. D. (2006). Gender and the meanings of adolescent romantic relationships: A focus on boys. *American Sociological Review, 71*, 260–87.
Harper, G. W., Gannon, Watson, C., Catania, J. & Dolcini, S. G. (2004). The role of close friends in African American adolescents' dating and sexual behavior. *The Journal of Sex Research, 41*(4): 351–62.
Hernandez, J., Lodico, M., & DiClemente, R. (1993). The effects of child abuse and race on risk taking in male adolescents. *Journal of the National Medical Association, 85*, 593–97.
hooks, b. (1990). *Yearning: Race, gender and cultural politics.* Boston: South End Press.
hooks, b. (2004). *We real cool: Black men and masculinity.* New York: Routledge.
Howard, W. L. (1903). The Negro as a distinct ethnic factor in civilization. *Medicine, 9*, 423–26.
Johnson, T. (2018). Challenging the myth of Black male privilege. *Spectrum: A Journal on Black Men, 6*(2), 21–42.
Kardiner, A., & Ovesey, L. (1951). *The mark of oppression.* Mansfield Center: Martino Publishing.
Kogan, K., Yu, T., Allen, K., Pocock, A. M., & Brody, G. H. (2015). Pathways from racial discrimination to multiple sexual partners among male African American adolescents. *Psychology of Men and Masculinity, 16*(2), 218–28.
Landor, A., & Simons, L. G. (2019). Correlates and predictors of virginity among heterosexual African American young adults. *Sexuality and Culture*, 943–61.
Leemiller, J., VanderDrift, L., & Kelly, J. (2011). Sex differences in approaching friends with benefits relationships. *The Journal of Sex Research*, 275–84.

Lewis, L. J. (2007). Contesting the dangerous sexuality of Black male youth. In G. Herdt, & C. Howe, *21st Century Sexualities: Contemporary Issues in Health, Education, and Rights* (pp. 24–28). New York: Routledge.
Manning, W., Giordano, P. C., & Longmore, M. A. (2006). Hooking up: The relationship contexts of "nonrelationship" sex. *Journal of Adolescent Research, 21*(5), 459–83.
Manning, W., Longmore, M. A., & Giordano, P. C. (2000). The relationship context of contraceptive use. *Family Planning Perspectives, 32*(3), 104–10.
Mathews, J. (2013). *Condom use and trust differences by relationship type: Friends with benefits, commited relationships, and casual sex*. Minneapolis: Walden University.
McGuire, H., & Lydston, G. F. (1893). *Sexual crimes among the southern Negroes*. Louisville, KY: Renz and Henry.
Mongeau, P. A., Knight, K., Williams J., Eden J., & Shaw, C. (2013). Identifying and explicating variation among friends with benefits relationships. *Journal of Sex Research, 50*(1): 37–47.
Oluwayomi, A. (2020). The man-not and the inapplicability of intersectionality to the dilemmas of Black manhood. *Journal of Men's Studies, 28*(2), 183–205.
Ott, M., Ghani, N., McKenzie, F., Rosenberger, J., & Bell, D. (2012). Adolescent boys' experiences of first sex. *Culture, Health & Sexuality: An International Journal for Research, Intervention and Care, 14*(7), 781–93.
Packer, M. (2011). *The science of qualitative research*. Cambridge: Cambridge University Press.
Pass, M., Benoit, E., & Dunlop, E. (2014). "I just be myself": Contradicting hyper masculine and hyper sexual stereotypes among low-income Black men in New York City. In B. C. Slatton, & K. Spates, *Hyper-Sexual, Hyper-Masculine? Gender, race, and sexuality in the identities of contemporary Black men* (pp. 165–81). Burlington, VT: Ashgate.
Reed, S. J., Bangi, A., Sheon, N., Harper, G., Catania, J., Richards, K., . . . Boyer, C. (2012). Influences on sexual partnering among African American adolescents with concurrent sexual relationships. *Research in Human Development*, 78–101.
Staples, R. (1978). Masculinity and race: The dual dilemma of Black men. *Journal of Social Issues, 34*(1), 169–83.
Staples, R. (1982). *Black masculinity: The Black male's role in American society*. San Francisco: Black Scholar Press.
Staples, R. (2006). *Exploring Black sexuality*. Lanham, MD: Roman & Littlefield Publishers.
Stein, M. (2015). *Measuring manhood: Race and the science of masculinity, 1830–1934*. Minneapolis: University of Minnesota Press.
Thorne, S. (2008). *Interpretive description*. Walnut Creek, MD: Left Coast Press.
Thorne, S., Kirkham, S. R., & O'Flynn-Magee, K. (2004). The analytic challenge in interpretive description. *International Journal of Qualitative Methods, 3*(1), 1–11.
Upchurch, D., Levy-Storms, L., Sucoff, C., & Aneshensel, C. (1998). Gender and ethnic differences in the timing of first sexual intercourse. *Family Planning Perspectives*, 121–27.
Wentland, J., & Reissing, E. (2014). Casual sexual relationships: Identifying definitions for one night stands, booty calls, fuck buddies, and friends with benefits. *The Canadian Journal of Human Sexuality, 23*(3), 167–77.
Williams, J. E., & Holmes, K. A. (1981). *The second assault: Rape and public attitudes*. New York: Praeger.
Williams, L., & Adams, H. L. (2013). Friends with benefits or "friends" with deficits? The meaning and contexts of uncommitted sexual relationships among Mexican American and European American adolescents. *Children and Youth Services Review, 35*, 1110–17.
Wolfgang, M., & Ferracuti, F. (1967). *The subculture of violence: towards an integrated theory in criminology*. London: Tavistock Publications.

*Chapter Three*

# Reverse Interest Convergence, Kaepernick, and Nike

*An Educational Lobbyist Playbook for Equitable Funding by Investment in Urban Public Education*

Aaron J. Griffen and Derrick Robinson

Who gets what in educational resources and equity? More specifically, how can we address the educational debt that is owed to Black and Brown children in urban public schools? This chapter reveals how race and economics inform the non-investability of public education and how a national movement of fortune 500 companies can reverse this frame of thinking. We build upon a previous study where reverse interest convergence is introduced as a strategy to impact and influence education for Black and Brown children academically, socially, and economically (Griffen, 2017). Reverse interest convergence occurs when the marginalized group, knowing the true economic interest and intent of the group in economic power, purposely feeds into the interests of that group or entity in order to further the marginalized groups agenda. Recommendations include how a few pairs of Nikes (i.e., other large corporations such as Under Armor, Adidas, Walmart, and Microsoft), for example, could bring new interests in the investability of urban public education.

If power and privilege cared about the national deficit, they would have resolved it by now. They also would invest more in the major interests of most U.S. citizens: health care, education, and a livable wage. Here, we respond to a recent Edbuild report that suggested that non-White school districts receive on average $23 billion less per year than White school districts, despite serving comparable students. If this is true, how can education be the great equalizer?

## WHY URBAN PUBLIC EDUCATION IS NOT INVESTIBLE

Urban public education generally does not carry an immediate economic return. Certainly, an educated body will enter the workforce, bringing skills to meet various demands. However, in the short term, it is not investible. Furthermore, urban public education is predominately Black and Brown, and high poverty. Conversely, the current legislative body, at the state and national level, is largely White and male.

The United States pretends to be a democracy, but operates like a patriarchal oligarchy. Ebenezer Falcon summarized it best when he declared there is no such thing as a democracy; every man ultimately will vote in his own best interest (Johnson, 1998). In terms of the public interest, educational lobbyists have found it difficult to pry funding for early childhood, Head Start, after-school programming, and mental health programs. It has become increasingly more difficult to increase pay for teachers.

Strikes in Oklahoma, Los Angeles, and Denver reflect problematic wages for educators. Teachers cannot afford rent in California and New York. Others purchase supplies out of their own pockets. This is especially tough on teachers and students in urban centers. It is easy to say that all lives matter until someone proposes legislation that would greatly benefit students in need.

One cannot simply approach decision makers with proposals that benefit only Black and Brown children (Griffen, 2017). For example, when the Powell Amendment was initially attached to the National Defense and Education Act (NDEA) of 1958, William Clayton Powell argued that federal funding should not be made available to segregated school districts. At the time, Clayton faced three main arguments against racial desegregation. First, some argued that society would not accept desegregation and violence would result. Second, some said that integration would cause White students to leave their schools, making desegregation much more difficult. Third, they argued that segregation would make life more difficult for African Americans students (Watras, 2008).

After much deliberation, the Powell Amendment was added to a 1956 federal funding bill. It failed. Eventually, the bill came to include assurances that integration would not be mandated to receive funding. Discriminatory language was excluded from the bill.

## AMERICA OWES AN EDUCATION DEBT

As described by Ladson-Billings (2006), the education debt is comprised of historical, racial, systemic, and sociopolitical components. The education debt is not to be confused with an education deficit. The education deficit view speaks to the politically and socially constructed achievement gap, and purports that Black and Brown children are less capable than their White peers. According to Toldson (2019), indicators of academic achievement are meaningless without a relationship to positive life outcomes.

## BRIBERY AND AFFIRMATIVE ACTION

Despite efforts to address the separate but equal education debt, the nation's economic motivation has been reintroduced. The inequitable truth is evidenced by fifty White and wealthy parents, coaches, entertainers, and executives who were arrested for defrauding the college admission process. To be clear, they did not merely attempt to defraud the system, they were entirely successful to the tune of $25 million for their children to receive enrollment into prestigious universities including Wake Forest, Stanford, Yale, and the University of Texas (Schuman et al. 2019). Ironically, the University of Texas and the University of California had been the site of affirmative action lawsuits where White students argued that their non-admittance resulted from the preferential admission of less deserving non-White students.

Critics of anti-affirmative action called for the same outrage. "I want the people who were up in arms about affirmative action to keep that same energy for rich people who pay to get their kids into Ivy League schools. These are the people who are stealing your kid's spot" (JenetAllDay, 2019). For Black and Brown children, meritocracy does not matter. Despite the hard work, one cannot escape the influence of race, money, and privilege. As such, we question the legitimacy of university endowments, legacy enrollments, and large donations.

## CRITICAL RACE THEORY IN EDUCATION

Derrick Bell and Alan Freeman introduced critical race theory (CRT) as an extension of critical legal studies. Racism is an integral, permanent, and indestructible component of society. CRT challenged racial oppression in law, employment, and education. CRT provided a lens to analyze how educators assume normative standards of Whiteness in the classroom, and how these values, attitudes, and behaviors impact the development and academic achievement of African American students.

Historically, U.S. education has included the religious indoctrination of indigenous people, the maintenance of a status quo between elite Whites and poor Whites, and racial division through literacy to exclude Black people. This chapter looks at the work of African American educational lobbyists on race in education (Griffen, 2015, 2017), including how CRT reveals how race matters when lobbying for the interests of Black and Brown children. We focus on three central propositions for CRT in education:

1. Race is a significant factor in determining inequity in the United States.
2. Society is based on property rights.
3. The intersection of race and property create an analytic tool through which we can understand educational inequities. (Ladson-Billings & Tate, 1995)

CRT's interest convergence reveals how *Brown v. Board of Education* benefitted Whites and staggered people of color. It desegregated schools and empowered White women who had endured discriminatory hiring practices based on gender. Some argued that Whites perceived it profitable or cost-free to serve, hire, admit, or otherwise deal with Blacks on a nondiscriminatory basis. If they had feared a loss, inconvenience, or disruption then discriminatory conduct would have followed (Bell, 1992). This was evident when Gucci and Prada promoted clothing featuring Black face. They communicated a disregard for the Black dollar. There is no expectation to become a Nike for urban communities.

Most urban schools are largely non-White. Contrarily, lobbying firms are largely White. This is where the property rights become a focus of CRT, and why urban education could benefit from a few pairs of Nikes. In schools lacking equitable funding, the intellectual property deficits result in fewer gateway courses, such as Advanced Placement, which enhance opportunities for students to go to college (Griffen, 2015).

## INTEREST CONVERGENCE AND COLIN KAEPERNICK

Interest convergence included Arizona declaring Martin Luther King Day as a strategy to maintain the Super Bowl and other major sporting events. Additionally, North Carolina enacted a gender-neutral bathroom law to attract revenue associated with the NCAA and other major sporting events. During the Montgomery Bus Boycott, African Americans protested the city's transit services for the purpose of civil rights, whereas the city succumbed to financial loss. Interest convergence is grounded in economics. The compromise occurs when the group in power acts to regain or increase profits. North Carolina stood to lose $3.76 billion dollars as a result of barring gender neutral bathrooms. Phoenix lost an estimated $200 to $250 million when the 1993 Super Bowl moved to California.

When Nike partnered with Colin Kaepernick to produce the "Stand for Something" campaign, their economic interests combined with his social justice interests. Some called it a ploy to maximize off Kaepernick's popularity. Others saw it as a historic day where a corporate giant stood in support of a marginalized group. The tangible reality is that the interest convergence increased Nike's revenue. Also, the "Stand for Something" campaign took root in African American communities nationwide. Despite the controversy surrounding Kaepernick's kneeling, Nike's stock recovered from a short dip and increased by billions of dollars.

## REVERSE INTEREST CONVERGENCE

Reverse interest convergence may be a way to mobilize interests for Black and Brown children. This occurs when the marginalized group accepts the proposition of the dominant group, in order to benefit the marginalized group. For example, Kaepernick could have accepted a contract in the Canadian football league, or stopped his protest all together to gain an NFL contract. Instead, he chose to sustain his platform.

## THREE TENETS OF REVERSE INTEREST CONVERGENCE

Here, reverse interest convergence is comprised of three tenets. First, educational lobbyists should intentionally advocate for African American and Latino school children. This sentiment may reflect the following attitude:

> When you see me coming, you know a Black or Brown child has been hurt. I am community focused and student driven. For that reason, I'm crying foul if a policy or rule has an adverse impact on students of color; no matter the risk.

This is similar to Kaepernick's sentiment "Believe in something even if it costs you everything." Some say it cost him nothing, but nothing is a relative term. For Kaepernick, it included being banned from the National Football League (NFL), which is why he received a settlement.

Second, educational lobbyists should predesign outcomes for the marginalized group. For example, include a strategically packaged deal for the marginalized group, within the larger package for the privileged group:

> In order to get an audience, package your issue within an issue that will affect all kids. If an issue that affects the African American community is packaged as an issue that affects all kids (or at least kids that are disadvantaged), it will increase the chances that policymakers will view the issue as a priority. (Griffen, 2015, 2017)

The goal here is to broker a deal to benefit the dominant group, while simultaneously ensuring that Black and Brown interests are served. This requires strategy on the part of urban public education systems, concerning who they accept as their new Nike.

Third, educational lobbyists should accept some dominant assumptions in order to gain an advantage. This might include criticism. Kaepernick did this well. He was called a race baiter. Critics contended that he was all about money. They said Black lives did not matter to Kaepernick. Furthermore, when reports surfaced about Nike's million-dollar donation to the Republican Party, critics asserted that Kaepernick had been used as a pawn.

Kaepernick, may have known that he was being used. He may have expected alienation from multiple groups, thus deciding to play his part in the ordeal by taking the money offered by Nike. The strategy is described by "Joy," an African American educational lobbyist. She used the perceptions to her advantage. As a triple asset she has knowingly accepted assumptions about race, age and gender to gain advantage, recognizing that she is sometimes called upon to be a token representative of diversity:

> If you want me for my expertise, I can talk to anybody. And, that's not related to or what color they are, what race they are. Sometimes that may be a benefit, and that's gonna cost you a little bit of extra because I may have some insight that you don't know. (Griffen, 2017)

In another sense, reverse interest convergence may be viewed as hegemonic, self-fulfilling prophecy. Participating in one's own oppression may increase the possibilities for fear and failure. However, well developed tactics may increase possibilities to advantage the marginalized group.

## COLIN KAEPERNICK AND REVERSE INTEREST CONVERGENCE

Kaepernick's protest became an international message of "sacrifice even if it means losing everything." On the other hand, converging with Nike's "Stand for Something" campaign afforded him a million dollar contract.

The packaging approach may benefit urban public educational interests and ultimately improve the funding inequity and the education debt (Ladson-Billings, 2004). To solicit support from corporate America, educational lobbyists need to enact purposive lobbying centered on the greater good (Griffen, 2015). Lobbyists need to explain the necessity for partnerships with corporate America.

To ensure the convergence benefits urban educational interests, the end must justify the means (in this case, the goal is equitable funding). Additional resources may include an increase in experienced teachers and technology. Budgets must include salaries to recruit and retain experienced teachers of color because they have a profound impact on all students (Thomas, 2018). In addition, the budget should provide greater benefits such as loan forgiveness, stipends, and tuition assistance to earn higher degrees. Graduate degrees should be encouraged and compensated. In urban areas like Chicago, teachers of color are promoted 3.5 years later than their White peers (Marchitello, 2018). Clear purpose and measurable outcomes are necessary to achieve reverse interest convergence. The goal will benefit all groups.

## EDUCATION NEEDS A FEW PAIRS OF NIKES

To address the aforementioned gaps, Texas, via Senate Bill 3, approved a $5,000 salary increase for teachers. The increase passed on the heels of teacher strikes in Denver and Oklahoma. In Colorado, Senate Bill 59 encouraged automatic enrollment in advanced courses if students demonstrate proficiency in the material or preceding course, whether measured by state tests or another metric determined by the school (Meltzer, 2019). There appeared to be public support for a living wage, but the action was defeated on a Colorado ballot that would have provided $1,600,000,000 and revised funding relating to preschool through high school public education. Consequently, resources were located and redistributed by cutting 150 administrative positions. One wonders how other states will handle the funding deficits in high poverty schools serving Black and Brown students.

## IMPLICATIONS FOR NIKES IN EDUCATION

When asked if she would hold schools accountable for discriminating against students with special needs, LGBTQ students, or students of color, Secretary of Education Betsy Devos indicated that schools should have a right to educate who they wish to educate. Devos has not actively supported all educators and the children they serve. As a result, the education platform is in need of a hero. The education platform needs a corporate body to invest in marginalized groups.

Investment should focus entirely on the educational capacity of persons impacted by centuries of redline policies, White flight, and economic deprivation. The goal is equity. When a major corporation earmarks funds for a specific community, the community's allies will support that corporation, thus creating interest convergence. In this case, Nike knew that Kaepernick was investible because of his ties to the Black community—the largest purchaser of the Nike brand. Conversely, Nike has allegedly donated millions of dollars to conservative groups who may or may not have supported Kaepernick.

## CONTEXTUALIZING NIKE AND THE BLACK COMMUNITY

To appreciate reverse interest convergence, we must understand the complex relationship between Nike and the Black community. Below we conceptualize Nike's history, and its involvement in the Black community. We also explore how corporate entities view Black communities.

With annual revenue over $36 billion, Nike positioned itself as a growth company built on talent and brand promotion (Nike, 2018a). The investor relations section of the Nike website is laden with photographs of Black and Brown athletes, including Black female athletes ranging from Serena Williams to Simone Biles. This study is based on nine months of viewing the Nike Corporation through two distinct lenses: (a) The Kaepernick effect, and (b) cause-related marketing, CRM.

The Kaepernick Effect: On September 4, 2018, Nike debuted the "Stand for Something" campaign featuring prominent athletes who self-identify as Black, female, disabled, LBGTQ, and youth. The advertisement was narrated by Colin Kaepernick. Amid controversy and criticism from the president of the United States, financial indicators revealed that Nike stock shares opened that day at 79.39, rose as high as 80.97, and closed at 79.60 (Yahoo Finance, n.d.). By September 11, Yahoo Finance reported that Nike shares closed at 83.63. For perspective, one year earlier shares closed at 53.01 and 53.03. Further, from September 3 to September 6, online product orders rose 27 percent, as opposed to a 2 percent fall experienced in the same time period in 2017 (Whitten, 2018, September 7).

On September 20, 2018, Harvard University selected Kaepernick to receive the W. E. B. Du Bois award presented by the Hutchins Center for African and African American Research (Bogage, 2018, September 20). On the same day, Nike stock shares opened at 85.09, rose to a high of 85.87, and closed at 85.37. On September 21, Nike shares opened at 86.00 and closed at 85.55 (Yahoo Finance, n.d.). While these may appear as small bumps in financial impact, Nike did particularly well in the quarter. According to the Nike investor relations FY2019 Q2 report covering September 1 to November 30, 2018, revenues and net income were up 10 percent, while earnings per share were up 15 percent from FY2018 Q2 (Nike, 2018a).

Furthermore, by February 15, 2019, Kaepernick and teammate Eric Reed reached a settlement with the NFL (Mangan, February 15). The announcement was tweeted from Kaepernick's attorney Mark Geragos at 1:59 p.m. Nike shares rose from 85.12 at 1:45 p.m., to 85.28 at 2:00 p.m., and closed at 85.38. According to Nike investor relations FY2019 Q3 report covering December 1 to February 28, 2019, revenues increased 7 percent, net income from −$921 billion to $1.1 billion, while earnings per share rose from −.57 to .70 per share from the FY2018 Q3, a year prior (Nike, 2019). These figures indicate that Nike's alignment with Kaepernick did not hurt corporation or investor earnings.

Cause-Related Marketing: Major corporations often engage in social causes. Framed as cause-related marketing (CRM), corporations make targeted attempts to generate resources for pro-social concerns (Berglind & Nakata, 2005; Lucke & Heinze, 2015). Research indicates an upward trend in CRM to foster pro-social goodwill and increase a corporation's bottom line and competitive position (Berglind & Nakata, 2005). Lucke and Heinze (2015) indicate that social issues are selected with little to no consumer input, or consideration for individual preferences. This suggests two realities: (a) corporations are not bound by their target audience, and (b) corporations are not beholden to national mood or trends.

A cursory review of the corporate website for Nike illustrated a concerted effort toward sustainability as its social cause. The Nike Sustainability Report Executive Summary indicated that in FY2016, Nike promoted sustainability worldwide (Nike, 2018b). Released on March 14, 2018, the Sustainable Business Report revealed efforts in material efficiency, clean water, waste conservation, and energy emissions (Nike, 2018b). Moreover, the report highlighted more than $54 million in donations to support children's health organizations such as Marathon Kids. Noticeably absent is the water crisis in Flint, Michigan, despite Nike's stated commitment to "cost-effective water recycling" (Nike, 2018b, p. 1).

Moreover, the report barely mentioned investment in education, except for training over 1,100 employees in unconscious bias awareness. This is particularly important when considering the level of brand loyalty that Nike has enjoyed with the Black community. Lyons and Jackson (2011) note that in 2007 Nike spent nearly $3 billion on Black celebrity endorsements and sponsorships, to maintain brand awareness with Black consumers. However, when it comes to CRM, the Black community receives no direct reciprocity to their social causes. As supported by Lucke and Heinze (2015), this decision indicates a disconnect from consumer and individual causes. Moreover, this recognition signals an opportunity for Black educational and community lobbyists.

## CONTEXTUALIZING BLACK CONSUMERISM

As we consider the potential of reverse interest convergence and the relationship to Nike, it is important to discuss Black consumerism. Below we provide the social context of the Black community to identify who drives consumption. We also frame different levels of consumption in connection to corporations such as Nike.

Who are Black consumers? According to the 2013 Nielsen report, Resilient, Receptive, and Relevant: The African-American Consumer, Black consumers include young mainstream influencers (Whiting, Campbell, & Pearson-McNeil, 2013). The report suggested that 73 percent of Whites and 67 percent of Hispanics recognized the Black community as drivers of mainstream culture. This report also revealed that 53 percent of Black consumers were under the age of 35, and 54 percent of Black consumers were female. Black women comprised 29 percent as head of household, 43 percent of annual spending, with 23 percent annual incomes over $50,000. As for 2013 revenue generation, 31 million African Americans were over the age of 16; 63 percent were in the labor force, and 52 percent of the labor force were women. Black women continue to be the majority in Black business ownership.

In 2017, the top 3 consumer products purchased in Black communities included ethnic hair and beauty aids at $54.4 million; women's fragrances at $152 million; and feminine hygiene products at $54.1 million (Neilson Insights, 2018). While Black households made eight more frequent shopping trips than the average consumer household, they made fewer trips to "grocery stores (3 trips less), warehouse clubs (3 trips less), and mass merchandisers (2 trips less)" (Whiting et al., 2013, p. 9). Black households included a recognizable younger population. Blacks and other people of color are considerable consumers of vegetables and grains at 50.18 percent, baby food at 42.76 percent, personal soap and bath needs at 41.64 percent, fresheners and deodorizers at 38.29 percent, and shelf-stable juices and drinks at 37.51 percent (Whiting et al., 2013; Neilson Insights, 2018).

Black consumers are high in status materialism and brand awareness (Lyons & Jackson, 2011; Mazzocco, Rucker, Galinsky, & Anderson, 2012; Podoshen, Andrzejewski, & Hunt, 2014). According to the literature and data, there is tremendous potential for corporations to enact cause-related marketing to a brand loyal community. Given Nike's history as an endorser of Black celebrity and athleticism, it is worthwhile for Nike to invest in the sustainability of the Black community.

Levels of Consumerism: Consumerism comprises two basic categories: (a) general consumption, and (b) conspicuous/vicarious consumption. In general consumption, Black communities devote considerable expenditures to household maintenance. There is particular devotion toward self-care, and any perceived overspending on personal household goods may be attributed to an overemphasis on brand loyalty (Lyons & Jackson, 2011; Neilson Insights, 2018; Podoshen, Andrzejewski, & Hunt, 2014; Whiting et al., 2013).

Conspicuous/vicarious consumption refers to items that connote the acquisition or appearance of higher status (Mazzocco et al., 2012). Arguably, given the historical legacy of social, political, and economic oppression, Black consumers have been late entrants into the world of consumption and the status gained or felt as a result of vicarious consumption. In a society that promotes material acquisition as a measure of success, Black participants may use high-status products as a means of identifying/promoting importance. Podoshen et al. (2014) suggested that conspicuous consumption associates materialism with a sense of personal growth and fulfillment. This is not to paint Black communities as foolish consumers. Rather, it is to say that Black communities are loyal consumers. The problem is when loyalty is one-sided and unrequited. It is time for Nike and other corporations to invest in the educational and social needs of their dedicated consumers.

## RECOMMENDATIONS

Some people argue against discriminatory spending and funding by corporations. Other people argue against wealthy school districts sharing property tax base revenue with communities in need. As such, we offer four recommendations. First, we recommend investment and expectation at both ends of the spectrum. Convergence requires corporations to give back to communities. Investment requires communities to meet standards which could include, but are not limited to, improved graduation rates, increased advanced placement and concurrent enrollment options, and before/after school care for teen parents.

In 2017, higher levels of education equated to higher rates of employment. For example, for a bachelor's degree or higher, the employment rate was 86 percent. For an associate's degree, the employment rate was 80 percent. For persons with a high school diploma, the employment rate was 72 percent (NCES, 2018). The data suggests that graduation, and access to college and certification via technology and health, contribute to the well-being of society.

Second, we recommend that educational lobbyists negotiate predesigned outcomes for marginalized groups, based on the principals of reverse interest convergence. The goal is to converge the economic and social mobility of marginalized communities, with the economic interests of corporate sponsors. These corporations will profit, communicate good will, and benefit from tax qualifications. The convergence will serve their economic interests. Moreover, corporate investment does not negate or replace additional federal funding necessary to maintain effective education in Black and urban communities.

Third, we recommend advocating specifically for Black and Brown children. Imagine if Adidas, Under Armour, Apple, McDonald's, Walmart, Target, Lane Bryant, Jordan, Chase Bank, and Ford Motor Company invested in high poverty communities and schools of color. We also suggest a pipeline of internships and policies to maintain and support current demographics and teachers of color. Teachers and administrators of color are essential to the viability of urban schools.

Fourth, we recommend caution against converging with interest groups that seek to redraw districts or rearrange school boundaries in order to gain a share of the funding.

## CONCLUSION

This paper began with two questions. Who gets what in educational resources and equity? And, how can we address the educational debt owed to the Black and Brown children in urban public schools? The research reveals the social construction of meritocracy, including bribery schemes for college admission, and a $23 billion gap in resources between non-White and White school districts. The "pull yourself up by your bootstraps" discourse has become more of a status-quo-keeper, rather than an access-to-mobility-creator. Through reverse interest convergence, this paper has shown how race and economics inform the non-investability of public education, and how corporations like Nike can reverse this frame of thinking for both their corporate interests and the social and economic interests of urban public education.

## REFERENCES

Bell, D. (1992). *Faces at the bottom of the well: The permanence of racism*. New York: Basic.

Berglind, M. & Nakata, C. (2005). Cause-related marketing: More buck than bang? *Business Horizons, 48*(5), 443–53.

Bogage, J. (2018, September 20). Harvard awards Colin Kaepernick top honor for African and African American studies. Retrieved from https://www.washingtonpost.com/sports/2018/09/20/harvard-awards-colin-kaepernick-top-honor-african-african-\american-studies/?noredirect=on

Carpenter, L. (2017). Colin Kaepernick has won: He wanted a conversation and Trump started it. *The Guardian*. https://www.theguardian.com/sport/2017/sep/24/colin-kaepernick-conversation-donald-trump-anthem-kneel

Edbuild (2019). 23 billion. Retrieved from: https://edbuild.org/content/23-billion

Griffen, A. J. (2015). Hearing the voices of African American educational lobbyists and their role in lobbying for education. [Dissertation]. Texas A&M University Office of Graduate Studies. Retrieved from: https://oaktrust.library.tamu.edu/bitstream/handle/1969.1/156268/GRIFFEN-DISSERTATION-2015.pdf?sequence=1

Griffen, A. J. (2017). Advantages of being invisible: African American educational lobbyists enact reverse interest convergence. *National Journal of Urban Education and Practices, 11*(2), 57–68.

JenetAllDay. (2019 May 3). Keep that same energy: Critics argue college admissions scandal is nothing new, reignite debate over affirmative action. [Twitter post]. Retrieved from https://www.cnn.com/2019/03/12/us/college-admission-cheating-scheme/index.html

Johnson, C. (1998). *Middle passage*. New York: Scribner.

Ladson-Billings, G. (2004). New directions in multicultural education: Complexities boundaries and critical race theory. In J. A. Banks and C. A. McGee Banks (Eds.), *Handbook of research on multicultural education* (pp. 50–68). San Francisco, CA: Jossey-Bass.

Ladson-Billings, G. (2006). From the achievement gap to the education debt: Understanding achievement in U.S. schools. *Educational Researcher, 35*(7), 3–13.

Ladson-Billings, G., & Tate, W. (1995). Toward a critical race theory of education. *Teachers College Record*, *97*(1), 47–68.

Lucke, S. & Heinze, J. (2015). The role of choice in cause-related—Investigating the underlying mechanisms of cause and product involvement. *Procedia—Social and Behavioral Sciences*, *213*, 647–53.

Lyons, R. & Jackson, N. (2011). Factors that influence African-American millennials to purchase athletic shoes. *The Sports Journal*, *14*(1), 1–7.

Mangan, D. (2019, February 15). Colin Kaepernick reaches settlement in national anthem kneeling collusion case against NFL. Retrieved from https://www.cnbc.com/2019/02/15/colin-kaepernick-reaches-settlement-in-collusion-case-against-nfl-lawyer-says.html

Marchitello, M. (2018). Pension problems: How gender and race complicate Illinois' teacher retirement woes. *Bellwether Education Partners*. [Report]. Retrieved from: https://www.teacherpensions.org/sites/default/files/Bellwether_TP_IL_GenderRace_Final.pdf

Mazzocco, P. J., Rucker, D. D., Galinsky, A. D., & Anderson, E. T. (2012). Direct and vicarious conspicuous consumption: Identification with low-status groups increases the desire for high-status goods. *Journal of Consumer Psychology*, *22*(4), 520–28.

Meltzer, E. (2019). Colorado bill aims to help close gap. *Chalkbeat*. https://chalkbeat.org/posts/co/2019/01/31/fewer-students-of-color-take-advanced-courses-this-colorado-bill-aims-to-help-close-that-gap/

NCES (2018). Fast facts: Employment rates of college graduates. Retrieved from: https://nces.ed.gov/fastfacts/display.asp?id=561

Neilson Insights. (2018, February 15). Black impact: Consumer categories were African-Americans move markets. Retrieved from: https://www.nielsen.com/us/en/insights/news/2018/black-impact-consumer-categories-where-african-americans-move-markets.html

Nike. (2018a). Select financials. Retrieved from https://s1.q4cdn.com/806093406/files/doc_financials /2018/ ar/select_financials.html

Nike. (2018b). FY2019 Quarter 2 Report. Retrieved from https://s1.q4cdn.com/806093406/files/doc_financials/2019/Q2/FY19-Q2-Combined-NIKE-Press-Release-Schedules-FINAL.pdf

Nike. (2019). FY2019 Quarter 3 Report. Retrieved from https://s1.q4cdn.com/806093406/files/doc_financials/2019/Q3/FY19-Q3-Combined-NIKE-Press-Release-Schedules-FINAL.pdf

Podoshen, J. S., Andrzejewski, S. A., & Hunt, J. M. (2014). Materialism, conspicuous consumption, and American hip-hop subculture. *Journal of International Consumer Marketing*, *26*(4), 271–83.

Schuman, M., Martin, J., Thompson, M. Del Valle, L., & Simon, D. (2019). Wealthy parents, actresses, coaches, among those charged in massive college cheating admission scandal, federal prosecutors say. *CNN*. Retrieved from: https://www.cnn.com/2019/03/12/us/college-admission-cheating-scheme/index.html

Thomas, D. (2018). Diversifying the teaching profession: How to recruit and retain teachers of color. *Learning Policy Institute Report*. Retrieved from: https://learningpolicyinstitute.org/product/diversifying-teaching-profession-report

Toldson, I. A. (2019). *No BS (bad stats): Black people need people who believe in Black people enough not to believe every bad thing they hear about Black people.* Leiden: Brill-Sense.

Whiting, S., Campbell, C., & Pearson-McNeil, C. (2013). Resilient, reception, and relevant: The African-American consumer [2013 Report]. Neilson, The African American Consumer Report. Retrieved from https://www.iab.com/wp-content/uploads/2015/08/Nielsen-African-American-Consumer-Report-Sept-2013.pdf

Whitten, S. (2018, September 7). Nike's online sales surge in days after Kaepernick ad debut. Retrieved from https://www.cnbc.com/2018/09/07/nikes-online-sales-surge-in-days-after-kaepernick-ad-debut.html

*Chapter Four*

# Outkasted Black Masculinity

*Shifting the Geographical and Performative Landscape of 1990s Hip-Hop*

Marquese McFerguson

When I fell in love with hip-hop culture as a teenager, I had no idea of the impact it would have on how I conceived and performed Black masculinity. Initially, like many listeners, I was hypnotized by the beats and mesmerized by the melodies. I would sit for hours in a trance-like state, bobbing my head to the rhythm and poetry of artists until I knew all the words to their songs. However, in the process of memorizing their lyrics, I also began to mimic their mannerisms and mentalities. In this autoethnographic chapter, I detail how mirroring the performance of Black masculinity present in hip-hop culture during my adolescence supported and simultaneously challenged hegemonic Black masculine images and canonical stereotypes ascribed to heterosexual Black men. In particular, I illustrate how hip-hop artist André 3000's performance of Black masculinity, through his lyrics, fashion choices, and music video appearances, complicated the narrow performative lens which Black men were viewed through within hip-hop and American popular culture. Ultimately, as Outkast led a sonic and cultural movement that expanded the geographical borders of where hip-hop could derive and the aesthetic boundaries of how hip-hop could sound, they also expanded my childhood understanding of the performative possibilities of Black masculinity.

## COOL POSING: BLACK MASCULINITY REHEARSAL SESSIONS

Picture this. It is the early 1990s and Dr. Dre drops *The Chronic* (Young, 1992). Every car cruising down my block has Dre's album, or Ice Cube's "It Was a

Good Day" (O. Jackson, 1992), reverberating through their sound systems. My friends are begging their parents to buy them Karl Kani, Cross Colours, and FUBU clothing. Fab Five Freddy is hosting the latest edition of *Yo! MTV Raps* in Paris, France. It is the early 1990s. I am a teenager. Hip-hop is barely twenty years old, yet it is an international and cultural phenomenon.

During my teenage years, due to my father's untimely death, I looked to hip-hop culture to understand and find exemplars of Black masculinity. I utilized hip-hop music and videos as my instructional soundtrack to Black manhood. When the block was too hot from the state of police surveillance or the state of southern summer heat, my bedroom became my cool place for my Black masculine rehearsal sessions. Like a b-boy practicing atop a piece of worn cardboard on a street corner, remaking and reimagining how his body could move, my bedroom became the space where I reimagined and reshaped my Black masculine identity through rehearsing my cool pose. My cool pose included posturing to communicate power, toughness, detachment, and style (Majors & Billson, 1993).

I stand in front of my bedroom mirror, singing the rap lyrics from songs like Nate Dogg and Warren G's "Regulate" (Hale & Griffin, 1994) and Snoop Dogg's "Gin and Juice" (Casey, Young, Finch, & Broadus, 1994). I mimic the swagger of the Black men in rap music videos. Their racially gendered gangster performances saturate hip-hop culture and represent the masculine posturing my friends and I rehearse and attempt to master. As I listen to Tupac's "Hit 'Em Up" (Shakur, 1996), the Luniz's "I Got Five On It" (Ellis & Husbands, 1995) and "Piru Love" (Carter, Carter, Dillon, Doby, & Faulks, 1993), I mimic the imagery in the songs. I practice puffing imaginary blunts, throwing up gang signs, sagging and perfecting an aggressive mean mug. I rehearse moving my body like the rapper's as if they are choreographers and I am their star pupil. I cannot afford to look weak or soft. On my block, to be seen as weak or soft is to be marked for perpetual bullying, insults, and social death. Thus, my aggressive posturing and me practicing my cool pose is a survival strategy.

## DO YOU BELIEVE IN ATLIENS?

In 1996, I was exposed to the music of the Atlanta based hip-hop group, Outkast. Better yet, in 1996 I fell in love with their music. I spent hours sitting on the edge of my bed, reciting songs from their album *ATLiens* (Benjamin & Patton, 1996a). The music was saturated with bass, soulful samples, and Southern drawl. I admired Outkast's rhyming ability and personas. I coveted the street toughness and swagger of Big Boi. However, I also admired the defiant and rebellious performance of Black masculinity brandished by André 3000.

As time went on, I began to listen to more of Outkast's music and less to other artists. I gravitated toward Outkast because they were unapologetically Southern. Their voices and dialect sounded like mine. They were unique among the hip-hop radio airwaves dominated by east and west coast artists. As André 3000 stated at the infamous 1995 Source Awards (Cantor, 2015), the South had something to say, and my adolescent ears were eager to listen. As Outkast expanded the geographical borders and aesthetics boundaries of hip-hop culture, they also expanded my understanding of the performative possibilities of Black masculinity.

When I started listening to Outkast, André 3000—one half of the music duo—was beginning a personal transformation. He was navigating away from contemporary hip-hop images of the pimp, gangster (R. Jackson, 2006), thug (Neal, 2013), and hyper-violent (Boylorn, 2017) rap persona popularized by his peers in the 1990s. During a time when fitted caps and baggy jeans were seen as markers of authentic urban masculinity (White, 2011), André defiantly donned turbans, tribal/floral patterned bell-bottoms, leopard print trousers, safari hats, and shoulder pads during music video shoots. As a teenager, I was intrigued by his eccentric fashion choices and willingness to go against the grain. His assured sense of identity caused me to question the small ideological box I'd placed my adolescent definition of Black masculinity within. Initially, I wanted to be hard like the gangsters within my city and the rap industry, but my mentality was slowly shifting. I admired André. His performance of masculinity juxtaposed the gangster, however, in my opinion, it did not make him less of a man or soft. In the process, his push challenged pejorative Black masculine tropes. Conversely, as I watched André 3000's music videos more and saw how he remixed music industry standards, I began to question the narrow scope through which I saw Black manhood.

## BLACK MASCULINITY AND AGGRESSION

During the '90s, André 3000 became a celebrated artist who curated his own style of Outkasted masculinity. He rarely conformed to hip-hop's norms. His personal growth was evident and inspired me to rethink the boundaries of my own Black masculine performance. Undoubtedly, André 3000's avant-garde style and nonviolent lyrical themes were instrumental in shifting and reshaping ideas of masculinity for many young Black men from the hip-hop generation (Rambsy, 2013). During the 1990s, when notable east/west coast emcees and record labels were embroiled in rap beefs and producing hyperaggressive music that instigated and glorified violence, André 3000's music served as a lyrical counter-narrative. During the bicoastal feud that claimed the lives of Tupac Shakur and the Notorious B.I.G., André 3000's verses on songs like

"ATLiens" and "Babylon," challenged Black men to put down guns and be empowered through consciousness and self-discovery (Benjamin & Patton, 1996a). As a teenager, as my infatuation with Outkast grew, I started questioning the hyperaggressive thug persona that was so prevalent in the media (Bogle, 1996) and began to seek out alternative representations of Black masculinity within hip-hop culture.

## BLACK MASCULINE INQUISITIVENESS AND KNOWLEDGE CONSUMPTION

> Friends, Romans, country men
> I come to bury Caesar,
> Not to praise him.
> —William Shakespeare (1599)

As an adolescent, many of my ideas were formed and policed by my peers. Our adolescent conversations were filled with three primary things: sports, music, and girls. The topics of our conversations mirrored the content we listened to in hip-hop music. Topics outside these parameters were often met with furrowed eyebrows, frustrated looks, and statements like "Bro, nobody wants to hear about that shit." For example, one day I was sitting on the porch with my friends, taking a break from playing the classic neighborhood game, "That's My Car." I attempted to start a conversation about the PBS documentary I watched the previous night. I enjoyed PBS broadcasts because I was naturally inquisitive and enjoyed learning about other cultures. This particular documentary was about French explorer Jacques Cousteau. When I mentioned the documentary, my friends replied, "Nobody wanna hear about some dude from France swimming in the ocean." A chorus of voices declared "Don't nobody wanna hear about that shit!" I was Outkasted. Moments like these conditioned my thinking. For my adolescent peers and I, knowledge consumption consisted of sports, music, and girls. That's what cool Black men talked about.

André 3000's lyrics eroded these topical boundaries. In my teenage mind, André was the epitome of cool. He was a platinum-selling artist who graced the covers of *Vibe* magazine and *The Source*. Furthermore, André 3000 routinely and creatively broached topics in ways that contrasted his contemporaries. For example, on the Goodie Mob song "Black Ice," André recites a verse that highlights the struggle of growing up in an urban environment. His verse opens with the words "Friends, Romans, countrymen, lend me your eardrums," which is a reference to Shakespeare's play, Julius Caeser. With the words in his verse, André 3000 introduced me to sixteenth-century Elizabethan Era literature and the beauty that can be found from exploring art from different cultures.

André 3000's global/cultural inquisitiveness is further exemplified on songs like, "Millennium." On this track, he provides listeners with a reflexive in-depth look into the factors that have contributed to the mental anguish he is currently feeling in his life. He raps "Me and everything around me is unstable like Chernobyl" (Benjamin & Patton, 1996b). Upon hearing this lyric, I played the track over and over again trying to figure out what was "Chernobyl." I'd never heard of the term. After doing some research, I discovered that Chernobyl is located in the Ukraine. In 1986, it was the site of a historic nuclear power plant catastrophe. As I continued to listen to the verse, I became even more impressed by André's ability to creatively describe his lived experiences and connect them to Soviet Union history. As I continued to listen to the verse, I began to think.... André 3000 is from the hood. André 3000 is one of coolest Black men in the rap industry and he consumes many different types of knowledge, from classical literature to world history. Why can't I?

## BLACK MASCULINITY AND ROMANTIC RELATIONSHIPS

My uncle was one of the first men to advise me on how to interact with women. Most of his advice was rooted in misogynistic mantras like "Ain't no woman like a new woman." The first time he uttered those words, I was shocked and confused. However, I emphatically nodded in agreement as if I knew exactly what he meant. I did not want him to think of me as less of a man.

Lying about sexual experiences became an ongoing theme in my teenage years. I was extremely shy and rarely talked to girls. However, I learned early if others knew I was a virgin, I would be ridiculed and shamed. So, I learned to lie. My cool points grew with each story about my fictional sexual conquests. In my teenage mind, manhood was connected to sex. I developed a patriarchal and misogynistic mentality that women were to be objectified.

Hip-hop music played an influential role in developing and challenging my misogynistic mindset. Although Tupac uplifted women on songs like "Keep Ya Head Up" and "Dear Mama," I emphatically recited the lyrics from his more sexually explicit songs like "How Do You Want It" and "I Get Around." Standing in front of my bedroom mirror, my hairbrush doubled as an imaginary microphone as I emphatically rapped Shakur's verses. I gravitated toward sexually explicit songs because their lyrics aligned with my uncle's misogynistic teachings. While rehearsing and perfecting my playa persona, I had no idea my behavior was supporting canonical and pejorative stereotypes that reduced Black men to hypersexual bodies that are constantly searching for women to satisfy their insatiable sexual appetites (R. Jackson, 2006; Boylorn, 2017).

I revered Tupac's promiscuous ladies' man image, but Outkast shifted my feelings about intimate relationships. For instance, on the track "Jazzy Belle," André 3000 rhymes about being in love with a woman and treating her like a queen. After professing his love for his partner, later in the verse André raps "Them folks might think you soft talking like that." However, he asserts that he doesn't care what others think of the love he shares with his partner. Moments like these were rare within the landscape of mainstream hip-hop. It was the first time I heard a rapper profess his love for a woman and advocate for being in a monogamous relationship.

André 3000's performance within the "Jazzy Belle" music video also left a lasting impression on me and complicated my hypersexualized framing of intimate relationships. In the music video he is shown washing the feet of his partner. André's servile actions within these scenes framed Black masculinity in a different light and advocated for Black men to be caring, nurturing, and faithful—a far cry from my uncle's teachings. Playing on repeat in my headphones, these themes challenged the misogynistic messaging prevalent within much of '90s hip-hop and promoted a reimagining of Black men's performatives possibilities within intimate relationships in my teenage mind.

Throughout this chapter, I celebrate André 3000's open mindedness and willingness to challenge normative behaviors prevalent in '90s hip-hop culture. However, there are also sometimes where the artist used his work to expand the ways we view Black men but restrict and police the ways we view Black women. For instance, "Jazzy Belle" is a derogatory term used to describe sexually promiscuous women. This verbiage perpetuates double standards concerning sexual behavior. In the same song where he uplifts his fictional significant other, André also raps that women who choose to have multiple sexual partners lessen the value of their bodies and are unfit for motherhood. Ironically, André never states that sexually promiscuous Black men are unfit for fatherhood. Furthermore, on the song, André criticizes women who engage in romantic relationships that extend beyond heteronormative parameters. Thus, on "Jazzy Belle," while André 3000 marks some Black women as queens, unfortunately, he also asserts that women who don't meet his problematic standards aren't fit to wear a crown.

## CONCLUSION

Undoubtedly, Outkast has left a lasting impression on hip-hop culture and my perception/performance of Black masculinity. As a youth, my performance of Black masculinity was a choreographed carbon copy of what I saw on city corners, television screens, and heard in rap music. When I was exposed to Andre 3000's music, it was like seeing a b-boy dance for the first time. I was amazed because I did know Black men could move (through the world) like that. Mirror the range of reimagining and contorting that that b-boys did with their bodies, from stylized footwork, shuffles, drops, spins, and freezes (Johnson, 2015), Andre 3000's reimagined the way Black masculine bodies could perform within '90s hip-hop culture. Benjamin's performance of Black masculinity created a break beat within hip-hop and my imagination that stretched, rather than restricted, how Black men could move, and allowed Black masculine bodies, including Black boys like me, to maneuver more freely throughout the dance floor of our days and be o.k. with dancing to the beat/notion of a masculinity that breaks normative standards of Black masculine performativity.

## REFERENCES

Benjamin, A., & Patton, A. (1996a). *ATLiens* [CD]. Atlanta, GA: LaFace Records.
Benjamin, A., & Patton, A. (1996b). Babylon. On *ATLiens* [CD]. Atlanta, GA: LaFace Records.
Benjamin, A., Gipp, C., Patton, A., & Sheats, D. (1998). Black ice. On *Still standing* [CD]. Atlanta, GA: LaFace Records.
Bogle, D. (1996). *Toms, coons, mulattoes, mammies and bucks: An interpretive history of Blacks in American films* (4th ed.). New York: Continuum.
Boylorn, R. M. (2017). From Boys to men: Hip-hop, hood films, and the performance of contemporary Black masculinity. *Black Camera, 8*(2), 146–64.
Cantor, P. (2015, August). How the 1995 source awards changed rap forever. *Complex*, Retrieved from https://www.complex.com/music/2015/08/how-the-1995-source-awards-changed-rap-forever
Carter, J., Carter, J., Dillon, W., Doby, S., & Faulks, R. (1993). Piru love. On *Bangin on wax* [CD]. New York: Warlock Records.
Casey, H., Young, A., Finch, R., & Broadus, C. (1994). Gin and juice. On *Doggystyle* [CD]. Los Angeles, CA: Death Row Records.
Ellis, J., & Husbands, G. (1995). I got five on it. On *Operation stackola* [CD]. Santa Monica, CA: Noo Trybe Records.
Hale, N. D., & Griffin, W. (1994). Regulate. On *Regulate . . . g funk era* [CD]. New York: Def Jam Records.
Jackson, O., Sr., (1992). It was a good day. On *The Predator* [CD]. Los Angeles, CA: Priority Records.
Jackson, R. L. (2006). *Scripting the Black masculine body: Identity, discourse, and racial politics in popular media*. Albany, NY: Suny Press.
Johnson, I. (2015). Hip-hop dance. In J. Williams (Ed.). *The Cambridge companion to hip-hop*. Cambridge: Cambridge University Press.
Majors, R., & Billson, J. M. (1993). *Cool pose: The dilemma of Black manhood in America*. New York: Simon and Schuster.
Neal, M. A. (2013). *Looking for Leroy: Illegible Black masculinities*. New York: NYU Press.
Rambsy, H. (2013). Beyond keeping it real: OutKast, the funk connection, and afrofuturism. *American Studies, 52*(4), 205–16.
Shakur, T., A., (1993). I get around. On *Strictly 4 my n.i.g.g.a.z.* [CD]. Los Angeles, CA: Death Row Records.
Shakur, T., A., (1996). Hit em up. On *How do you want it* [CD]. Los Angeles, CA: Death Row Records.
White, M. (2011). *From Jim Crow to Jay-Z: Race, rap, and the performance of masculinity*. Champaign, IL: University of Illinois Press.
Young, A. (1992). *The Chronic*. [CD]. Los Angeles, CA: Death Row Records.

*Chapter Five*

# The Killing of Black Boys

*A Collaborative Critical Autoethnography on "the Talk"*

Mark C. Hopson, Gina Castle Bell, and Richard Craig

Black children are doubly displaced within White institutional spaces. Historically, they are not seen as children, but adultified. Race, gender, and age can be used against them. For example, America's masculine dispensation constitutes White boys as being naturally naughty. Conversely, Black boys are discerned as willfully bad. The consequences are dire. There is a need to look more closely at this displacement (Ferguson, 2000). The following chapter is a response to racialized and gendered discourse pertaining to Black boys in the United States. More specifically, we examine the talk surrounding the killing of Black boys.

We apply collaborative critical autoethnography to delineate racial and cultural talk emanating from the 2012 murder of Trayvon Martin and the 2013 acquittal of George Zimmerman. The talk works to frame racial identity for individuals and groups. Thematically, the talk is a form of critical intercultural communication largely used in three ways: (1) to manage and survive historic conflict; (2) to construct race in mass media; and (3) to inform dialogue around race and racism in the United States.

This chapter is organized according to specific objectives. First, we introduce collaborative critical autoethnography as a methodology to explore our respective observations of a tragic phenomenon. Second, we offer a brief synopsis of the unfolding events. Third, we historically conceptualize the talk surrounding Black boys killed in the United States. Fourth, we present the heuristic value of the study.

## METHODOLOGY: COLLABORATIVE CRITICAL AUTOETHNOGRAPHY

Autoethnography is used to foreground the researcher's engagement with a specific cultural context. It is the intentional analysis of a lived experience, for the purposes of explicating and articulating symbolic meanings associated with an experience. Within autoethnographic methodology, the researcher is positioned to observe unfolding events and make known the ways in which these events relate to larger cultural narratives (Jones, 2005). This is a reflexive activity regarding the lives of individuals and groups, including the analyses of their dynamic social connections.

Furthermore, critical autoethnography is formed at the nexus of anthropology and cultural critique (Marcus & Fischer, 1986), and takes into account personal experiences which contribute to our knowledge of power and social inequality. It is a method to transform systems of power by discursively highlighting the ways in which our personal lives intersect, collide, and commune with others—as we critically reflect upon, combine, and thematize our personal narratives. It is an academic engagement to dismantle inequities of power structures by exposing narratives that would otherwise remain muted (Spry, 2011). Arguably, critical autoethnography should not be taken at face value but instead be interrogated for the social positions they entail (Reed-Danahay, 2017). This is precisely the purpose of our chapter.

Our collaborative critical autoethnography calls attention to the factors surrounding a specific moment in time, thereby creating space for critical inquiry. Our close observations interrupt what is otherwise taken for granted. By examining a specific historical context (i.e., terrorism perpetrated against Black people), we highlight communicative factors surrounding the talk about past and current racialized interactions within the United States. Researchers and learners are empowered by the ways theory can help us heal (hooks, 1994). We interrupt the master narrative by critically reflecting back on who we are, where and when (Spry, 2011). In the spirit of critical collaborative autoethnography, we question social progress toward peace and freedom for all.

Our collaborative critical autoethnography is a reflection of our engagement within a specific context. Our methodology is suitable because our goal is to better understand the ways that individuals discuss, dismantle, and transform the inequities of power structures.

We self-identify as two Black/African American men and one White/ European American woman. Also, we are scholars with sons. Separately, we pondered, journaled and engaged critical reflexivity on the tragic shootings of Black boys and men including Ahmaud Arbery, Botham Jean, De'Von Bailey, Sean Bell, Oscar Grant, Jordan Davis, Eric Garner, Michael Brown,

Philando Castile and others, many of whom died as the result of police-related violence.

A glaring anti-Black racism surrounds police-related violence. For example, by October of 2019, the police shootings database reported sixty-two shooting deaths of Black men under 29 years old—including three persons under 18 years old (WashingtonPost.com, October 31, 2019). By comparison, the police shootings database reported fifty-one shooting deaths of White men under 29 years old—none under the age of 18. At the time, Black/African American boys and men were approximately 7 percent of the U.S. population, while White/European American boys and men were approximately 32 percent of the U.S. population. Per capita, Black boys and men were a minority in the U.S. population, and yet they were the majority population killed in police-related shootings.

The scope of this chapter is focused on Black boys and men. However, we cannot overlook the tragic deaths of Black girls and women including Breonna Taylor, Atatiana Jefferson, Korryn Gaines, India Kager, Rekia Boyd, Yvette Smith, Sandra Bland, Muhlaysia Booker and others. The nation must respond to their tragic deaths. Justice for all is our collective responsibility. #SayHerName, #BlackLivesMatter, and other organizational efforts call attention to police-related violence and gun violence overall. Simultaneously, we recognize that in some cases violence and death occurred at the hands of Black men. Additionally, we recognize police-related shootings against White/European Americans and others. For example, on November 9, 2004, a Kenosha police officer shot Michael Bell on the day before Bell was to testify at a court hearing regarding a previous incident with the same officer who stopped him that last fatal time.

The year 2020 revealed an epidemic within a pandemic, by foregrounding the ongoing disrespect for the Black body within the context of White supremacy ideology. The killing of George Floyd forced the United States to reexamine the ways in which Black life is treated as disposable and disregarded with false justification. Boys, girls, men, and women—it did not matter, police-related deaths exemplified the ultimate disrespect for Black life.

Additionally, police violence revealed disturbing levels of irresponsibility on the part of city, state, and federal leaders. Many leaders expressed their concern, yet the issues continued. Their concern lacked responsibility. Their concern lacked action.

Finally, police violence was predictable. By 2020, Black death ran the risk of being normalized had it not been for the Black Lives Matter movement and other efforts to raise awareness and action. The killing of Black boys and men is not a new phenomenon. We saw it with Emmett Till and George Stinney Jr. We saw it with Tamir Rice and Trayvon Martin.

This chapter is based on the murder of Trayvon Martin and the acquittal of George Zimmerman. Three primary themes emerged from our analysis: (1) "the talk" is a metaphor for discussing historic racial conflict and terrorism against Black Americans; (2) "the talk" is used to construct racialized images in mass media; (3) "the talk" may contribute to dialogue.

The next section offers a brief description of the death of Trayvon Martin and the acquittal of George Zimmerman.

## A BRIEF SYNOPSIS OF EVENTS STARTING WITH FEBRUARY 26, 2012

In February 26, 2012, George Zimmerman shot and killed Trayvon Martin. Martin was a 17-year-old, Black/African American male, high school student. Zimmerman was 28-year-old and self-identified as a mixed-race Hispanic American male. He volunteered as a neighborhood watch coordinator for a gated community in Sanford, Florida where Martin was visiting with his father. Zimmerman called authorities prior to the altercation (Zorn, 2012). He was instructed not to initiate contact with Martin. But he did so anyway, resulting in the fatal shooting. Police arrived on the scene within minutes of Zimmerman's call, only to find Martin dead.

Zimmerman was taken into custody by the Sanford Police Department. He was treated for head injuries, and questioned and released approximately five hours later. According to the police department, there was no evidence to refute Zimmerman's claim of self-defense. Additionally, authorities declared that Florida's stand-your-ground law prohibited an arrest because Zimmerman was within his rights to use lethal force (T. Lee, 2012).

News of Zimmerman's release made mainstream media. Concerned individuals and groups used social media to promulgate attention. Communities across the country were outraged with questions: No arrest? No further investigation into the death of a citizen lawfully passing through the Sanford neighborhood? How can Zimmerman shoot in self-defense when the teen did not have a weapon? Protestors called for Zimmerman's arrest and a more extensive investigation (*CNN*, 2012). He remained free for approximately forty-six days after the shooting.

After a large public outcry and protests across the nation (Mathew, 2012), Florida's governor appointed a special prosecutor to examine the circumstances surrounding Martin's death. Consequently, on April 11, 2012, George Zimmerman was charged with second-degree murder. The trial began on June 24, 2013, and was presented to the jury for deliberation on July 12, 2013. On July 13, 2013, the jury found Zimmerman not-guilty.

## SETTING THE STAGE FOR THE TALK

*From an early age, Black boys are taught about race and racism. I had the talk with my father. I've also had it with my son because I understand the necessity for guidelines for self-preservation pertaining specifically to him.*

The talk is a metaphor for managing conflict. In all cultures, young people receive lessons in preparation for adulthood. These lessons may focus on work-ethics, firm handshakes and eye contact, and sex education. However, for many young Black men these lessons also include strategizing for survival in White spaces where non-White individuals and groups are marginalized and threatened (Jackson & Hopson, 2011; Orbe, 1998; Orbe & Harris, 2008). The talk may focus on driving while Black (DWB), which is a theory based on the high probability of being targeted for traffic stops due to racial profiling (Hopson, 2011). The talk about DWB includes strategies to avoid driving through predominantly White neighborhoods. For example, when stopped keep your hands on the steering wheel or otherwise visible, and observe badge numbers. As unrealistic as it might seem, these are a few of the strategies taught to young Black men who risk paying the price of White racism in the twenty-first century.

*Any young Black man could have been in Trayvon Martin's shoes that evening. The result would have been the same. I feel vulnerable. My thoughts turn to worry. Many questions come to mind regarding the stereotypical construction of my son's Black body. How safe is he? Will his clothing impact how others perceive him? As long as prejudice and racism continue, he is not exempt from potential danger.*

Trayvon Martin's death and George Zimmerman's acquittal reignite talk about race, gender, culture, and the U.S. justice system (NY *Daily News*, 2013). The talk occurs at public demonstrations, churches, barbershops, and college campuses. Public memory is jarred with each reference to past injustices. Media personalities, educators, and citizens grapple with the topic. Parents discuss the issue with their children. All interrogate the central questions: How does something like this happen? And what can be done about it?

*I ponder these questions as I look at my son's picture. My son is now a young man. I am both proud and nervous about his maturation. We've had many talks in preparation for these days. Yet all of these killings have reinforced my deepest fears.*

Race and racism matter in the United States. The words themselves are entangled in the midst of stark controversy, but race and racism are different concepts. Race is largely a social construct often mistakenly associated with biological difference (Hopson, 2011). Race is not entirely real although racial and cultural experiences are certainly tangible. Racism on the other hand is painfully real and refers to socially constructed identities organized hierarchically within institutional structures (e.g., employment, health, education, incarceration) (Allen, 2009). An informed dialogue about race requires clarity about these terms. Definitions minimize ambiguity and increase intercultural competence. Versions of the talk occur much too often as the result of tragedy, at which time any hope for understanding is lost in oppositional rhetoric. How long will the United States continue to miss the point?

## HISTORY MATTERS

It is important to discuss Martin and Zimmerman as part of a larger sociohistorical issue. The shooting and subsequent trial are not isolated incidents. To disconnect history from the here-and-now is a set-up to ignore valuable lessons and ultimately repeat history.

Trayvon Martin's death is laden with symbolic meaning. He was a young Black man in a country where his race and gender are disproportionately displaced across miseducation, incarceration, and violent death. Martin was born and killed in February, Black History Month—the celebration of struggle, success, and hope for the future. His death symbolized an attempt to extinguish the next generation of African American hope. Moreover, Martin's death occurred approximately forty-four years after the assassination of Dr. Martin Luther King Jr., and shortly after the second inauguration of the 44th U.S. president, Barack Obama. Some people argued that White terrorism increased as the result of the historic presidency, similar to the rise of White terrorism after the Civil War.

President Obama was criticized for his remarks on the controversy: "If I had a son, he'd look like Trayvon. When I think about this boy, I think about my own kids" (Condon, 2012). The president encouraged the nation to engage in a talk about race for the sake of progress. Arguably, Obama's presidency would become the backdrop of increased shootings and other forms of violence against Black men and women. The killing of Black bodies spoke to race relations of the past and present.

After Martin's death, efforts were made to protect the civil rights of a young man who was unable to speak for himself. Ultimately, Martin's voicelessness was used to substantiate the acquittal. Marginalized communities questioned Florida's stand-your-ground law—used to justify deadly force in the reasonable belief of threat. The law has long existed in various forms across forty-six states. Scrutiny is heightened by accusations of the law's racist applications.

In May 2012, Florida resident Marissa Alexander was sentenced to prison for firing a warning shot to scare off her abusive husband (Osunsami, 2012). Alexander, a Black woman, was unsuccessful in her claim of self-defense under the stand-your-ground law. The warning shot did not injure anyone, but a jury convicted Alexander of aggravated assault after just twelve minutes of deliberation (www.cbsnews.com/news/fla-mom-gets-20-years-for-firing-warning-shots/). Like Trayvon Martin, Alexander's story gained attention via social media. The next year an appellate court released Alexander on bond in preparation for a new trial. She was released after three years of incarceration.

In November of 2012, Jordan Davis, a 17-year-old Black male, was shot and killed by Michael Dunn, a 45-year-old White man from Brevard County, Florida (Broward & Hannan, 2013). Reportedly, Dunn was at a gas station when he confronted a group of teens about their loud music. Dunn claimed the teens brandished a gun, to which he responded by firing eight shots into their car, killing Davis. According to the Jacksonville Sheriff's Office, there were no guns found inside the teens' car.

The stand-your-ground statue extends an old English doctrine that a man's home is his castle and worth protecting. However, when considering Martin, Alexander, Davis, and other Black bodies, the following questions must be asked: Whose home is this? Who is protected in the United States? More specifically, Zimmerman's murder trial increasingly critiqued Trayvon Martin's character, stirring more questions: Whose trial is this? Didn't Martin have the right to stand his ground? The talk involves clearly articulating which individuals and groups are protected. History matters when examining the lynching of Black children and adults.

National memory is jarred with references to historic injustice. We remember the 1963 church bombing that killed four little girls in Birmingham, AL. The children had arrived for Sunday morning service at the Sixteenth Street Baptist Church. They played, laughed, talked, and lived until they were met with an unexpected attack on humanity. Moments before the explosion, the church phone rang. A child answered to hear an unidentified voice on the other end: "Three minutes." Moments later, Denise, Carol, Addie Mae, and Cynthia perished under collapsed bricks, mortar, steel, and glass. Other children and adults were injured. Families were torn apart.

We also remember 1955 when a jury of White men tried and acquitted two White men for the murder of 14-year-old Emmett Till (Metress, 2002). Till was tortured and killed after being accused of whistling at a White woman. He was beaten, stabbed, shot, and thrown into the Tallahatchie River. When Till's body was found, it was a horrific sight. The talk about U.S. race relations intensified when Mamie Till allowed *Jet* magazine to publish photographs of Emmett's body. She allowed the world to see what they did to her son. Reportedly, the sheriff, coroner, and local media of Money, Mississippi, assisted in exonerating J. W. Milam and Roy Bryant from the murder of the Black child. Two years later, *Look* magazine paid Milam and

Bryant $4,000 for their confessions. These historic representations inform the collective memory we are experiencing today.

Mass media is required to create awareness around such issues. Imagine how many Black lives have been taken without a headline or hashtag. Most of America had not heard of Oscar Grant until his story was told in the 2013 Hollywood film "Fruitvale Station." Fewer people know that Sean Bell died in 2006, in a hail of bullets fired by five New York City police officers. Bell did not have a weapon at the time of the shooting (Buckley & Rashbaum, 2006). In 1999, similar efforts were necessary to call attention to the shooting death of Amadou Diallo after he fell victim to NYPD bullets (Cooper, 1999). Diallo did not have a gun.

Returning to Emmett Till and Trayvon Martin, both were surrounded by media sensationalism. Without extreme coverage, they could have been reduced to cases where Black people are killed with little attention and false justification. Till and Martin represent the historic irony of Black masculinity. Till was viewed as criminal while visiting Money, Mississippi. Likewise, Martin was framed as a criminal in Sanford, Florida. Their legitimacy was questioned without evidence of wrongdoing. Any possibility of culpability was hearsay at best.

Moreover, both boys were adultified within White America. Their age became a topic of debate. The talk about Till's age fluctuated between 14 years old and 15 years old. The goal was to situate him as less of a child and more of an adult threat. Similarly, talk about 17-year-old Martin concerned whether he was a boy or a man. Age seemed to determine the extent of America's sympathy, as if to deny that children had been killed.

Their Black bodies were put on display for the world to see. Photographs of their corpses flooded the news. The only difference was the year and medium. From *Jet* magazine to Facebook, the images were reminders of White terror inflicted upon Black Americans.

The historic reality dates back to the Night Riders (also known as the Ku Klux Klan) who covered their faces and terrorized free Black men and women during the Reconstruction period. White vigilantes used violence and murder to reinforce Black codes. These groups organized well into the late nineteenth century and early twentieth century, including the White Camelia, Red Shirts, and the White League. All tried to suppress voting rights, land ownership, education, and other civil rights for Blacks. More than 3,400 Blacks were lynched between 1882 and 1951 (Gibson, 1979), which begs the question: How many race based murders went unrecorded?

## CONSTRUCTING RACE IN THE MEDIA

Black Americans are overwhelmingly represented as perpetrators of crime. Popular media perpetuates the image in many ways. Competing talk works to reconstruct race in popular media. During the time of Zimmerman's trial, Trayvon Martin was racially profiled on talk shows and in the news. He was dehumanized. His story was never told, but countless stories were told about him. The trial reached the popularity of a sporting event. Jurors sat near life-size cardboard cut-outs of an intimidating figure meant to represent Martin, and a much smaller figure meant to represent Zimmerman. Martin's physicality fluctuated with every cruel description.

Zimmerman's attorneys based their strategy on threatening images of Black men. At the peak of the bizarre ride, the defense played a video of an animated black body attacking a white body. Literally, it was a cartoon—a fictional representation of societal fear. The cartoon was enhanced with accusations of drug use, potential burglary, school disciplinary action, and a propensity for violence. This was a ready-mix stereotype. Just add water.

Coverage of Martin's death became surreal. There were countless justifications for the shooting. *FOX News* commentator Geraldo Rivera proclaimed that Trayvon Martin's hooded sweatshirt was "as much responsible for Martin's death as George Zimmerman was." Rivera added, "I'll bet you money that if he didn't have that hoodie on, that nutty neighborhood watch guy wouldn't have responded in that violent and aggressive way" (M. Lee, 2012).

Rivera's comments twisted culpability in the eyes of the world. He was seen by millions of viewers. Did he really mean to suggest that Black youth transfer onto themselves the responsibility for racial profiling? That wearing a particular article of clothing can get them killed? Rivera's blame-the-victim attitude spoke to stereotypes that make the talk imperative. His words fed into a racial schema that young Black men did not create for themselves, especially when considering the degree to which popular culture promotes and applauds the athletic gear sought by millions of young people. Geraldo Rivera and others failed to mention that hoods, like those worn by the KKK, were first associated with White terror.

In a rhetorical attempt to reverse oppressive power, a "Million Hoodie Movement" spread across the nation. Hooded sweatshirts became a method to demonstrate solidarity and keep the pressure on authorities. Representative Bobby Rush, D-IL was thrown off the House floor for wearing one (Seitz-Wald, 2013). The hoodie came to represent victims of injustice. "I am Trayvon" was an overwhelming attitude among agitators in cyberspace and on the streets. The symbolic outcry added to the collective call for justice. It is not enough to focus solely on clothing, they argued. The problem is White racism and a political system that justifies the killing of Black boys and men.

## RACE IS EVERYWHERE AND NOWHERE SIMULTANEOUSLY

The trial itself included disturbing intercultural and interracial interactions. Race was everywhere and nowhere simultaneously. For example, Judge Nelson ruled against using the term racial profiling (Bloom, 2013). Yet, the term spoke to the heart of the issue. After the trial, Juror B-37 suggested that character witnesses for the defense connected with the jury in ways that witnesses for the prosecution did not (Ford, 2013). The juror connected with Zimmerman, and affectionately called him George, which suggested common experiences (e.g., education level, socioeconomic position, and style of English vernacular). Some attempted to craft a narrative of Blacks vs. Hispanics. Others called for justice denied to a child. It was a call to see and hear the problem.

> As defense attorney O'Mara questioned Rachel Jeantel, I wondered why the prosecution didn't discuss the legitimacy of Black English. Why wouldn't they contextualize Jeantel's style of speaking and viewpoint? I wanted to question the prosecution, "Did you ever stop to think that jurors who culturally relate to the defendant may hurt your case?" The jury needed instruction on cultural competence.

In terms of hyper-racialized stereotypes, the prosecution's witness, Rachel Jeantel, was framed during the televised trial. Jeantel was a 19-year-old woman of Black/Haitian and Dominican descent. She had been on the phone with Martin at the time of his run-in with Zimmerman. Her testimony had the potential to offer a new dimension of understanding. However, the defense attorney West (and jury) placed more emphasis on how Jeantel spoke rather than what she said.

Her testimony was questioned and discounted as the result of her race, ethnicity, education, and overall social identity. She was framed as unintelligent and criticized later for speaking Ebonics or African American English. She used phrases like "creepy ass cracker" when discussing Martin's description of being followed by Zimmerman. Also, she was questioned about using the word "nigga." Attorneys drew her into back-and-forth banter about pronouncing the word with "er" or with "a." Like the majority of her viewers, Jeantel's understanding of the word was generational and cultural (Caputo, 2013). The attorney spent extra time on the old debate. By framing Jeantel as a racialized being (as opposed to human being) he took the attention off Zimmerman. The attorney's approach was fueled by cynicism. Attitudes erupted. He talked about race without blatantly talking about race. This racial dimension was not supposed to exist in Judge Nelson's court, but it did. For mainstream America in general, and the jury specifically, connecting with Jeantel was like trying to fit a square peg into a round hole.

In that moment, the internet lit up with scathing comments about Jeantel. Hateful language described a young woman who had been thrust into the public eye. They disrespected her perception of the world. They used dominant language structures and dominant worldviews to evaluate her intelligence.

While on the stand, Jeantel was interrupted repeatedly. Defense attorneys took strategic advantage of the scrutiny. They demanded that she speak louder, slower, and more clearly. Even the court recorder began to ask for clarification. Their requests were enough to rattle any young adult. Attorneys undermined Jeantel by asking if she understood English. Jeantel spoke English, Spanish, and French. In any other context, her multilingualism would have been applauded. The defense worked to frustrate her. They portrayed the witness as unintelligent, illiterate, and uncommunicative. Jeantel could not win. Later, when witness Selma Mora spoke through an interpreter, her credibility was hardly questioned. The court reporter had no issues with Mora. English was the primary language spoken during the trial, but it was dismissed when associated with Blackness. Black intelligence was misconstrued over and over again.

> *I am not quite sure how to describe my reaction to the verdict. Outwardly, I probably appeared stoic, but internally I was unsettled. I experienced frustration, dejection, anger, sorrow and powerlessness. An array of negative emotions clouded my thoughts. Though I had hoped justice would prevail in this circumstance, I was not surprised the law had overridden justice when dealing with the death of a Black male.*

Bright lights and big personalities helped distract people from the cause of Martin's death. Manufactured conflict kept viewers tuned into networks and publications. NBC was accused of falsely editing Zimmerman's 911 call (Martinez, 2012). Other sources associated Martin's likeness with marijuana and truancy. Bill Maher reported, "I don't blame Black people for thinking the law is a little bit of a license to shoot Black people." He argued that Whites are more likely to be justified for killing a Black person, than a White person killing a White person. Maher also argued that when Blacks are killed, perpetrators walk free 73 percent of the time.

Maher's comments refer to the foundation of the talk. White privilege is the stark difference in lived experiences. Black Americans may travel in the same spaces and conduct themselves similarly, yet White Americans face considerably less risk of violent or fatal exchanges with the authorities. Confronting inequality begins with awakening consciousness within those who are oblivious to its harsh realities.

Trayvon Martin was objectified and consumed across all aspects of media, as if his Black body was something other than human. His tragic death is a reminder of America's deprivation of peace and freedom. Persistent societal imbalances impact people in very real ways. There is no peace without freedom.

Black boys are doubly displaced within White institutional spaces. The consequences are dire. We need to continue to interrogate this displacement.

## CREATING INTENTIONAL DIALOGUE

The spirit of Trayvon Martin lives on in dialogue about race and racism in the United States. Trayvon lives on in the talk about George Floyd, Breonna Taylor, and Eljjah McClain. We remember Trayvon when we speak of Levena Johnson, Vanessa Guillen, and Brayla Stone. We remember Trayvon when we remember Shukri Abdi. The talk can be painful. At best, our informed dialogue can raise consciousness about oppression, but trading words is not enough. There is a need to move beyond sensitivity to taking collective responsibility for how the past impacts the present. The talk begins with our daily interactions. Societal change begins with individuals. For example, educators cannot afford to avoid controversial issues for the sake of minimizing potential conflict. Transformational environments require multiple viewpoints. The key is to construct time and safe space for different perspectives.

> *I consider my position as a White, middle-class, female, college professor. I consider genuine, unconditional, empathic conversations with other Whites about the role of race in America. I realize that creating a space for dialogue is part of my responsibility. Each of us has a responsibility to move beyond ourselves and educate others.*

Responsibility does not mean that we have all the answers. Responsibility does not relieve feelings of guilt. Responsibility requires that we contribute to difficult discussions. Responsibility requires that we examine the degree to which our respective societal roles promote or hinder peace and freedom.

This chapter is part of a larger project on dialogue. Within this particular chapter we created intentional dialogue using the following strategic steps:

a. Listen
b. Speak with honesty
c. Try not to make assumptions
d. Take action and work toward societal health and well-being

These steps occurred cyclically, not necessarily linearly. We returned to each step more than once. Additionally, these steps informed a larger imperative required for educators and learners alike.

> *As an African American man I embrace the tragedy, empathize the loss, and question the legalities of who is not protected under the law. For me, the talk has to take place in the classroom. As an educator, I feel obligated to explore social norms, different realities, and the consequences of our attitudes and*

*actions. I have to be willing to explore these matters. Where better to initiate an informed dialogue?*

History lives in the present. History lives in us. We carry the legacies of previous generations. The talk can be used to teach history pertaining to social identity for individuals and groups. Also, the talk can be used to analyze the ways in which race is constructed in mass media. Finally, the talk may inform dialogue around race and racism in the United States.

## CONCLUSION

This collaborative critical autoethnography is our attempt to engage controversial issues. The talk represents our feelings of loss and hope. The collaboration created a space for our critical inquiry and collective understanding. In the process of sharing, we empower ourselves and others. The talk is a metaphor for how to engage conflict. It is a dialectic laden with possibilities: positive and negative; liberate and oppress; move and restrict; connect and disconnect; and build and destroy.

Racial profiling includes biased perceptions of in-group and out-group members. Perceptions inform actions. Indifference will cause inaction. This chapter reveals the power of communication to interpret and experience intercultural environments. The world is more than Black and White. Race and racism impact everyone. Again, there is no peace without freedom. Knowledge is essential to move from sensibility to responsibility, and from debate to dialogue.

This chapter represents the ideas of three authors. We do not claim to speak for any other person or group. Our contributions are informed by our personal observations and experiences. This project brings together general (not essential) truths. Concurrently, our exploration of the talk will resonate with readers from various backgrounds. Together we are empowered by the unique ways in which theory helps us heal (Spry, 2011). By questioning twenty-first-century critical intercultural communication, we can build new ways to move forward. Rest in power, Trayvon.

## REFERENCES

Allen, B. J. (2009). *Difference matters: Communicating social identity*. Long Grove, IL: Waveland Press.

Bloom, L. (2013, July 16). Zimmerman prosecutors duck the race issue. *New York Times*. Retrieved from: http://www.nytimes.com/2013/07/16/opinion/zimmerman-prosecutors-duck-the-race-issue.html?pagewanted=all.

Broward, C., & Hannan, L. (2013, April 10). Michael Dunn remains adamant in police interview about killing Jordan Davis. *Florida-Times Union*. Retrieved from:http://www.jacksonville.com/news/crime/2013-04-09/story/michael-dunn-remains-adamant-police-interview-after-killing-jor dan-davis.

Buckley, C., & Rashbaum, W. (2006, November 27). A day after a fatal shooting, questions, mourning and protest. *New York Times*. Retrieved from: http://www.nytimes.com/2006/11/27/nyregion/27shot.html?_r=0.

Caputo, M. (2013). Zimmerman trial witness to CNN: "nigga," "cracka" not racist terms. *Miami Herald*. Retrieved from: http://www.miamiherald.com/2013/07/16/3502851/racheljeantel-on-cnn-talks-about.html.

Castle Bell, G., Hopson, M. C., & Craig, R. (In Press). Exploring Black and White accounts of 21st century racial profiling and prejudice: Riding and driving while Black. *Qualitative Research Reports in Communication*.

*CBS NEWS*. (2013, July 15). Fla. mom gets 20 years for firing warning shots. Retrieved from: http://www.cbsnews.com/news/fla-mom-gets-20-years-for-firing-warning-shots/.

CNN Political Unit. (2012, March 26). Majority call for arrest in Trayvon Martin Shooting. *CNN*. Retrieved from/l http://www.cnn.com/2012/03/26/justice/florida-teen-shooting-poll/.

Condon, S. (2012, March 23). Obama: If I had a son he'd look like Trayvon. *CBS NEWS*. Retrieved from: http://www.cbsnews.com/news/obama-if-i-had-a-son-hed-look-like-trayvon/.

Cooper, M. (1999, February 5). Officers in Bronx fire 41 shots, and an unarmed man is killed. *New York Times*. Retrieved from: http://www.nytimes.com/1999/02/05/nyregion/officersin-bronx-fire-41-shots-and-an-unarmed-man-iskilled.html?pagewanted=all&src=pm.

Ferguson, A. A. (2000). *Bad boys: Public schools in the making of Black masculinity*. Ann Arbor: University of Michigan Press.

Ford, D. (2013, July 15). Juror: No doubt that George Zimmerman feared for his life. *CNN*. Retrieved from: http://www.cnn.com/2013/07/15/justice/zimmerman-juror-book/.

*FOX News Latino*. (March 26, 2012). Trayvon Martin attacked George Zimmerman, report says. Retrieved from: http://latino.foxnews.com/latino/news/2012/03/26/trayvon-martin-attacked-george-zimmerman-report-says/.

Gibson, R. A. (1979). The Negro Holocaust: Lynching and race riots in the United States, 1880–1950. Yale-New Haven Teachers Institute. Retrieved from: http://www.yale.edu/ynhti/curriculum/units/1979/2/79.02.04.x.html.

hooks, b. (1994). *Teaching to transgress: Education as the practice of freedom*. New York: Routledge.

Hopson, M. C. (2003). For Cynthia, Denise, Carole and Addie Mae: Gazing at Whiteness in Spike Lee's "4 Little Girls." *Journal of Intergroup Relations, 30*(3), 39–55.

Hopson, M. C. (2011). *Notes from the talking drum: Exploring Black communication and critical memory in intercultural communication contexts*. Cresskill, NJ: Hampton Press.

Hopson, M. C., Castle Bell, G., & Craig, R. (2018). DWB, crime and race. In X. Hou & R. Dennis (Eds.) *Encyclopedia of race, ethnicity and nationalism*. Indianapolis: Wiley-Blackwell.

Jackson, R. L., & Hopson, M. C. (2011). *Masculinity in the Black imagination: Politics of communicating race and manhood*. New York: Peter Lang.

Jones, S. H. (2005). Autoethnography: Making the personal political. In N. K. Denzin & Y. S. Lincoln (Eds.), *The SAGE handbook of qualitative research* (pp. 763–92). Thousand Oaks, CA: Sage.

Lee, M. J. (2012, March 27). Geraldo Rivera apologizes for "hoodie" comment. *Politico*. Retrieved from: http://www.politico.com/news/stories/0312/74529.html.

Lee, T. (2012, March 22). Trayvon Martin case: Police chief Bill Lee under Fire with "no confidence" vote. *Huffington Post*. Retrieved from: http://www.huffingtonpost.com/2012/03/22/trayvon-martin-case-george-zimmerman-bill-lee_n_1371635.html.

Marcus, G. E. & Fischer, M. F. (1986). *Anthropology as cultural critique: An experimental moment in the human sciences*. Chicago: University of Chicago Press.

Martinez, M. (2012, December 7). George Zimmerman sues NBC Universal over edited 911 call. *CNN*. Retrieved from: http://www.cnn.com/2012/12/06/us/florida-zimmerman-nbclawsuit/.

Mathew, S. (2012, March 23). Thousands in city join Million Hoodie March. Retrieved from: http://articles.philly.com/2012-03-23/news/31230023_1_land-mines-neighborhood-watchvolunteer-basketball-game.

Metress, C. (2002). *The lynching of Emmett Till: A documentary narrative*. The University of Virginia Press.
Moore, F. (2012, April 7). NBC fires producer of misleading Zimmerman tape. *Huffington Post*. Retrieved from: http://www.huffingtonpost.com/2012/04/06/nbc-fires-producer-of-misleading-tape_n_1409405.html.
NY *Daily News* (2013, July 15). Attorney general Eric Holder calls Trayvon Martin killing "tragic" and "unnecessary" as justice department weighs civil rights charges. Retrieved from: http://www.nydailynews.com/news/national/eric-holder-trayvon-martin-killing-unncesssary-article-1.1399117.
Orbe, M. P. (1998). *Constructing co-cultural theory: An explication of culture, power, and communication*. Thousand Oaks, CA: Sage Publications.
Orbe, M. P., & Harris, T. M. (2008). *Interracial communication: Theory into practice*. Thousand Oaks, CA: Sage Publications, Inc.
Orbe, M. P., & Roberts, T. L. (2012). Co-cultural theorizing: Foundations, applications & extensions. *Howard Journal of Communications, 23*(4), 293–311.
Osunsami, S. (November 12, 2013). Florida woman sentenced to 20 years for firing a warning shot wants bail. *ABC News*. Retrieved from: http://abcnews.go.com/US/florida-woman-sentenced-20-years-firing-warning-shot/story?id=20859087.
Reed-Danahay, D. (2017). Bourdieu and critical autoethnography: Implications for research, writing, and teaching. *International Journal of Multicultural Education, 19*(1).
Seitz-Wald, A. (March 28, 2013. Congressman gets kicked off house floor for wearing hoodie for Trayvon. ThinkProgress. http://thinkprogress.org/politics/2012/03/28/453744/bobby-rush-hoodi/.
Spry, T. (2011). Performative ethnography. In N. K. Denzin & Y. S. Lincoln (Eds.). *The SAGE handbook of qualitative research* (pp. 497–511). Thousand Oaks, CA: Sage.
*Washington Post*. (2012). Audio: Calls from Zimmerman, neighbor capture last minutes of Martin's life. Retrieved from: http://www.washingtonpost.com/wp-srv/special/nation/last-minutes-trayvon-martin-911-calls.
Zorn, E. (2012, May 12). Trayvon Martin shooting death—Initial police reports and "911" call transcript. Retrieved from: http://blogs.chicagotribune.com/news_columnists_ezorn/2012/03/trayvon-martin-shooting-death-initial-police-reports.html.

*Chapter Six*

# A Conversation on Black Masculinity with Principal John Hawkins Snowdy of Baltimore Collegiate School for Boys

## Kimberly Moffitt

In 2015, just four months after the "Baltimore Uprising,"[1] after a city's rage, frustration, and neglect following the death of Freddie Gray, emerged a glimmer of hope for young Black males. Baltimore Collegiate School for Boys (BCSB), a public charter school founded by Jack Pannell Jr., opened its doors to 180 "Collegiate Gents" in grades 4–6. As the founding parent of this school, a venture pursued on behalf of my own son and many others like him in the city, I envisioned along with Mr. Pannell an academically rigorous learning space that also communicated the notion of Black masculinity as a continuous spectrum, rather than a limited space, where all boys could see themselves reflected.

What follows here is an in-depth conversation with the school's principal John Hawkins Snowdy, who leads the school of 440 boys. Principal Snowdy presented his perspective on Black masculinity among this vulnerable yet vibrant segment of a population in one of our nation's struggling urban centers.

Three primary questions guided our discussion: (1) What is Black masculinity? (2) How do you see Black masculinity manifested and performed among students in your building? and (3) What lessons have you given or learned as your staff strives to convey the broad idea of Black masculinity? Using the words of the seasoned school administrator who is also a Morehouse College graduate (an all-male historically Black college in Atlanta, Georgia), we are provided insights to the representations of young Black boys by others and of themselves, and the challenges and successes experienced inside the walls of this all-male academic setting.

What is most striking about this conversation is Principal Snowdy's willingness to view the school and his role in it as an ever-evolving work-in-progress, striving toward excellence on behalf of his students. He shares his "open book" for all of us to see the constraints of masculinity, while also exploring the complexity around familial relationships and those with other men. Finally, he discusses what he considers the "secret sauce" of Baltimore Collegiate because of the school's intentionality around a culture of success.

## CONSTRAINED MASCULINITY

Scholars (Jones, 2016; Brown, 2005; Jackson & Dangerfield, 2002; and, Jackson, 1997) articulate Black masculinity as a constrained and contested space with a complex set of political, social, and cultural agendas attached. As a result, the definition is always influx and embedded in stereotypes often embraced or rejected by those claiming Black and masculine identities. This definition seems to initially counter the perspective given by Principal Snowdy who suggests instead that "Black masculinity is the same as masculinity across the board with every other race and demographic" (J. H. Snowdy, personal communication, November 13, 2017). He sees masculinity as a shared experience imposed upon all men in our society. Trujillo (1991) discusses this as hegemonic masculinity and explains that every culture creates a notion of what it expects of its men. In U.S. society, it is often presented as one who is invested in patriarchy, exhibiting the physical and intellectual control of men over women, and men of color and who are unquestionably heterosexual.

When I press him further on that definition the school leader affirms that the constraints of Black masculinity do appear differently among other races; thus, aligning his understanding of the term to that of the scholars in the field:

> I think Black men have more pressure than any other group to fit into a particular space of what a Black man should be. . . . [For instance] if you attend schools that are diverse, a lot of people say, "Black guys don't do that, Black guys don't say that, Black guys do this." There is not as much leeway or diversity in the type of person you can be if you are in that type of space. (J. H. Snowdy, personal communication, November 13, 2017)

The lack of diversity resides in the limited representations of Black men and boys in the media, specifically the tendency to present a monolithic depiction of [this] multifaceted population (Jackson & Hopson, 2011). Jones (2016) purports, "it is impossible to define Black masculinity without addressing the stereotypes that are attributed to the portrayals of Black men in our society." Such stereotypes render this population violent, exploitable, hypersexual, incompetent, and uneducated (Jackson & Dangerfield, 2002). As it relates to

Black males and education, the early work of Kunjufu (1983) explicates this idea of the 4th grade failure syndrome, in which he raises specific connections between the lack of educational success of young Black boys and the shift in perception by the adults in our school buildings toward those students. Principal Snowdy describes it this way:

> The media really has a huge impact on how black boys perceive themselves. They're either athletes, rappers, and they're presented in very few other ways. Even with President Obama, he just became President Obama. He wasn't a type or it wasn't like okay, there's the athlete, the rapper, the actor, the politician. It didn't become an archetype itself. He just became an exception which I would like to have seen the ripple effect of it being a goal that little kids aspired to be the same way they aspire to be athletes. (J. H. Snowdy, personal communication, November 13, 2017)

Additionally, Principal Snowdy acknowledged a cool pose embedded in the complexity of Black masculinity (Majors & Billson, 1993). When asked about the ways in which students perform masculinity, he offers examples that specifically reference a "ritualized form of masculinity that entails behaviors, scripts, physical posturing, impression management, and carefully crafted performances that deliver a single, critical message: pride, strength, and control" (p. 4):

> [When] they hear the constant messages of "Be a man." "Be tough." "Don't cry." "Don't show emotion." "Don't talk." It really makes them very angry. A lot of our boys are extremely mad, extremely angry and they don't understand why. I think they think being angry is what men are and that attaches to their interpretation of masculinity. Like, "when I see my dad, he's mad, and that's what men do. I get mad and when I get mad, I have to show everyone that I am mad and the way I can do that is by using profanity, by fighting and by threatening." (J. H. Snowdy, personal communication, November 13, 2017)

Posturing can be physical in nature. Also, posturing can appear to disregard what others find important or relevant:

> I think a lot of times our boys think that masculinity means not caring or showing indifference in particular to academics or getting in trouble. "I don't care. Call my mother, I don't care." "Call the school police, I don't care." And [it is] being tough enough to survive whatever is thrown at them as a result. I think a lot of times the indifference is what really scares me because it's posturing. It's not authentic because they do care. They do want better for themselves. They do see what happens and the negative outcomes as a result. But "I'm not a punk, I can't care." Or, "if I don't want to be seen as soft, I can't care." (J. H. Snowdy, personal communication, November 13, 2017)

The impact of posturing has real and material consequences for students. The principal recognizes that several of the students have to manage significant responsibilities in their home life or community, which further fosters a façade that academic performance is inconsequential:

> Many of our boys are holding adult responsibilities. . . . We have some 9 and 10-year-olds who catch the bus by themselves and navigate the city effortlessly. Or 11 and 12-year-olds who go pick up siblings and care for them throughout the night. Granted, these are things which, around the world people do all the time, but they don't live in large metropolitan cities with the same levels of danger that are here. So, it's different for our boys. (J. H. Snowdy, personal communication, November 13, 2017)

The pursuit of academic success could be interpreted by some as having sold out or opting to act White (Fordham, 1996; Ogbu, 1990), as those efforts may appear peculiar to those of the community. Therefore, to avoid being ostracized by peers, some students underachieve in their school performance (Noguera, 2003) and choose to place greater emphasis on skills of survival or toughness that have larger consequences or significance in their daily lives.

## MOTHERS AND SONS

U.S. Census (2016) data report most Black American households (~65%) are headed by single mothers. This suggests that a significant number of women rear their children, and in this case, sons, alone. The statistic is reified in a single-gender school environment where mothers are visibly the strongest supporters of their sons whether the activity is educational or sports-related in nature.

Regardless of socioeconomic status or educational attainment, Black mothers are often present and engaged in a multitude of ways to advocate for their children (Allen & White-Smith, 2017), especially during the elementary years of schooling. And while the parental involvement may be limited by the inability to volunteer in the school building, mothers find alternative ways to be ever-present in the educational experiences of their children. This engagement was of particular concern for Mr. Snowdy as he broached the topic of interactions of mothers with their sons. He immediately disclaimed that he was not "picking on mothers," but he offered a strong opinion on how this parent-child relationship impacts young boys and their school performance:

> Our 4th graders, I don't think they really understand what masculinity means because they're 9. I think, they're very much young boys who are trying to break away from their mothers but still need that level of nurturing and look for it everywhere they can. I believe a number of boys have been emasculated and that starts very early . . . and I see that a lot throughout the school but

particularly with the younger boys in the way that they always need to be reinforced. (J. H. Snowdy, personal communication, November 13, 2017)

The school leader extends this point by highlighting specific concerns regarding how some mothers communicate with their sons:

> Some of our younger boys only respond to certain levels of reinforcement. Like if I tell you that I need you to sit down, if I say it in a respectful, calm way you may not respond to that because you're used to being spoken to with profanity and malice in a voice that often times comes from a female adult at home. I recall the scene from *Boyz in the Hood* a great deal when the boy is brushing his hair and his mother says, "You ain't s***, you ain't gon' be s*** because your daddy wasn't s***. Look at you . . . you ain't s***." Sometimes the mothers come into the school like that and they associate all of the negativity that they are seeing with their sons to a man that may or may not be around. And the only male figure often times that our boys can relate to is constantly being berated and talked down upon and equated with something that's less than, which in turn, they internalize and begin to feel that way about themselves. (J. H. Snowdy, personal communication, November 13, 2017)

Mr. Snowdy raised concern about the tone of this communication, which at times is demoralizing to his students, yet he also acknowledged that mothers pacify the boys and, hence inhibit their development into positive manhood:

> They are also being infantilized by not being pushed to do anything more. Not being held to high standards or expectations, making excuses for them and their behaviors; not being held accountable and not being expected to act appropriately which is really destructive for them because it puts them in a position where they never feel empowered to control their actions, or what they do, or what they can do. It then goes from their grades, to their academic performance, to their behavior, and to their interactions with peers. (J. H. Snowdy, personal communication, November 13, 2017)

The principal notes a significant shift in interactions with middle school students. Most mothers seem to approach their teenage sons with a different strategy that does not placate them:

> Once they are in middle school or in our case, in the 8th grade, I hear mothers, primarily, say: "I put my hands up, you're a man now. This is your life and I can't make you do anything different." But they're still 13! These boys experience a premature masculinity in that the roles typically ascribed to men are often given to the boys. Some of the parents who had their sons really young, specifically mothers, I know this is controversial, but they position their sons like a surrogate boyfriend or provider. They're their companion; they're their friend; they're their buddy. But you can't hold your buddy accountable the same way that you could hold your child accountable; so, pushing them to be men prematurely and take on male responsibilities while also not having an

appropriate scaffolding of, or not having enough of a gradual release in terms of what they are able to do, is unwise. (J. H. Snowdy, personal communication, November 13, 2017)

The result here is a conflicting message regarding what is expected of these young men. Forcey (1987) suggests that mothers are affected by the adage "damned if you do, damned if you don't," or a "Catch-22." It places them in the precarious role of supporting their sons, even to a determent, while also demanding certain manly behaviors, despite their inability to carry out such tasks at a young age (Burleson, 2015). Randolph (1995) surmised that Black males in single-mother households may be overwhelmed trying to fulfill the role of absent father, which might also preclude their efforts to excel in school.

## HOMOPHOBIA

An area of concern within the school building centers around the issue of sexual orientation, or more specifically, the homophobia exhibited among students. Scholars have historically referenced "African Americans [as] more likely to think of homosexuality as a moral failing" when compared to other racial/ethnic groups (Connell, 2016, p. 601). These stances may be grounded in religiosity, stigma, or even concerns of ambivalence associated with the institution of marriage. While numerous studies (Bonilla & Porter, 1990; Egan & Sherrill, 2009; Hunter, 2013; Lewis, 2003) acknowledge the disapproval of Blacks regarding homosexual relationships, it also noted that this population is "more likely to approve of gay rights protections, including employment nondiscrimination policies, than their white and Latino counterparts" (Connell, 2016, p. 601). Nonetheless, the microcosm of an all-male, largely Black student population would reflect that larger population regarding issues of sexual orientation and to that end impact the school community in uncertain ways:

> I think we have a lot of people who are being playfully discriminatory with saying who's gay and who's not gay. And that seems like with the 8th graders, that's all they're talking about, "Oh, he's gay." "Oh, he's not gay." One of the main ringleaders of the boys, during detention he said, "Mr. Snowdy, can I tell you something?" And he had a smile on his face when he said, "I'm gay. I need to come out of the closet." He made this huge thing of it and the other boys are just laughing, laughing, laughing, right? It's this joke that is pervasive in that grade level, specifically, but statistically, about 10 to 15 percent of them at least, if not more, are gay or may not know it yet, and are struggling and questioning [their sexual orientation]. How does that make them feel when everyone is making a joke about how I feel about the guy that's sitting next to me? (J. H. Snowdy, personal communication, November 13, 2017)

This is a pivotal growth moment for the school leadership and the Collegiate Gents. I recall in our first year as a charter school that one of our middle school teachers, who also was a former undergraduate student of mine, wanted to share with his 6th grade students that he, in fact, was gay. Many of the administrators struggled with this decision for fear it would become a distraction to the students and an impediment to the learning process. The teacher ultimately agreed and chose not to have those conversations with the boys but did take advantage of opportunities with the students to redirect language or discussions that proved denigrating to LGBTQ communities. Principal Snowdy continues:

> We haven't figured out yet how we [address], outside of just consequencing it, but that's not going to change the behavior. It's just going to drive it underground. Also knowing the negative effect it has on those who are having those feelings but don't want to be ridiculed is something that we need to do a better job of addressing. We need to make sure our boys feel safe and also let them know that their masculinity is fine. One of my old supervisors, he was gay, and he was one of the meanest, toughest guys I've met. Sexuality is separate from that. He's very much, if you look at strength and confidence and ability to speak your mind, what we believe masculine men do. But he's also gay . . . and they're not one and the same. (J. H. Snowdy, personal communication, November 13, 2017)

He speaks candidly about this limitation yet seems motivated to provide educational moments for the students to be educated further. Mr. Snowdy kept repeating the need to be intentional in his actions to convey what must be done differently within the school community:

> I am working with a teacher to do an equality campaign where we'll have equality signs through all the classrooms. We will spend a week on morning meetings specifically addressing it. I don't know to what extent that's going to address it. I don't know to what extent that's going to be successful. I don't know if we failed by allowing the playful homophobia to go too far. My master's thesis was actually about whether attending single-gendered institutions promote homophobia because during my senior year at Morehouse [I witnessed] a guy I was in class with, nearly kill a gay guy who peeked at him in the shower. He went to his room and got his baseball bat and ended up serving nine years in jail for that. So, his homophobia was to the point that he was willing to kill somebody for it. I don't think our boys are afraid. I don't think they're violent as a result of it. They're not fighting each other because they think someone else is gay. They think it's the biggest joke in the world and they play and talk about it, which is extremely insensitive to those who are in that community or not sure whether they're in it or not. (J. H. Snowdy, personal communication, November 13, 2017)

This level of intentionality by the principal and staff is necessary to address a concern that likely impacts a segment of the student body. It also serves as a reinforcement of the school's commitment to enable every child to be known and loved in our building, as often stated by BCSB's founder and executive director, Jack Pannell. The most effective way to communicate that expression is assuring the all Collegiate Gents are comfortable with their identity, regardless of where it falls on the spectrum of Black masculinity.

## "ARE YOU A WINDOW SHOPPER?"

An area of pride for the school leader focused on the messaging around success. Principal Snowdy noted that over the three years of the school's existence that administrators, teachers, and support staff alike convey messages of motivation and encouragement that also afford the boys to consider a new, broader interpretation of Black masculinity:

> I think often times we're kind of creating the school that we want in terms of the cool, masculine, tough guy, where the cool guys are the guys who do really well academically, or have options, those are the ones who are cool. The ones who are not doing well in school, whose options are going to be limited, I mean they're still cool because you can hang out with, joke around here and there with, but they're not the cool ones that are going to be successful and everyone knows it. Their cool masculinity comes from that indifference [mentioned earlier] as opposed to the other cool masculinity of ambition and I think it goes both ways. (J. H. Snowdy, personal communication, November 13, 2017)

Mr. Snowdy uses the hip-hop song, "Window Shopper" by 50 Cent to convey this point further with students:

> I played it and I was like "some of you guys are just going to be window shopping. You're going to be walking around and wishing that you had other things or looking at what other people have in their life and wishing that you could have it because you didn't put the work to get it yourself." Some of our boys are putting in the work now to be rewarded later and the fact that they are getting rewarded and they are going to be rewarded gives them an elite status in our school that others aspire to. The ones in the middle aspire to, but the indifferent ones remain indifferent. (J. H. Snowdy, personal communication, November 13, 2017)

He also speaks to the students about the secret sauce which he believes exists within each Collegiate Gent but may not be tapped. His goal is to teach the boys about hard work in order to be afforded choices:

I think the key is you reward the students who do well. Not only with just lauding them with praise, but you set them up as models, as examples. You reward them with opportunities that everyone values, and you directly link it to their hard work and achievement. People aspire to have what they have. I think we are fostering something that doesn't really happen until after high school—a secret sauce of sorts. So now, boys are seeing these amazing private schools and public schools that people value and want to go to. Some kids are getting these opportunities and others are not. If you want to be like the ones who have access and are getting these opportunities, you need to do a number of different things. For example, two guys go to a car dealership and one guy can buy any car on the lot; he's cooler than the guy who only can buy the one car that he qualifies for. That's a real life! What's cool; what's masculine; what's tough; what's IT is having choices. It's not cool to have to live in one place because you can't live anywhere else. And we talk about that all the time. (J. H. Snowdy, personal communication, November 13, 2017)

The school leader recognizes this secret sauce is not so secret or unique at all; but in fact, a value he works to instill in each student. Due to their respective challenges, he knows that the secret sauce has to be conveyed intentionally for each student to grasp and understand their ability to succeed. The goal is that all Collegiate Gents become more than window shoppers.

## CONCLUSION

The work at Baltimore Collegiate School for Boys is a part of a larger movement by educators, charter school management organizations, and community leaders to address the educational pitfalls of Black boys in urban settings. Schools such as Urban Prep Academies (IL), Eagle Academy for Young Men (NY), and Middle College at NC A&T State University (NC) were early innovators of academic success with this population of students of which BCSB benefitted. There remain detractors of this work who are not in favor of single-gender educational settings as well as those who speculate that such environments reinforce antifeminist pedagogies (Lindsay, 2018). While there may be merit to those critiques, the educational statistics for Black boys in Baltimore remain dim; for example, 41 percent of Black boys in Baltimore City Public Schools scored a "1" on the English/Language Arts component of the annual standardized test, which is the lowest possible score on the assessment, suggesting an inability to read and comprehend literature texts (Maryland State Department of Education, 2018). As a result, efforts such as these have provided a generation of students and their families an opportunity to shine.

This conversation with Principal Snowdy offered an opportunity to explore an all-male educational setting, while considering the concept of Black masculinity among its students. The school leader highlighted ways in which the school saw masculinity expressed or performed within the walls of BCSB and shared the challenges and successes experienced when striving to convey Black masculinity to the Collegiate Gents. What seems apparent is that this concept remains undefined and constrained, but is most aptly understood by how it is expressed:

> John McWhorter wrote a book called, *Black Authenticity*. I read that probably shortly after I graduated from college and essentially he was discussing what does it mean to be authentically Black? What does that mean in terms of how you carry yourself or how you conduct yourself or your level of education and what you want to do and how we get pigeonholed and I think black masculinity fits into that as well. (J. H. Snowdy, personal communication, November 13, 2017)

The challenges and successes are clearly articulated. Specifically, Principal Snowdy shared that the relationship between mothers and sons could hamper the development of the young boys. He expressed concern that the challenges around the role of a single mother might add undue pressures on their sons and, in effect, impact the students' trajectory to succeed in their academic performance.

Additionally, the school leader noted the issue of sexual orientation as another challenge area. Although often presented in the form of jokes, homosexuality was conveyed in a derogatory fashion and not a welcomed environment for all students. Principal Snowdy desired to create a school culture that was more intentional about supporting all students, regardless of sexual orientation. In his effort to expand the Collegiate Gents understanding of masculinity, Mr. Snowdy exhibited one of the school's strengths as well. The notion of cool is redefined in this space to enable students to see the possibilities before them when they strive to excel. Cool is not just the male student who is physically aggressive or exhibits a demeanor of indifference, but in fact, the cool kids are those who do more than window shop because they have several options before them.

BCSB promoted its first class of students, the Vanguard Class, to high school in June 2018. Over half of the seventy Collegiate Gents were admitted into merit-based public high schools or selective independent schools. Additionally, several of the students traveled internationally to Montreal, Canada, and London, England, to commence their time at BCSB. This educational space, while ever-evolving, has experienced tremendous success in its first three years of operation. It is clear that Principal Snowdy believes that exists because students "have more freedom to define masculinity beyond being a physical threat. You can just be cool."

## NOTE

1. On April 12, 2015, Freddie Gray, a 25-year-old Black male, was arrested for possession of an illegal knife and transported in a police van for booking. Upon arrival he was found unresponsive and in need of medical attention. A week later he succumbed to his injuries in what many believed was purportedly at the hands of the six Baltimore City police officers who arrested and transported him. His death led to several days of protesting known as the "Baltimore Uprising." The cases against the officers charged with his death were unsuccessful and eventually dismissed.

## REFERENCES

Allen, Q. & White-Smith, K. (2017). "That's why I say stay in school": Black mothers' parental involvement, cultural wealth, and exclusion in their son's schooling. *Urban Education, 53*(3), 409–35. https://doi.org/10.1177/0042085917714516

Bonilla, L. & Porter, J. 1990. A comparison of Latino, Black, and Non-Hispanic White attitudes toward homosexuality. *Hispanic Journal of Behavioral Sciences, 12*, 437–52. https://doi.org/10.1177/07399863900124007

Brown, T. (2005). Allan Iverson as America's most wanted: Black masculinity as a cultural site of struggle. *Journal of Intercultural Communication Research, 34*, 65–87.

Burleson, C. A. (2015). *Media representations and perceptions of Black "mama's boys:" A creative ethnography*. (Unpublished master's thesis). California State University, Northridge. Northridge, CA.

Connell, C. (2016). Contesting racialized discourses of homophobia. *Sociological Forum, 31*(3), 599–618. https://doi.org/10.1111/socf.12265

Egan, P. J. & Sherrill, K. (2009). *California's Proposition 8: What happened, and what does the future hold?* National Gay and Lesbian Task Force Policy Institute. Retrieved May 20, 2018: http://www.local2.thetaskforce.org/downloads/issues/egan_sherrill_prop8_1_6_09.pdf

Forcey, L. (1987). *Mothers of sons: Toward an understanding of responsibility*. New York: Praeger.

Fordham, S. (1996). *Blacked out: Dilemmas of race, identity, and success at Capital High*. Chicago, IL: University of Chicago Press.

Hunter, M. A. (2013). Race and the same-sex marriage divide. *Contexts, 12*, 74–76. https://doi.org/10.1177/1536504213499884

Jackson, R. L. (1997). Black "manhood" as xenophobe: An ontological exploration of the Hegelian dialectic. *Journal of Black Studies, 27*(6), 731–50. https://doi.org/10.1177/002193479702700601

Jackson, R. L. & Dangerfield, C. (2002). Defining Black masculinity as cultural property: Toward an identity negotiation paradigm. In L. Samovar and R. Porter (Eds.), *Intercultural communication: A reader* (pp. 120–36). Belmont, CA: Wadsworth.

Jackson, R. L. & Hopson, M. C. (2011). Introduction. In R. L. Jackson and M. C. Hopson (Eds.), *Masculinity in the Black imagination: Politics of communicating race and manhood* (pp. 1–6). New York: Peter Lang.

Jones, M. (2016). Defining Black masculinity. Odyssey. Retrieved on May 22, 2018: http://www.theodysseyonline.com/defining-black-masculinity

Kunjufu, J. (1983). *Countering the conspiracy to destroy Black boys*. Chicago, IL: African American Images.

Lewis, G. B. (2003). Black-White differences in attitudes toward homosexuality and gay rights. *Public Opinion Quarterly, 67*, 59–78. https://doi.org/10.1086/346009

Lindsay, C. (2018). *In a classroom of their own: The intersection of race and feminist politics in all-Black male schools*. Urbana-Champaign, IL: University of Illinois Press.

Majors, R., & Billson, J. M. (1993). *Cool pose: The dilemma of Black manhood in America*. New York: Simon and Schuster.

Maryland State Department of Education (2018). *PARCC: English Language Arts Current Year Data (2018)*. Retrieved on March 20, 2019: https://msp2018.msde.maryland.gov/Graphs/#/Assessments/ElaPerformance/1EL/17/6/3/3/3/3/3/3/3/3/3/3/30/XXXX

Noguera, P. (2003). *The trouble with Black boys: The role and influence of environmental and cultural factors on the academic performance of African American males*. Urban Education, 38, 431–59. https://doi.org/10.1177/0042085903038004005

Ogbu, J. (1990). Literacy and schooling in subordinate cultures: The case of Black Americans. In K. Lomotey (Ed.), *Going to school* (pp. 3–21). Albany, NY: SUNY Press.

Randolph, S. (1995). African American children in single-mother families. In B. Dickerson (Ed.), *African American single-mothers: Understanding their lives and families* (pp. 117–45). Thousand Oaks, CA: Sage Publications.

Trujillo, N. (1991). Hegemonic masculinity on the mound: Media representations of Nolan Ryan and American sports culture. *Critical Studies in Mass Communication, 8*, 290–308. https://doi.org/10.1080/15295039109366799

U.S. Census. (2016). Table C3. Living arrangements of children under 18 years and marital status of parents, by age, sex, race, and Hispanic origin and selected characteristics of the child for all children: 2016. Retrieved on May 25, 2018: www.census.gov/data/tables/2016/demo-families/cps-2016.html

*Chapter Seven*

# (Re)Educating Boys and Men of Color by Shaping Community Support

Kenneth Brown

Many research articles explore issues plaguing African American males, including studies on economic, social, and political gaps, and negative societal images. This chapter does not aim to add to that literature. The purpose here is to discuss how mentoring programs can be used to uplift African American males. Also, I call attention to skills needed to develop positive mentoring relationships. Limited attention is devoted to depressing data recorded in policy reports, briefs, and research studies. Instead, I focus on Black masculinity and resiliency, the importance of education, and best practices to foster mentoring relationships for boys of color.

According to the Schott 50 State Report on Public Education and Black Males, the national graduation rate for African American males is 47 percent (Weldon, 2015). More often than not, schools with African American majority enrollments are underfunded, lack contemporary technology, have short-tenured superintendents and principals, and high turnover rates among teachers (Fenwick, 2013). The Schott Report also concluded that within schools with talented, caring teachers, well-trained support staff, and challenging curricula, African American males graduate at significantly higher rates (Weldon, 2015).

African American males' suspension rates more than double their representation in schools across the country (Government Accountability Office Report, 2018). They tend to be suspended, expelled, and sent to the office, which causes them to miss valuable instruction time and indirectly affects levels of support. African American males are also disproportionately represented in special education programs across the country. On average, they receive an education that is less rigorous because the focus is typically on emotional and behavioral issues or learning disabilities, with little attention directed toward academic excellence, capacity development, or preparation to contribute to society. The lifelong implications of special education for this specific group includes higher rates for dropouts, arrests, and incarceration, as well as lower rates for college attendance, socioeconomic well-being, and life expectancy (Kunjufu, 2005; Rueda, Klingner, Sager, & Velasco, 2008; Skiba, Simmons, Ritter, Gibb, Rausch, Cuadrado, & Chung, 2008).

In 2017, Bridge and colleagues found that among children ages 5 to 11, and adolescents ages 12 to 14, those who took their own lives were more likely to be male, African American, and dealing with stressful relationships at home or with friends (Nutt, 2018). African American males account for more than 70 percent of all new male AIDS cases (Centers for Disease Control and Prevention, 2019). Nationwide, many African American males are unemployed and underemployed, lead the nation in homicides both as victims and as perpetrators, and have the highest incarceration, conviction, and arrest rates among comparative ethnic groups (Noguera, 2003). They have the highest probability of dying in the first year of life and face the reality of being the only group in the United States experiencing a decline in life expectancy (Noguera, 2003).

Masculinizing practices are situated within American families, school, and social settings. Families, male peer groups, and schools are consistently cited as having the most significant impact on the development of masculine identities for boys (Harper, Harris, & Mmeje, 2005; Kimmel & Messner, 2007; Kimmel, Hearn, & Connell, 2005). Gender-related messages consumed by boys in schools are remarkably consistent with those reinforced within families and peer groups. Scholars note that tasks that lead to academic success do not necessarily complement the activities in which boys engage to achieve a masculine identity (Harper, 2014). The relationship between masculine identity and academic success is further fundamentally incompatible, given the processes of socialization for boys (Harper, 2014). Often, learning and studying are equated with femininity.

Black masculinity is an ideology that influences the perception of African American males throughout society. African American males redefine manhood in order to respond to feelings of social alienation from dominant society. They do not accommodate standard traditional roles of masculinity largely equated to prejudice and racism. To compensate, African American males have highlighted attributes such as toughness and sexual promiscuity (Majors & Billson, 1992; Oliver, 1989). Physical posture, speech, and style of clothing all function as mannerisms consistent with alternative masculinity for African American men.

Harris (1995) states that behaviors include suppression of emotions, denial of vulnerability, and a predominant heterosexual focus. These attitudes are consistent with Majors and Billson's (1992) definition of cool pose, which refers to African American males' reliance on hypermasculine roles, values, and presentation of self to deal with stressful conditions (Roberts-Douglass & Curtis-Boles, 2013). According to Gause (2005), young African American males see power as stylizing their bodies over space and time in such a way that their bodies reflect uniqueness and provoke fear in others. To be bad is good because it subverts the language of the dominant White culture, and imposes distinctive chaos and attention that makes others pull back with trepidation (Gause, 2005). Black heterosexual masculinity is hero worship in the case of rappers, naturalized and commodified bodies in the case of athletes, symbols of menace and threat in the case of African American gang members, and noble warriors in the case of Afrocentric nationalists (Gause, 2005). Black men are typecast as entertainers, clowns, and super-athletes. While these images are seen throughout all facets of media, competing claims arguing for and against the need for Black masculinity lie solely on the backs of the African American men who deal with it.

Stigmas are embraced by people of other races, and by African Americans, but Black men see themselves as provider and protector of their families and communities. They feel misunderstood and believe that limited media portrayals are used to represent all African American men. When displaying self-advocacy their voices are stifled quickly. Conversely, their White counterparts can challenge any injustices they see fit without the same recourse.

Black men prepare Black boys for the double standards of White society. Lessons include maneuvering through school and the community, advocating for themselves and others, and overcoming social obstacles. Masculine identity development can be especially stressful due to environmental factors that confine manhood. White culture perpetuates negative imagery of Black males in media, film, and music. As such, we must eradicate negative representations, and showcase positive representations of the Black community.

Many African American men assert their masculinity in ways that differ from the expectations of the majority. The counter-narrative is necessary to foster pride and resiliency. Institutionalized racism, poverty, and media representation have contributed to the development and commodification of the images of African American men (Patrick, 2014; Milton, 2012). In response, some communities have begun to invest resources into mentoring programs. Mentoring is a way for African American men to address key issues while serving as role models in their communities. In addition, mentoring programs help adolescents navigate dominant culture while reinforcing their sense of identity and self-worth. Generally, mentoring is based on relationships with positive adult male role models. However, the influential role may be held by women as well. The goal is to promote intellectual growth, emotional support, and training toward social, academic, and professional goals.

## MENTORING PROGRAMS FROM A HISTORICAL PERSPECTIVE

Recent decades reveal an emergence of mentoring programs for African American males. The national government has recognized disparities in the quality of life for African Americans in comparison to other racial subgroups. In 2014, President Obama launched a new initiative to provide greater opportunities for boys and men of color. My Brother's Keeper enabled the White House to partner with businesses, nonprofit organizations, foundations, and African American fraternities to address disparities in education, criminal justice, and employment (Lee, 2014).

My Brother's Keeper is meant to help young men of color at critical moments in their lives. The initiative addresses early literacy, the school-to-prison pipeline, and young adulthood (Lee, 2014). It is based on connecting boys and young men of color, and providing support networks needed for higher education and employment (Lee, 2014). President Obama launched the initiative in the shadow of Trayvon Martin's death and George Zimmerman's acquittal. Local and national organizations immediately joined on. Considering the factors mentioned earlier in this chapter, mentoring programs are a necessity for survival.

For more than one hundred years, mentoring programs have been essential in the development of young African American males. For example, Big Brothers Big Sisters of America was established in 1904, initially mentoring goals focused largely on strategies to help children stay out of trouble. Gradually, mentors began to focus on one-on-one relationships based on trust and friendship, to help mentees reach their potential (www.bbbs.org). Today Big Brothers Big Sisters of America provides mentoring for children through partnerships with businesses, fraternities, and sororities, and nonprofit organizations.

In the last ten years, National CARES became a nationally recognized movement providing mentoring services to African American boys, girls, and young adults. It is uniquely designed to improve participants' self-esteem. The program is located in twenty-one states, and continues to grow. In addition, National Cares has influenced other programs, such as the Harvard Mentoring Project, which uses public service announcements to recruit mentors and raise awareness about the value of mentoring.

In recent years, many organizations have prioritized mentoring programs designed to serve African American males. Objectives include increased rates of graduation and interventions to incarceration, violence, and death. Data show that African American males are at the top of most negative categories (Patrick, 2014, Staples, 1982). Mentoring programs serve as one of the remedies to this epidemic.

Founded in 2006 as Essence CARES, the National CARES Mentoring Movement is a fast-growing coalition of some of the nation's most trusted organizations, high-profile African Americans and caring supporters. In

2008, Susan L. Taylor, then editor-in-chief of *Essence* magazine, left the company to lead the National CARES Mentoring Movement. Taylor has forged partnerships with the National Urban League, Children's Defense Fund, United Negro College Fund, NAACP, National 100 Black Men of America, and many other organizations. Currently in approximately forty-seven cities, National CARES is the only organization dedicated to providing mentoring, healing, and wellness services on a national scale for Black children (www.caresmentoring.org).

The National CARES signature program is called The Rising. Piloted at four high schools (one on the South Side of Chicago, two in Fort Lauderdale, and one in Detroit), the program focuses on the cultivation of cultural pride and high self-esteem, the development of critical thinking and literacy skills, and a love for learning among young Black parents (www.caresmentoring.org). The Rising is designed to help students learn about their heritage in an effort to help them succeed in school and in life.

Through the years, other organizations have made similar effort. The national nonprofit America's Promise/The Alliance for Youth has created mentoring programs to help boys and girls strategize around issues plaguing the communities. In addition, churches, schools, and community organizations began tailoring their mentoring programs to meet the needs of their community's children. These organizations recognize the benefits in mentoring the youth. Most have begun to streamline their services to focus on the individual needs of the children.

To increase awareness, January was dubbed National Mentoring Month. The annual high-profile campaign is also designed to recruit volunteers to serve as mentors. Throughout the month social media pages highlight events, provide information about programs, display pictures and videos, and recruit mentors.

Word continues to spread. Within the past twenty years, articles, local news, major networks like CNN, and successful talk shows like The Oprah Winfrey Show and Steve Harvey Show, have increased their coverage on mentoring programs. Additionally, ABC, CBS, Fox, and NBC have produced public service announcements that enable viewers to call for information on mentoring opportunities in their local communities (www.Harvard.edu). Currently, twenty-eight cable networks report commitment to airing public service announcements during prime time. And television shows have included episodes with dialogue or story lines dealing with mentoring. The increased media exposure has shed light on an effective way to impact the lives of children.

Mentoring programs have gained national attention. However, African American fraternities have provided mentoring services for over sixty years. These fraternities have contributed to communities throughout the United States and around the world. Most were founded in the early 1900s as a way for African American students to support each other. Soon thereafter, these fraternities added national programs and collaborations with other organizations to address the needs of children. Currently, each organization focuses on community outreach. Mentoring is at the core of their national programs.

## BEST PRACTICES TO DEVELOP POSITIVE MENTORING RELATIONSHIPS

How one defines mentoring will affect the type of mentor/mentee relationship that is established. Throughout the literature, mentoring is defined differently, but key ideas influence relationships between mentors and mentees. For example, one common criticism is the absence of a clear definition of mentoring for everyone involved (Benishek, Bieschke, Park, & Slattery, 2004). Mentoring is described as a relationship where an experienced friend is there to help in any number of ways (www.mentoring.com). It is a positive contribution by a non-parental adult to the life of a young person (Baker & McGuire, 2005; DuBois & Rhodes, 2006). Often, mentoring involves regular dyadic meetings between a child and an older person who provides guidance, support, attention, and caring over an extended period of time. Additionally, a mentoring relationship may include constant and consistent meetings, direction, and long-term commitment. Mentorship infers an existence of activities, such as tutoring, field trips, or extracurricular activities in which observable guidance and support occur. Simultaneously, it is a process that cultivates a relationship that is less observable, and dependent upon perceptions and expressions of both parties. A mentor can be a volunteer role model, or a leader, that is committed and consistent in helping the mentee. Mentors tend to be counselors, teachers, coaches, bosses, coworkers, community members, relatives, or friends.

Identification is an important component of academic success. Academic identification is the extent to which academic pursuits and outcomes form the basis for self-evaluation (Osborne, 1999). Students who identify with academics are motivated to perform because self-esteem is closely tied to their ability to excel academically. They see themselves as significant members of the community, accepted and respected in school, and include school as a part of their self-definition (Voelkl, 1996).

African American adolescent boys may feel stereotyped and alienated due to negative experiences encountered in school. Thus, their self-evaluation may disconnect from their academic performance (Osborne, 1999). African American males are tracked disproportionately into low-ability groups, are socially and economically isolated from their classmates, receive more frequent and harsher disciplinary actions, and tend to be held in lower academic regard by teachers in classrooms throughout the country. They are expected to succeed academically in what may feel like a hostile environment that arouses defensive reactions that interfere with intellectual performance.

To change the way we perceive, talk about, and interact with African American boys, is to promote their academic and social development (Goings, Smith, Harris, Wilson, & Lancaster, 2015). Mentoring programs help reinforce strategies to decrease the effects of stereotyping and alienating experiences, and provide an outlet to express frustrations with the system. A mentor's narrative can counter the negative perceptions of African American males. Also, a mentor can encourage the self-esteem and confidence needed to achieve socially, academically, and financially.

African American males require culturally responsive programs based in appropriate knowledge, prior experience, frames of reference, and performance styles of ethnically diverse students. Topics taught must connect to their lived experiences. Majority group members make an easier connection due to constant images that reflect their heritage. Typically, in predominantly White systems, Black students experience some level of disconnect. Culturally responsive programs encourage confidence, pride, responsibility, and critical consciousness (Jackson, Sealey-Ruiz, & Watson, 2014).

A good mentoring program will develop long-standing relationships. The quantity of time and quality of interactions significantly impact young peoples' perceptions of interpersonal relationships. Indeed, the mentor-youth bond is essential to their perceptions of relationships (Thomson & Zand, 2009). For example, a national evaluation of Big Brothers Big Sisters programs reveals that mentored youth show increased trust in their parents, increased emotional support from peers, and are less likely to use alcohol and drugs at an early age (Grossman & Tierney, 1998).

Another study by Rhodes, Grossman, and Resch (2000) revealed that mentored youth show increased improvements in parental relationships, value for school, self-worth, and academic achievement (Thomson & Zand, 2009). In both studies, positive outcomes were realized most by youth who saw mentors as important in their lives. Mentors challenge negative views that adolescents may hold about themselves or adults, and demonstrate positive, caring relationships. Enduring positive interactions modify adolescents' general perceptions of relationships, and terminate interactions not in their best interest. In addition, programs support African American males with challenges they face in academic settings. For example, the Guide Right Program by Kappa Alpha Psi Fraternity, Inc., Big Brothers Big Sisters of America, and 100 Black Men of America, Inc. were created to support students outside traditional educational settings.

A safe space is necessary to encourage trust between mentees and mentors. Safe space also lends to open dialogue. Participants must be able to share personal feelings and experiences, and show emotion and care in a culturally appropriate and gendered cipher (Jackson, Sealey-Ruiz, & Watson,

2014). These conversations create opportunities for friendship, knowledge, personal identity and increased self-esteem. Trust leads to respect. Within African American communities respect is important to relationships. Communication will not occur without respect. Once respect is established, participants can engage in a reciprocal thought and communication.

Mentors and youth approach the mentoring relationship with their respective expectations. As such, effective programs respond with protocols to assign individuals based on their respective needs (Rhodes, 2002). Mentors should be trained on best practices to foster relationships. Also, mentors need to be knowledgeable about applicable content. The dynamics of adolescent behavior will influence the mentoring process. The mentor must respond accordingly.

Effective programs enact a range of practices necessary for healthy mentoring. For example, some mentors use technology to communicate more often. Others meet in person, but less frequently. Both approaches can incorporate fun and interesting activities. Other important aspects include training and ongoing supervision of mentors, clear expectations, program-sponsored activities, and parental support and involvement (Randolph & Johnson, 2008). Participants need to understand their roles and obligations in the mentoring process. Training should include knowledge about mentors and mentees, including background, motivation and feelings, and strategies for support (Britner, Balcazar, Blechman, 2006).

Although mentor training is critical to a program's success, DuBois and Rhodes (2006) argue that it is equally important to provide training and technical assistance to administrators and staff responsible for implementing mentoring programs. They are often responsible for setting goals and measuring effectiveness. Everyone should be in agreement with the administration and implementation of the program.

## CONCLUSION

African American mentors positively inform the lives of African American adolescents. Mentees tend to be more receptive of mentors who are from similar backgrounds. Empathy and share of common knowledge may translate into skills needed to navigate oppressive structures. Conversely, shared experiences alone will not guarantee positive mentoring relationships. There is no extant formula for accomplishing this work (Jackson, Sealey-Ruiz, & Watson, 2014).

Black masculinities vary based on background. Personal experiences differ from mentor to mentor. African American males are not a monolithic group. Mentors and mentees must begin with their respective goals. Everyone involved has the potential to contribute to, and benefit from, mentoring programs.

## REFERENCES

Baker, D. B. & Magruire, C. P. (2005). Mentoring in historical perspective. In D. L. DuBoise & M. J. Karcher (Ed.) *Handbook of youth mentoring*. Thousand Oaks, CA: Sage.

Benishek, L. A., Bieschke, K. J., Park, J., & Slattery, S. M. (2004). A multicultural feminist model of mentoring. *Journal of Multicultural Counseling and Development, 32*, 428–42.

Big Brothers Big Sisters of America. www.bbbs.org.

Bridge, J. A., Iyengar, S., Salary, C. B., Barbe, R. P., Birmaher, B., Pincus, H. A., Ren, L., & Brent, D. A. (2007). Clinical response and risk for reported suicidal ideation and suicide attempts in pediatric antidepressant treatment: A meta-analysis of randomized controlled trials. *Journal of the American Medical Association, 297*(15), 1683–96.

Britner, P. A., Balcazar, F. E., & Blechman, E. A., (2006). Mentoring special youth populations. *Journal of Community Psychology, 34*(6), 747–63.

Centers for Disease Control and Prevention. (2019). HIV in the United States and dependent areas. Retrieved from https://www.cdc.gov/hiv/statistics/overview/ataglance.html

DuBois, D. L. & Rhodes, J. E. (2006). Youth mentoring: Bridging science with practice. *Journal of Community Psychology, 47*(6), 647–55.

Fenwick, L. (2013). Upending stereotypes about Black students. *Education Week, 33*(7), 28–32.

Gause, C. P. (2005). The ghetto sophisticates: Performing black masculinity, saving lost souls, and serving as leaders of the new school. *Taboo: The Journal of Culture and Education, 9(*1), 17–31.

Goings, R. B., Smith, A., Harris, D., Wilson, T., & Lancaster, D. (2015). Countering the narrative: A layered perspective on supporting black males in education. *Perspectives on Urban Education, 12*(1), 54–63.

Grossman, J. B., & Tierney, J. P. (1998). Does mentoring work? An impact study of the Big Brothers/Big Sisters program. *Evaluation Review, 22*, 403–26.

Harper, S. R. (2014). (Re)setting the agenda for college men of color: Lessons learned from a 15-year movement to improve Black male student success. In R. A. Williams (Ed.) *Men of color in higher education: New foundations for developing models for success* (pp. 116–43). Sterling, VA: Stylus.

Harper, S. R. and Associates. (2014). *Succeeding in the city: A report from the New York City Black and Latino male high school achievement study*. Philadelphia: University of Pennsylvania, Center for the Study of Race and Equity in Education.

Harper, S. R., Harris, F., & Kenechukwu, M. (2005). *A theoretical model to explain the overrepresentation of college men among campus judicial offenders: Implications for campus administrators.* University of Pennsylvania: GSE Publications.

Harvard School of Public Health. (1998). 33 TV networks join national campaign to recruit mentors for at-risk youth. Press Release. www.harvard.edu.

Herrera, C., Grossman, J. B., Kauh, T. J., Feldman, A. F., & McMaken, J. (2007). *Making a difference in schools: The Big Brothers and Sisters school-based mentoring impact study.* Philadelphia, PA: Public/Private Ventures.

Jackson, I., Sealey-Ruiz, Y., & Watson, W. (2014). Reciprocal love: mentoring Black and Latino males through an ethos of care. *Urban Education, 49*(4), 394–417. doi: 10.1177/ 0042085913519336.

Kimmel, M. S. & Messner, M. A. (2007). *Men's Lives*. New York: Paerson.

Kimmel, M. S., Hearn, J., & Connell, R. W. (2004). *Handbook of studies on men and masculinities*. Thousand Oaks, CA: Sage Publications.

Kunjufu, J. (2005). *Keeping Black boys out of special education*. First Edition, Tenth Printing. United States.

Lee, T. (2014). President Obama expands "My Brother's Keeper" initiative. http://www.msnbc.com/msnbc/obama-expands-my-brothers-keeper-initiative.
Majors, R., & Billson, J. M. (1992). *Cool pose: The dilemmas of black manhood in America.* New York: Lexington Books.
Milton, T. (2012). Class status and the construction of Black masculinity. *Ethnicity and Race in a Changing World, 3*(1), 17–31.
National CARES website. www.carementoring.org.
Noguera, P. (2003). The trouble with Black boys: The role and influence of environmental and cultural factors on the academic performance of African American males. *Urban Education, 38,* 431–59.
Nutt, A. E. (2018, May, 21). Suicide rate for black children twice the rate of white children, new data show. Retrieved from https://www.washingtonpost.com/news/to-your-health/wp/2018/05/21/suicide-rates-for-black-children-twice-that-of-white-children-new-data-show/.
Patrick, L. (2014). Outside insiders: Remember the time. *The Journal of Pan African Studies, 7*(6), 106–27.
Randolph. K., & Johnson, J. (2008). School-based mentoring programs: A review of the research. *Children & Schools, 30,* 177–85.
Rhodes, J. E. (2002). *Stand by me: The risks and rewards of mentoring today's youth.* Cambridge, MA: Harvard University Press.
Rhodes, J. E., Grossman, J. B., & Resch, N. L. (2000). Agents of change: Pathways through which mentoring relationships influence adolescents' academic adjustment. *Child Development, 71,* 1662–71.
Roberts-Douglass, K., & Curtis-Boles, C. (2013). Exploring positive masculinity development in African American men: A restrospective study. *Psychology of Men & Masculinity, 14*(1), 7–15.
Rueda, R., Klingner, J., Sager, N., & Velasco, A. (2008). Reducing disproportionate representation in education: Overview, explanations, and solutions. In T. C. Jimenez & V. L. Graf (Eds.) *Education for All: Critical Issues in the Education for Children and Youth with Disabilities.* New York: Jossey-Boss.
Skiba, R. J., Simmons, A. B., Ritter, S., Gibb, A. C., Rausch, M. K., Cuadrado, J., & Chung, C. (2008). Achieving equity in special education: History, status, and current challenges. *Exceptional Children, 74*(3): 264–88.
Staples, R. (1982). *Black masculinity: The Black male's role in American society.* San Francisco: Black Scholar Press.
Thomson, N. R., & Zand, D. H. (2009). Mentees' perceptions of their interpersonal relationships: The role of the mentor-youth bond. *Youth & Society, 41*(3), 434–45.
U.S. Department of Education. (2005). 27th annual report to Congress on the implementation of the Individuals with Disabilities Education Act. Washington, DC: Author.
United States Government Accountability Office Report (2018). K–12 education discipline disparities for Black students, boys, and students with disabilities. (Report No. GAO-18-258). Retrieved from the U.S Government Accountability Office website: https://www.gao.gov/assets/700/690828.pdf.
Voelkl, K. E. (1996). Measuring students' identification with school. *Educational and Psychological Measurement, 56*(5), 760–70.
Weldon, T. (2015). Study: Graduation rate gap exists between black, white males. Capitol Ideas, The Council of State Governments Insights & Innovations, 6. www.csg.org.

*Chapter Eight*

# "We Demand an Equal Show upon Matters Effecting Our Industrial Welfare"

*Black Manhood and Labor Activism in Early Jim Crow Illinois*

Alonzo M. Ward

In 1897, during one of the most violent decades in the history of labor relations in Illinois, former African American assemblyman Jacob Amos of Cairo, Illinois, wrote a series of editorials for the *Illinois Record* newspaper. The editorials focused primarily on the economic and political conditions among African Americans throughout the state. Amos was particularly incensed over the lack of interest in the labor condition of Illinois African Americans, and the racial exclusiveness of the nation's major labor unions. "Almost every branch of skill[ed] labor is organized," he wrote, "and most of their constitutions require . . . that an applicant must be a white male twenty-one years of age" (p. 5). Amos directed much of his angst toward politicians for their atrocious behavior for allowing racial exclusion. To emphasize his point, he invoked commonly used Victorian age gender discourse: "it is for manhood and [womanhood] that we demand protection against such selfish scoundrels as the labor leaders who set themselves up as the bridge between one set of labor and the Negro" (p. 5). He concluded by insisting that the "infamous treachery" end, and demanded immediate action: "As a people we demand [an] equal show upon matters affecting our industrial welfare" (p. 5).

By the 1890s, while Illinois African Americans were fighting against rampant racial exclusion from labor unions, they were simultaneously being pushed out of skilled and semi-skilled occupations throughout the state. As

White workers demanded that racial meanings be applied to the larger labor movement during the latter portion of the nineteenth century—that is, the racialization of labor—African American workers were forced to choose whether they would continue to vie for labor movement involvement or fight against it from the outside. Most Black men were provided with little choice and were forced to battle against the labor movement as strikebreakers. Yet the story of Black workers in Illinois during the early days of Jim Crowism is not one that follows a simple narrative. By the end of the first decade of the twentieth century, working-class White Illinoisans were convinced that African Americans were indeed a scab race. That narrative is not only misguided, but it also only tells a portion of the history of African American workers in the Prairie State. As Assemblyman Amos lamented, Illinois African Americans were, in fact, being shut out of labor unions at an alarming rate. However, in the face of rampant and often violent racism, Amos and many other Black people refused to accept their predetermined inferior position. Instead, African American leaders, like Amos, utilized the Victorian Age discourse of masculinity to demand their rights as workers and citizens.

## A NATION STEEPED IN A "NEW MASCULINITY"

White Americans had long associated virile manhood with White supremacy. According to historian Gail Bederman, by the last decades of the nineteenth century, middle class White Americans were discovering various ways to link male power to race. Sometimes they linked manly power to the racial supremacy of civilized White men, or in other contexts, they attached manhood to savagery of non-White peoples. Part of the need to reshape masculinity had to do with the notion that White men had become too civilized and were thus in danger of embracing an unmanly racial sloth instead of virile manhood. Bederman noted that White leaders, such as Theodore Roosevelt, insisted that American men needed to embrace a strenuous life in order to fully achieve the apex of civilization.

It was not happenstance that the redefinition of White masculinity coincided with Jim Crowism in the United States. While men like Roosevelt helped to reshape White masculinity in order to justify foreign colonial possessions over inferior and effeminate darker peoples in other nations, White Americans took their cue from this racialized outlook. The new racial viewpoint degraded domestic racial others by suggesting that these groups were under-evolved and therefore under-civilized (effeminate) races that were incapable of achieving the masculine level of White Americans. With limited masculine (civilized) traits, these groups were also distinguished from White Americans through a lack of gender differences within the race—that is, male and female societal roles and physical characteristics were less distinguishable.

As the racial hierarchy solidified, it gradually encompassed all facets of American life for its non-White subjects. While African Americans suffered from overwhelming exclusionary practices, legalized segregation (*Plessy v. Ferguson*, 1896), and extensive terrorization throughout the United States, they not only invoked commonly used tropes of masculinity and manhood rights, they acted upon them as well. As new industrial workers (including so-called native Whites) jockeyed for advantageous positions within the chaotic and rapidly growing industrial economy of the late nineteenth century, they struggled to adjust to the modernization of the workplace. Yet Illinois African Americans were also compelled to adjust to a system of racialization within a workplace that castigated them as stereotypically ineffectual workers that would somehow degrade the labor of White workers. This process resulted in frequent conflicts with European American workers who, in their effort to secure their own tenuous position as laborers within the chaotic political economy, competed against Black workers for even the lowliest occupations. The devastating consequence of this racialization process by the beginning of the twentieth century led to the idea that Illinois African Americans were anti-union and unsympathetic to the plight of the rights of workers. Rather than submit to overwhelming odds against them, Assemblyman Amos and other Illinois African Americans refused to be subjected to hapless victimhood. Instead, they openly combatted, debated, and protested racist treatment in the workplace as well as any idea they were less than a manly race.

## BLACK RESISTANCE TO LABOR EXCLUSION

In the context of heightened racial exclusion and violence against African Americans throughout the United States, Tuskegee Institute president and orator Booker T. Washington (Washington, 1901) urged African Americans to accept segregation and disenfranchisement in exchange for opportunities to harness their collective industrial skills. His most famous articulation of his vision for the African American worker was at the Atlanta Exposition in 1895 where he carved out a defined place for African Americans during a time when their exclusion from industrial labor and labor unions had become largely accepted. In his 1895 address, Washington argued that the best avenue for economic success for African Americans was to remain in the South where they should put brains and skill into the common occupations of life. Instead of pursuing civil and political rights, African Americans should secure their constitutional rights through the gradual and indirect process of first becoming successful businessmen in order to gain the respect of White Americans. Considering the widely held notion of the inferiority of African

Americans during the Progressive era, it is hardly surprising that White America lauded Washington's message.

Washington initially garnered strong support among African Americans for his achievements at Tuskegee and message of accommodation at the 1895 exposition. However, criticism mounted among African American intellectuals who called into question the manliness of his philosophy. The Washington Bee (September 14, 1901) chided Washington for his anti-protest philosophy: "If accepted as the greatest speech ever delivered by a negro, then it was a standing rebuke to the sturdy manhood; the eloquent protest against outrage and the life work of the immortal Frederick Douglass, and a refutation of the exposures of barbarism and wholesale murder of negroes, echoed through two continents by Ida B. Wells" (p. 1). Among his harshest critics was burgeoning scholar and activist, W. E. B. Du Bois, who derisively referred to the speech as The Atlanta Compromise. Du Bois noted that Washington insisted on thrift and self-respect, but also insisted on silent submission to civic inferiority, which he argued, was bound to sap the manhood of any race in the long run. Although Washington showed a remarkable ability to garner the approval of Southern and Northern Whites, Black support for accommodation was, at best, mixed.

African Americans were left with few viable options at making a living during the late nineteenth century—through pseudoscientific thought, they were validated as an unmanly and inferior race that was incapable of full evolution and justifiably relegated to second class citizenship. Since they were alleged inferior people, they were viewed as the problem in virtually all aspects of American life. By accepting Washington's accommodationist philosophy, many African Americans argued that it would sap the race of its manhood by accepting second-class status. Instead, Illinois African Americans largely rejected his conciliatory philosophy and battled against the normalization of racism. They refused to act as passive victims, and instead, often took matters into their own hands through a variety of strategies intended to counteract racist labor policies. As historian Sundiata K. Cha-Jua noted, the thread of self-defense runs through the African American experience, and the notion of the weak old Negro was largely a mythical idea.

To alleviate the hardships African American workers faced, newspaper editor and activist T. Thomas Fortune formed the National Afro-American League in 1887 to battle against racial discrimination and against the atrocious and appalling labor conditions of African American workers, their wages, and the overcrowded nature of labor in general. During his opening address in Chicago in 1890, Fortune set forth the organization's masculine and aggressive agenda through a combination of preeminent philosophy of self-help and racial solidarity with the protest tactics of legalism, direct action, and violent manhood self-help.

We propose to accomplish our purposes by the peaceful methods of agitation, through the ballot and the courts, but if others use the weapons of violence to combat our peaceful arguments, it is not for us to run away from violence. A man's a man, and what is worth having is worth fighting for. (Blackpast, 2007)

While Washington advocated virtual silence among African Americans to advance his agenda, Fortune not only demanded more protest among the masses, he advocated physical violence during a time when the lynching of Black men had reached an all-time high. Following Fortune's lead, Afro-Illinoisans refused to remain silent when their rights were trampled upon. Unfortunately, during the years before the Great Migration, African Americans were given plenty of opportunities to express angst over their rapidly deteriorating status.

## STRIKEBREAKING AS MASCULINE LABOR ACTIVISM

By the 1890s, strikebreaking had become a commonly used weapon against the labor movement. As Black workers were increasingly excluded from labor unions and as the trend of White workers refusal to work alongside Black men increased, employers sought to exploit the racialization process by hiring African Americans as strikebreakers. Historian Stephen H. Norwood suggested that strikebreaking appealed to many African Americans because it provided them with their best opportunity to assume a tough, combative posture in public and to display masculine courage while risking serious physical injury or even death. Furthermore, strikebreaking allowed Black men to challenge openly White society's image of them as obsequious, cowardly, and lacking the ability to perform well under pressure.

Black leaders often expressed mixed feelings about African American strikebreaking. T. Thomas Fortune correctly placed the blame on the shoulders of both White union workers and Northern industrialists for this growing phenomenon. "It is hard to find fault with the poor colored men for the part they have taken in these inroads; but for the capitalists who have brought them to the North there should be nothing short of positive popular condemnation." Every effort, he continued, "must be made to assert the rights of the colored," but they should be "loudly warned" against being used as strikebreakers to disrupt Northern labor conflicts. He argued that the onus to educate Southern African American workers was on Northern organized labor. However, he maintained that Black workers could not afford to "undermine white laborers when they make organized resistance to unjust wages or treatment at the hands of employers" (Blackpast, 2007).

Although he argued against antagonizing the interests of white laborers because their interests were identical in every particular with Black workers, he displayed an acute understanding of the need to become a strikebreaker in the face of overwhelming discrimination:

> it is not to be marveled at that colored men should embrace the inducements to better their condition held out to them by labor agents. These laborers are not always acquainted with the real condition of things in a district until after they have reached it, and when they have either to go to work or break the contracts and starve or suffer the effects of starvation in their efforts to reach again their Southern homes. It is a work of self-protection for the labor organizations of the North to educate the colored laborers of the South on the true conditions of the labor problem in the North. (Blackpast, 2007)

Fortune's stance on strikebreaking would be tested during the American Railway Union (ARU) strike of 1894. Secretary of the East St. Louis, Illinois, branch of the Afro-American League offered two hundred African American workers to replace the freight handlers, and twenty-five more to replace the firemen and brakemen. The effects of the Pullman strike, wrote the *Christian Recorder*, are "to give a chance to men who had no chance or small chance before, and the power of the government, can be in no better business than opening a path to work for men to whom it was before closed." While Fortune may have disapproved of the general concept of strikebreaking, he understood that African American workers were virtually forced to use what few weapons they could in self-defense.

Progressive era leader Eugene Debs formed the industrywide ARU with the goal of uniting all railroad workers into one union regardless of race or skill level. He warned the members that racial restrictions would be disastrous for the union, and further explained that he was ready to stand side by side with African Americans, and help them whenever he had the power to do so. Yet when given the opportunity to remove the Whites only clause from their constitution, ARU members scoffed at the idea because they believed it would cause a significant drop in union membership, and the organization would be destroyed. One delegate stated bluntly that the South would rebel against Black membership and lose five white members for every colored man taken in. Even if the proportion reversed, the union could not afford to take the step. The Southern states, he continued, would have never organized had they believed the colored men were to be admitted to membership with them. Other members said they would be willing to accept African Americans into the general body of the union, but they should be given a separate organization.

Undaunted by member rejection, Debs continued to strive for an egalitarian union because he understood that if they did not procure Black membership, it would adversely affect the union. In response to ARU members' insistence on racial exclusion, he stated:

It is not the colored man's fault that he is black; it is not the fault of 6 million negroes that they are here. They were brought here by the avarice, cupidity, and inhumanity of the white race. The father of our country was an owner of slaves. Bind down the white race for centuries and their intellects would become stunted, their refinement would disappear. If we do not admit the colored man to membership the fact will be used against us. I am not here to advocate association with the negro, but I am ready to stand side by side with him, to take his hand in mine, and help him whenever it is in my power. (Debs, 1894)

Deb's warning to the ARU predictably fell upon deaf ears, and when they went on strike against the Pullman Company in 1894, the strike quickly ended in disaster due to their exclusionary policies. The largest White railroad brotherhoods, known as the Big Four, did nothing to assist the ARU, and actually collaborated with railway management. The strike exposed the gulf between labor leaders like Debs, who advocated industrial unionism, versus the Big Four and their insistence on maintaining craft unions. Notions of racial hierarchy were inscribed not only onto the railroad brotherhood's ideological outlook, but onto their personal and occupational identities and onto the organizations they constructed and joined as well. From the Big Four's inception, race was written into the very definition of their unions' membership.

Representing the industry's overwhelmingly White, native born male constituency, the brotherhoods adopted explicit provisions in their constitutions to ensure continued racial, ethnic, and gender homogeneity. White workers were perfectly willing to sacrifice the potential for higher wages for what W. E. B. Du Bois referred to as the psychological wages of being White.

While White workers were given public deference and titles of courtesy because they were White, the wages for both Blacks and Whites remained artificially low, and White workers always feared that they would be replaced with Black laborers.

Illinois African Americans played a major role in disrupting the ARU strike of 1894—they not only worked as strikebreakers, but in retaliation to the union member's racist stance against African American workers, they formed an anti-strike union whose express purpose was to fight the ARU and replace White strikers. Anti-strike union president L. B. Stevens explained that his organization had no desire to antagonize the interests of those who were endeavoring to improve their condition. However, Black workers were compelled to take action against the ARU because they had declared war against the Black man and they had no intention of being driven to the wall without a struggle. Stevens was even more defiant when it came to the question of the value of Black labor—especially when compared to the labor of the European immigrant:

> Our labor has contributed largely to make this country great and prosperous, and now . . . we do not intend to be starved out of the country nor driven to the wall by the American Railroad Union and like organizations, largely composed of foreigners who have not been in America long enough for the ink to dry on their naturalization papers. (Tuttle, 1969)

Stevens maintained that African American workers had the ability to contribute largely toward breaking the backz of [the ARU], and they would exert themselves to accomplish their deed. Feeling that Black railroad workers were left with no alternative, he explained that the attitude of labor unions had become so aggressive and menacing as to cause revulsion in public sentiment. If industrialist had given employment to American-born Blacks instead of European immigrants, who were not in sympathy with and incapable of comprehending American institutions, many of the labor difficulties that now afflict the country would have been avoided. Blinded by the illogic of Progressive-era White supremacy, White workers consistently undermined their own efforts by restricting Black workers.

Unwilling to acknowledge their racist shortcomings, White workers refused to unify with Black workers even though such unification would have been to their benefit. In a massive show of solidarity with their White comrades of the ARU, throngs of White packinghouse and slaughterhouse workers walked off their jobs and conducted a sympathetic strike with the struggling ARU. Between one and two thousand cattle butchers left their work, partly in sympathy with the railroad workers but also in support of their own demand for a wage increase.

The packers were divided from the beginning—the butchers remained on strike, while other departments took no part in the conflict. Violence did not take place immediately—but when the militia arrived, rioting was almost continuous from that point on. The militia's arrival coincided with the arrival of imported strikebreakers, which riled up the packers even more.

Although many of the strikebreakers were in fact non-Black workers, the mere sight of a few African American strikebreakers was enough to cause an exaggerated reaction from European American workers. One after the other, White managers quit their jobs because they refused to work with African Americans. Armed guards, hired to protect the packinghouses, were not enough to combat the racial animosity of the White workers who, not only set numerous fires in the stockyards to frighten the African American workers, they also attacked them outside the gates as they left the stockyards. At the entrance of the workplace, an effigy of a Black worker swinging from a telegraph pole at the corner of Root and Halsted streets, with a note attached to the breast of the figure bearing a skull and crossbones with the word "nigger scab" in bold letters.

Black men willing to risk their lives in order to make a living were not alone in expressing manly indignation over foul treatment. The African American press also took umbrage with White union workers at the stockyards: "The moment a trade union man," wrote the *Indianapolis Freeman*, "dares to even threaten to say nothing of laying violent hands upon a fellowman who desires to take up the work he has laid down, that moment he should be restrained by authority and made to understand without the loss of time that the same liberty he arrogates to himself to quit work is just as sacred to the man who desires to work." The *Richmond Planet* commended President Grover Cleveland for sending troops to Chicago and declaring martial law, but criticized Illinois governor John Altgeld for protesting against this action. "It is indeed a peculiar condition of affairs when a Democratic governor should enter into a contention with a Democratic president as to the right to order U.S. troops to aid in the execution of the laws." To the dismay of Afro-Illinoisans, Altgeld, himself the son of German immigrants, would confirm his position as a pro-immigrant governor during labor issues.

Employers eventually defeated the strikers because of violence and chaotic in-fighting—which was essentially what employers envisioned when they recruited African American men to replace them in the first place. Economist Warren Whatley explained that one of the reasons industrialists hired Black workers as strikebreakers was because the predominantly White workforce were less likely to fraternize with African American workers, and a violent reaction was more of a possibility due to their racist attitudes (Whatley 1993).

## LOSING "NEGRO JOBS" AND STRIKEBREAKING AS THE NEW NORMAL

By the end of the nineteenth century, Illinois African Americans began to lose their grip on the service occupations. Industries that had traditionally employed African Americans and had largely been noted as "negro jobs" were being taken by White and immigrant workers. In their adherence to Booker T. Washington and his accommodationist philosophy, the *Chicago Tribune* argued that African American workers were to blame, and referred to them as "foolish" because they fought for their rights as workers during the numerous strikes in the restaurant industry in the 1890s. Rather than defend themselves against nebulous employers who inevitably underpaid and overworked them, or fired them without just cause, African American workers, according to the *Tribune*, should be steady, trustworthy, faithful workers who did not repudiate arbitration awards and violate agreements they had entered into. Conversely, when White workers fought against employers they were expressing their "manliness" as workingmen against the ferocious industrialist. However, when Black workers expressed the same resolve, they were "foolish" workers who were seduced into it by white employees. Race prejudice, of course, was the major factor in the replacement of African American workers in trades they traditionally held. Yet, it scarcely made any difference whether Black workers agitated or not—when White workers demanded the jobs of African American workers, they usually took them.

For example, in the late nineteenth century, many African Americans worked as barbers and coachmen, but by the early twentieth century, Whites had replaced most of them in these capacities. Thus, in the years just prior to the Great Migration, African American workers were largely left with occupations discarded by White workers that were generally low-paying jobs that carried the stigma of unmanliness, servility, and offered few opportunities for advancement.

As more African Americans lost jobs that they once dominated, their collective occupational choices by the close of the century continued to wither—strikebreaking increasingly became the most viable option. Yet Illinois African Americans refused to meekly accept the seeming inevitability of being shut out of desired occupations. "Our people are wage workers, and should be deeply interested in all that points to the question," said Lloyd Wheeler, an African American lawyer. He argued that Afro-Illinoisans could achieve better employment if they "united their energies in that direction." Another commentator warned White workers and employers that there were negative ramifications for all Americans if they continued to exclude African Americans from respectable labor. "Shut our young men out of the factories and throw them into brothels and club rooms, and you dwarf their manhood and ruin their morals" (Wesley, 1967).

With more Black men unemployed or underemployed, they increasingly reverted to strikebreaking as a viable option for supplementing their meager incomes. The 1890s marked a substantial rise in the use of African American strikebreakers in Illinois (compared to previous decades), it was the mid to late 1890s that witnessed not only a dramatic rise in Black strikebreaking, but also its most tumultuous period. Before 1890, there were only ten strikes in which African American workers were utilized; between 1890 and 1920 there were twenty-one strikes. Seemingly, as these events occurred, Illinois African Americans not only reacted against the interests of the labor movement, they also spoke out in defiance of racially exclusionary practices that relegated them inferior occupational positions.

When news first surfaced about an attack on the African American community in Spring Valley, Illinois, in August 1895, Black Illinoisans called for immediate action to aid the families that remained in desperate need of help. The initial reports stated that Italian American coal miners attacked African American miners and their families, and killed at least thirty people, including women and children. While it was later confirmed that these reports were exaggerated, African Americans expressed dismay over the idea that Italian Americans—many who were initially strikebreakers themselves—had the audacity to commit such violent acts. Leading Afro-Illinoisans immediately sprang into action upon hearing the news about the Spring Valley mob attacks. John "Indignation" Jones headed the Afro-Americans Citizens' Protective League whose duty was to resist mob violence and lynch law, as well as pledge themselves to bring the guilty perpetrators of these atrocious acts to justice. Even traditionally conservative African Americans expressed a need for violent retaliation against the attackers. A Chicago pastor believed that the Spring Valley mayor should step in to protect the Black families. If he failed to act, he advised Black Chicagoans to protect them. "This ain't Mississippi!" he exclaimed. "This is Illinois and should this matter be dropped by the powers that be I am in favor of a fight," he assured. Black Chicago activists, led by Ferdinand L. Barnett, sent a telegram to Illinois Governor Altgeld to call his attention to the murderous assaults upon colored men, women and children at Spring Valley, Illinois, and the further threat of extermination against the colored people of that district. Their goal was not only to express their outrage over the conflict, but also to demand that the governor protect the Black people in the region.

Working-class Afro-Illinoisans angrily demanded action from the governor. Throughout the state, Black citizens enthusiastically attended indignation meetings to express their anger over the attacks. At a meeting in Chicago, men discussed carrying rifles. "As American citizens we should insist upon our rights and not turn out of our tracks for these foreigners, the scum of Italy," said an irate African American barber from Chicago, who also insisted that Black men carry rifles to Spring Valley to defend the victims. Another meeting attendee invoked the honor of African Americans: "You cannot die at a better time for the glory of the negro race. . . . I counsel peace, but if there is no peace, let us die by our guns" (Weaver, 1946).

Smaller indignation meetings, often led by working-class African Americans throughout the state were held at residential houses rather than large churches. Men and women eagerly attended meetings in smaller cities and towns, with many attendees pledging to defend the victims. Black men in Rockford, Elgin, and Moline, Illinois, met to denounce the attacks, and volunteered to act in conjunction with regiments from Chicago, as well as pledge to extend moral and financial aid to the families under attack. A motion was supported to send a regiment of armed men from Peoria, Illinois, to Spring Valley who were willing to fight if need be. In Evanston, Illinois, seventy-five African American residents gathered and passed a resolution denouncing the sheriff and mayor of Spring Valley, and set forth an agreement to be obedient to the law and not take matters into their own hands. On the heels of labor violence in Chicago's stockyards the previous year in which Black men were regularly attacked, Afro-Illinoisans expressed an especially urgent desire for revenge against their Spring Valley assailants. It is very likely that they expressed more desire for vengeance because their attackers were foreigners who had a long history of job competition with African Americans. Further, retribution against recently arriving European immigrants had less serious ramifications due to their own precarious status in their new country.

During the 1898 strike in Virden and Pana, Illinois, the African American press unleashed their vitriol against Illinois governor John Tanner. The harshest criticism against the Illinois governor came from the *Illinois Record*—the official organ of the Afro-American Protective League. The *Record* argued that the governor was derelict in his duties, and was the cause of the Virden/Pana riot and subsequent deaths of the miners.

> The bombardment of the train loaded with human beings and the shooting down of laboring men was all uncalled for and would not have happened if Governor Tanner had been true to his oath of office and carried out the law which reads, "Duty of the Governor" whenever there is in any city, town or county a tumult, riot, mob or body of men acting together by force with attempt to commit felony or to offer violence to persons or property or by force or violence, to break or resist a law of the state or when such tumult, riot or mob is threatened, and the fact is made to appear to the Governor, it shall be his duty to order such military force as he may deem necessary to aid the civil authorities in suppressing such violence and executing the law.

Early in the conflict, the *Illinois Record* exclaimed in bold letters: "THE FIGHT ON TANNERISM MUST CONTINUE TO THE END." From the newspaper's viewpoint, the governor was a shifty politician who repeatedly refused to send in troops to protect the African American miners because they were imported labor, and gave orders to protect property, but not the lives of the Black miners. The *Record* agreed that the importation of labor was a bad thing, but Tanner should have been more concerned with stopping the thousands of paupers who were coming from Europe and degrading American labor before he railed against the few Black workers who were shut out from nearly every avenue of industry by a caste prejudice, relentless as fate. Even when the Illinois governor finally called for the National Guard to maintain order shortly after the shootings, the *Illinois Record* questioned not only the timing of the order, but also the purpose: "Who needed protection? Suppose the angry whites had begun to massacre the blacks, what would the troops have done?" The *Record* suggested that the governor's troops would not have helped the African American miners because the governor would not allow them, and he would have been an accessory before the fact to the murder of every man that was slain. The governor took his stand against the weaker side, hoping thereby to gain a transient popularity, but the "fair-minded, intelligent citizens of all races will reward him with their contempt." Like his predecessor, Governor Tanner was a champion for the working-man. Also like his predecessor, aid to the workingman was primarily limited to European American workingmen.

Afro-Illinoisans had learned lessons from the previous conflicts and were immediately suspicious of Tanner's willingness to help African American workers. They not only contested the Tanner administration's handling of the conflict, they also offered assistance to the African American miners. Five Black miners from Alabama were invited to meet at Quinn Chapel in Chicago during an indignation meeting. The men were introduced and they explained that they had come to Illinois "under no misrepresentation; that they came expecting to take the place of men who had broken their contract; that they had expected the protection of the government; and that, in their failure to secure this, they appealed to their race." An address, signed by 113 miners of Pana and Virden, Illinois, was then read, claiming the protection of the law in their labor. Resolutions at the meeting were adopted that extended the sympathy of Black Chicagoans to the miners, denouncing the charge that the men were convicts, and refuting the charge that they were taking the place of other miners. Part of Tanner's unwillingness to aid the Black workers in Pana came from the notion that the miners were ex-convicts from Alabama. Anti-lynching crusader Ida B. Wells met with Tanner days earlier to present him with evidence proving the African American miners were not ex-convicts. After he presented his evidence that the men had come from the State Mine Inspector, she read a letter from the inspector in which he denied having found any convicts among the miners.

## CONCLUSION

Illinois African Americans were relentless in their defiance against the racialization of labor during the early Jim Crow era. To prove themselves in the context of various forms of terrorism and intimidation, Black workers in Illinois refused to accept their predetermined status as inferior workers. Meanwhile they were constantly seeking the means to prove their racial manliness during an era when their manliness was repetitively called into question. Strikebreaking, of course, was only a single avenue for African Americans to fight for a better position within a late nineteenth-century racial hierarchy that was designed to maintain their degraded position on the economic ladder. It served as a viable form of working-class activism for African Americans as they sought to collectively strengthen their economic position during the labor upheaval of post-Reconstruction America. As historian Eric Arnesen explained, decisions by African American workers to become strikebreakers were often informed choices, rationalized by a complex and changing worldview that balanced their experiences as industrial workers, farmers, and African Americans. Indeed, these Black men were neither willing tools nor ignorant serfs—rather, they were poor and ambitious men who were often recruited by coal company agents, sometimes under false pretenses. During the nineteenth century, African Americans were never the only workers to break strikes in Illinois or any other Northern state.

Moreover, they were never the most used strikebreakers. However, African Americans were usually the most visible strikebreakers because of American racism, and therefore, they were almost always the easiest targets for White working-class rage during the tumultuous labor disputes of the late nineteenth century.

## REFERENCES

Alexander, S. L. (2008). *T. Thomas Fortune, the Afro-American agitator: A collection of writings, 1880–1928*. Gainesville: University Press of Florida.

Armfield, F. L. (2000). Fire on the prairies: The 1895 Spring Valley race riot. *Journal of Illinois History, Vol.3*, no. 3.

Arnesen, E. (2001). Like Banquo's ghost, it will not down: The race question and the American railroad brotherhoods, 1880–1920. In E. Jenkins and D. C. Hine. (eds.) *A question of manhood: A reader in U.S. Black men's history and masculinity*, Vol. 2, *The 19th century: From emancipation to Jim Crow*. Indianapolis: Indiana University Press.

Arnesen, E. (2003). Specter of black strikebreakers: Race, employment, and labor activism in the industrial era. *Labor History, Vol 44*, no. 3.

BlackPast (2007). (1890) T. Thomas Fortune, "It Is Time To Call A Halt". Retrieved from https://www.blackpast.org/african-american-history/1890-t-thomas-fortune-it-time-call-halt/

Barrett, J. R. (1990). *Work and community in the jungle: Chicago's packinghouse workers 1894–1922*. Urbana: University of Illinois.

Bederman, G. (1995). *Manliness and civilization: A cultural history of gender and race in the United States, 1880–1917*. Chicago: University of Chicago Press.

Cha-Jua, S. K. (1998). A warlike demonstration: Legalism, armed resistance, and Black political mobilization in Decatur, Illinois, 1894–1898. *The Journal of Negro History, Vol. 83*, no. 1.

Debs, E. (1894). Draws a race line: Question of color before the American Railway Union. *Chicago Tribune, Vol. 53*, 170, pg. 12.

Dolinar, B. (2013). *The Negro in Illinois: The WPA papers*. Urbana: University of Illinois Press.

Du Bois, W. E. B. (1990). *The souls of Black folk*. New York: Vintage Books.

Du Bois, W. E. B. (1998). *Black reconstruction in America, 1860–1880*. New York: Free Press.

Gaines, K. (1996). *Uplifting the race: Black leadership, politics, and culture in the twentieth century*. Chapel Hill: North Carolina Press.

Harris, W. H. (1982). *The harder we run: Black workers since the civil war*. New York: Oxford University Press.

Herbst, A. (1932). *The Negro in the slaughtering and meat packing industry in Chicago*. Boston: Houghton Miffin Co.

Hornsby-Gutting, A. (2009). *Black manhood and community building in North Carolina, 1900–1930*. Gainesville: University of Florida Press.

Joens, D. (2012). *From slave to state legislator: John W. E. Thomas, Illinois' first African American lawmaker*. Carbondale, Southern Illinois University Press.

Meier, A. (1966). *Negro thought in America, 1880–1915*. Ann Arbor: University of Michigan Press.

Mullane, D. (1993). *Crossing the danger water: Three hundred years of African American writing.* New York: Anchor Books.

Norwood, S. H. (2002). *Strikebreaking and intimidation: Mercenaries and masculinity in twentieth century America.* Chapel Hill: North Carolina Press.

Portwood, S. J. (1996). African American politics and community in Cairo and Vicinity 1863–1900. Archives at Northern Illionois University. http://www.lib.niu.edu/1996/iht329613.html.

Ross, M. (2004). *Manning the race: Reforming black men in the Jim Crow era.* New York: New York University Press.

Summers, M. (1996). *Manliness and its discontents: Black leadership, politics, and culture in the twentieth century.* Chapel Hill: North Carolina Press.

The Washington Bee (September 14, 1901). Professor Booker T. Washington, President of the Negro Leauge of the United States. The Afro-American Council is a farce and dangerous for any Negro to touch.

Thornbrough, E. L. (1961). The national Afro-American league, 1887–1908," *The Journal of Southern History, Vol 27,* no. 4.

Tuttle, W. M. (1969). *Labor conflict and racial violence: The Black worker in Chicago, 1894–1919.* Labor History.

The Washington Bee (September 14, 1901). Professor Booker T. Washington, President of the Negro League of the United States. The Afro-American Council is a Farce and Dangerous for any Negro to Touch.

Washington B. T. (1901). *Up from slavery.* New York: Doubleday, Page & Co.

Weaver, R. C. (1946). *Negro labor: A national problem.* New York: Harcourt, Brace and World.

Wesley, C. (1967). *Negro labor in the United States, 1850–1925: A study in American economic history.* New York: Russell and Russell.

Whatley, W. C. (1993). African American strikebreaking from the civil war to the New Deal. *Social Science History, Vol. 17,* no. 4.

*Chapter Nine*

# The Essence of the Black Man

*An Exploration of Black Masculinity through Double Consciousness in* Native Son

Isaih Dale

In this chapter, I examine masculinity in Richard Wright's *Native Son* (1940/1993a) via the lens of W. E. B. Du Bois's double consciousness. The "othering" of Bigger Thomas begins with the opening book entitled "Fear." Othering induces double consciousness which creates a fear for personal safety, family permanence, and societal detachment. Scholars argue that Bigger's fear stems from centripetal forces like racism, unjust laws, and the spatial form in which he lives. I argue that the trauma of not grasping double consciousness leads to Bigger's incomprehension of masculinity, which inevitably causes his demise. During the early to mid-twentieth century, as shown in texts like *Native Son* and Frantz Fanon's *Black Skin, White Masks* (1952), some African American men presented themselves as insolent, emotionless, insular beings. This, I argue, stems from conforming to the White world, bringing the African American man damaged pride and tenuous social competence. Moreover, Wright's invisible burden regarding double consciousness refers to the distress of living in a Eurocentric world, and to the distress of being raised without ideals of Black masculinity.

Richard Wright's naturalist novel *Native Son* (1940/1993a) proclaims that Black males carry an invisible burden in a Eurocentric world. The burden includes trying to conform to a White world that does not accept him. Consequently, if Black men are to survive, they must integrate with the cultural majority. Du Bois's double consciousness receives an earlier embodiment in Shakespeare's *Othello*. As Othello indicates, "Haply, for I am black. And have not those soft parts of conversation." Othello is aware of the anxiety and somatization that comes with being a Black man in a predominantly White environment. Ta-Nehisi Coates (2015) argues that Black men have developed a lost essence resulting from oppression, slavery, and discrimination. Moreover, Sheena Myong Walker (2013) found much more complexity to double consciousness:

> Black men who failed to integrate and only identified with one's Blackness and those who made drastic changes in one's reality by taking on characteristics of the Eurocentric world view, were expected to have higher levels of psychological distress. (p. 205)

Failure to integrate also resulted in issues with defining Black masculinity. Many Black men believed in White masculine tropes. Wright's invisible burden of double consciousness refers to the distress of living in a Eurocentric world, and the distress of being raised without an understanding of Black masculinity. W. E. B. Du Bois, Richard Wright, Frantz Fanon, and Ta-Nehisi Coates provide unrelenting and sometimes contrasting definitions of the lived experience.

Here, I draw from Mary Hamilton's concept of Black masculinity emphasizing familial connectivity, community leadership, and collectivity (Howard-Hamilton 1997; Pelzer 2016). Surely, Richard Wright's invisible burden, Frantz Fanon's suffocating reification, and Ta-Nehisi Coates's lost essence are three phrases which Black men endure while navigating the White man's world. But Wright's novel illustrates how double consciousness and Black masculinity are intertwined, specifically within the protagonist Bigger Thomas.

Most contemporary studies focus on melancholic projections of slavery and oppression, or they focus on the process of reframing Black masculinity to assemble a communal identity. There has been little study relative to double consciousness. I do not prescribe studying Blackness through a lens of oppression or an overemphasized communal identity. Instead, I suggest focusing on the analyzing of self. That is, the familial Black self.

## EXODUS AND BLACK SAVAGERY

Richard Wright's *Native Son* and other twentieth-century African American novels are deeply violent. Jeffrey B. Leak (2005) concluded that novels such as these portray "myths of inferiority, sexual prowess, criminality, and cultural depravity" (xii). Indeed, many of Wright's contemporary critics, including James Baldwin, fixated on stereotypes at the expense of the novel's internal anguish. Frantz Fanon (1952) refers to this phenomenon in "The Black Man and Psychopathology":

The Essence of the Black Man    131

> Since the racial drama is played out in the open, the black man has no time to unconsciousnessize it. The white man manages it to a certain degree because a new factor emerges i.e. guilt. The black man's superiority or inferiority complex and his feeling of equality are conscious. He is constantly making them interact. He lives his drama. There is in him none of the affective amnesia characteristic of the typical neurotic. (p. 129)

Fanon insists that a Black man must constantly think about his own life and the White life that surrounds him. In other words, Black men must subscribe to being the other. This is a dialectic between pain and dignity. Wright's protagonist is aware of being the other, but he works to resist the position. He is caught within a neurotic mindset. Ultimately, he moves to become savage-like.

This invisible burden is partially attributed to double consciousness in a White world. However, Bigger's invisible burden is also the absence of Black masculinity. The story's underlying theme is Sigmund Freud's Oedipus complex. According to Freud, the father controls the male child's expression of aggressive impulses by allowing the child to cast aspersion onto him. This theory does not consider institutionalized racism and other factors that impact the Black community. Yet, Bigger abides by this theory. He abandons or rather blots out his Blackness to become like the White family, the Daltons. In doing this, Bigger prescribes to the Oedipus complex which leads him to neurotic tendencies of anxiety and anger. By blotting out his own race, Bigger collapses his ego, and his actions become destined by Whiteness. Bigger has become a White man, thus he has inherited White supremacist values. Black masculinity is left to mourn.

African American literature underscores a larger political argument. Mourning is the act of not forgetting. African American literature aims to remember violence perpetrated against Black people. For Bigger, mourning occurs alongside a violent response. Murder is an act of self-creation. He can only become a man through violence. Bigger admits to being filled with elation after killing Mary Dalton. Black violence should not be shocking because White violence has long been ingrained in Western civilization. The essence of American manhood is reflected in the words of Patrick Henry: "Give me liberty or give me death." The declaration is inherently violent, yet in 1949 the *Chicago Daily Tribune* called Henry the greatest orator of all time.

Bigger sees himself as a hero. But White culture does not align with Black masculinity. As Fanon states, when Black men try to mimic their White peers, they lose themselves and turn to violence. Bigger strives for White masculinity, resulting in amnesia for his own race. Bigger's illusion results in the rejection of himself. White hegemonic masculinity was never meant to benefit African American men.

## CENTRIPETAL BLACK MASCULINITY

There is great confusion regarding the dichotomy between being fearless and being fearful. In 1970, in a Chicago *Daily Newspaper* article entitled "Views and Opinions: Fearless Black Men," Sister Michele writes that Black men are afraid to send their kids to schools because of Black gangs. She argues that Black gang members fear White men, so they imitate White men, which inevitably causes gang members to hate their Black brothers and sisters.

Bigger acts like a fearless Black man, but he feels socially incompetent. In the opening scene, he kills a rat. This suggests bravery. However, when arguing with his mother, Bigger's voice is filled with nervous irritation. He is more fearful of his mother than of a rat. He has total power over the rat. By contrast, he has no power over his mother. She does not fill the void of his absent father. Bigger hates his family. He wishes he could escape through the walls. They represent the Black body he wants to reject. This corresponds to Ta-Nehisi Coates's self-understanding:

> I knew that my portion of the American galaxy, where bodies were enslaved by a tenacious gravity, was black and that the other, liberated portion was not. I felt, but did not yet understand, the relation between that other world and me. And I felt in this cosmic injustice, a profound cruelty, which infused an abiding, irrepressible desire to unshackle my body and achieve the velocity of escape. (p. 21)

Bigger is bound by the profound cruelty of racism. It is all around him, starting with the ghetto where he and his family live. He turns to a velocity of escape centripetally. Due to the inability to escape shackles, he treats his body as a porous weapon. Before the Black man can escape, he must first survive. Fear is the driving force behind his anger. Anger masks Bigger's low sense of control, absence of stability, damaged pride, and social incompetence.

One may assume that Black violence is necessary to survive the White world. This is a psychotic experience. Bigger moves between thoughts of violence and total inaction. He suffers from Black paralytic syndrome. He is convinced that every movement must respond to, defeat, or vanquish White oppression.

## THE BLACK PSYCHE

Double consciousness and Black masculinity inform the psyche of Black men. *Native Son* is a literary representation of the ways in which Black men navigate hegemonic society. The Black male psyche is caught between the binaries of minority and majority. Black identity may change depending on cultural location (Hunter & Davis, 1992). Definitions of White/European

American masculinity include the accumulation of education, wealth, and mobility. These are stereotypical traits of the ideal American man. However, Black men must negotiate racism and discrimination no matter their place in society (Hunter & Davis, 1992). Wright states:

> His [Bigger's] hope toward a vague benevolent something that would help and lead him, and his hate toward the whites; for he felt that they ruled him, even when they were far away and not thinking of him, ruled him by conditioning him in his relations to his own people. (1993a, p. 115)

Bigger lives in hatred which he directs toward the people around him—Black people. He cannot act on his hatred for White people, because they are too powerful. Instead, he releases it on weaker people. Fanon (1952) suggests this is not uncommon, rather it is the norm: "A normal black child, having grown up with a normal family, will become abnormal at the slightest contact with the white world" (p. 122). The White world creates a collective aggressiveness, from films to social media. For example, historically, Black Americans and Native Americans have been framed as savages. To accept the frame is to fall victim to the dichotomy: support the Black villain or identify with the White hero. Both options speak to a distorted reality.

Bigger is trapped in this dichotomy. In the beginning of the novel, he strives to be White, and associates himself with White heroes. However, Bigger also chooses the role of the Black villain. As a third option, Bigger is stuck in the middle, feeling that some day there would be a Black man who would whip the Black people into a tight band and together they would act and end fear and shame. Bigger is both hero and villain. He speaks to potential freedom, but his method is violent. "Whipping" implies the actions of a slave master. Is Bigger simply confronting the issue of weakness? Is this his response to White terror?

Seemingly, Bigger is irritated with emotion and sensitivity. For example, he alienates himself from spiritual traditions, including his mother's singing. At one point, he hears singing in a nearby church. The singing filled his ears. He describes it as complete, self-contained, and mocking his fear and loneliness. The singing inspires within him an unwanted yearning for wholeness. Bigger rejects these feelings. He believes that church folks are "whipped." Thus, he rejects the spirit of his ancestors.

Historically, Black folks sang to voice their hope and signal plans for freedom. For example, in the song "Steal Away," Jesus is represented as resistance to American slavery. The song contains symbolism and praxis. It is a message and a plan. Ironically, Bigger's resistance to spiritual music is his psychological disassociation from Blackness. He is not concerned with Black tradition. He views religion as opposition to masculinity. He rejects passivity, domesticity, and Black cultural spaces. Bigger's Black psyche reflects his desire to hold a greater voice in the White world.

## THE BLACK MALE CHILD

Jean-Paul Sartre (1963) wrote, "Someday they must learn the truth: sometimes from the smiles of those around them, sometimes from rumor or insult. The later the discovery, the more violent the shock" (p. 75). Bigger learns this truth as an adolescent. In the beginning of the novel, readers learn that Bigger shares a room with his sister, brother, and mother. It is a small, almost suffocating, one-bedroom apartment. Bigger's world is much like his room. Furthermore, the story takes place in Chicago's Black Belt. The Black Belt is a chain of neighborhoods on the south side of Chicago where most African Americans lived in the mid-twentieth century. It is a compact suffocating environment.

Growing up, Bigger wants to escape this environment. He does not realize that Black bodies face similar challenges throughout the country and the world. Bigger will not learn this truth until it is too late. In the beginning of the novel, Bigger and his friend Gus watch a pigeon fly away. Bigger states, "Now, if I could only do that." But it is almost impossible to escape the poverty and oppression of the Black Belt.

His strategies for escape include a plan to rob the local store. Once again, he relies on violence. Fanon writes that "the dreams of the native are always of muscular prowess; his dreams are of action and aggression" (1952, p. 52). The Black child will come to understand violence and aggression as a way to manage life. Bigger is violent toward his friend Gus; his family; Doc, the pool owner; and his girlfriend Bessie. However, he is hardly violent to White people, at least not consciously. There are multiple reasons behind the killing of Mary Dalton, but it is still an accident. In Bigger's world, Whites are not concerned with the killing of Blacks. He is safe to act out against members of his own race. This is his double consciousness.

Wright's novel delineates a spectrum between boys and men. At times, Bigger's thinking mirror that of an adolescent. He wants to be a man. His family pushes him to become a man. He resists through anger. The Black child feels forced to mature at a faster rate than his White peers. Research reveals that stereotypical expectations endanger the health of Black boys (Hill, 1999). Bigger's mother is not to blame for his mistakes, but her expectations may be too much. He is raised to seek power seemingly possessed by White people. Yet, he is not taught to thrive in Blackness.

## BIGGER AND FILMS

Bigger does not recognize male role models. In the rare instance where he compliments a man, it is while watching the *Trader Horn* (1931) film about a White explorer living among African Tribes. Bigger observes naked Africans and smart White people. He wants to be smart too, but his Blackness is an obstacle. It is a cruel predicament. He experiences the chronic need to possess manhood, to the extent that murder is an act of self-creation. He is guided by Eurocentric ideologies of heroism.

Bigger mimics the violence of America. To better understand his perception, readers simply need to turn to films of the 1930s and 1940s. For example, the film *Stagecoach* (1939) shows John Wayne's character shooting and killing "savage" Native Americans. Bigger, one might argue, sees Native Americans as weak and White cowboys as heroes. Conforming to White manhood has created within him a moral monster. Masculinity tropes denigrate his sanity and morality.

Double consciousness is reinforced at the movie theater. White people and Black people are portrayed differently. Films of the mid-twentieth century reflect how people walk, talk, and think. Bigger learns how to act around White people. He learns to believe they are smarter and more gifted. One could argue that films contributed to the murder of Mary Dalton. He first sees her in a theater environment. He and his friends are captivated by her beauty. According to Jack, if Bigger plays his cards right, the rich White woman will sleep with him. After hearing this, Bigger embraces a fantasy of sex with Mary.

## BLACK PARALYTIC COMPLEX

Bigger justifies his thinking as a response to those around him. Every move is a reaction to his environment. This is his Black paralytic complex. Bigger is fixated on White people. He blames them for his crimes. He wants people to believe that he is in control. This sentiment has also been expressed by scholars. For example, Ta-Nehisi Coates states, "The Earth is not our [blacks] own creation. It has no respect for us. It has no use for us. And its vengeance is not the fire in the cities but the fire in the sky" (150). Bigger's life is based on pessimism. The Black man is fixated on who created the earth, and who the earth respects. Elsewhere, Kadeshia Matthews (2014) writes:

> Bigger is indeed a native son, but as the closeness of his first name to the epithet "Nigger" implies, his blackness renders the American manhood he has achieved unrecognizable precisely because it is a manhood that depends on the maintenance of racial difference. (2014, p. 295)

Bigger rejects Blackness, and develops characteristics of White American masculinity. In the process he is an object and an executioner of the White gaze.

Fanon writes "the environment had allowed him [the Black man] to manifest his humanity only in a negative form. . . . It had given him only the choice of becoming either a slave or a rebel; he had chosen the latter" (1963, p. 263). These archaic binaries inform a conflicted mindset. For example, according to James Baldwin, Tom, in *Uncle Tom's Cabin*, is not a hero because he did not fight back. Yet Baldwin also takes issue with Bigger, who fought back. Baldwin believes Bigger lacked morality thus his fight was essentially wasted. I ask then, if the Black man cannot be passive or violent, what other option does he have? For an answer, we turn to Zora Neale Hurston (2018):

> I am not tragically colored. There is no great sorrow dammed up in my soul, nor lurking behind my eyes. I do not mind at all. I do not belong to the sobbing school of Negrohood who hold that nature somehow has given them a low-down dirty deal and whose feelings are all but about it. Even in the helter-skelter skirmish that is my life, I have seen that the world is to the strong regardless of a little pigmentation more or less. No, I do not weep at the world. (2018, 2)

Hurston sees life through a lens of double consciousness, but she does not prescribe to a Black paralytic mindset. In fact, the world belongs to the oppressed. For Hurston, double consciousness does not mean conformity. It is a strategy for survival, not a permit to concede. Consequently, Black men can be hyperaware of White racism, and simultaneously maintain Black masculinity.

## CONCLUDING THOUGHTS

James Baldwin said "To smash something is the ghetto's chronic need. Most of the time it is the members of the ghetto who smash each other, and themselves" (2017, p. 42). Bigger feels a need to create something, even if its violence against other Black people. He is no hero. Nor is he always the victim. The Black man feels dammed in what he perceives as a White world. Within his Black community, internal conflicts inform his view of manhood.

Bigger's view of masculinity is representative of a larger view. This chapter explored double consciousness within the Black experience, through the lens of the Black self and the White gaze. Violence is an ongoing theme and a form of societal power and control. Bigger's actions symbolize his attempt to gain, or his loss of, power. This dialectic informs another theme—his paralytic mindset. Every (in)action is based on his perceptions of the

White world. Whiteness informs his distorted view of people around him, including Mary, his mother, his community, and most of all, himself.

Wright's *Native Son* is an imaginary exploration of the Black male psyche. It is not a full panoramic view. There is more to see. This chapter does not offer an exhaustive criticism of the novel. However, I argue that some of Wright's themes continue today. Black men have not yet realized free subjectivity. Black men occupy spaces of social death. There is a continued need to examine the ways in which race and gender inform masculinity. Writer Wole Soyinka called for Black men to address the issue of gender roles created under colonial rule and the postcolonial era, and the problems created by this confusion (Salamone 2007). This chapter responds to that call.

## REFERENCES

Baldwin, J., & Peck, R. (2017). *I am not your Negro*. New York: Magnolia Pictures.
Coates, T. (2015). *Between the world and me*. New York: Spiegel & Grau.
Fanon, F. (1952). *Peau noire, masques blancs. Black skin, White mask* (translation). New York: Grove Press.
Fanon, F. (1963). *The wretched of the earth*. Trans. Constance Farrington. New York: Grove.
Fanon, F. (1968). *Peau noire, masques blancs. Black skin, White mask* (translation). New York: Grove Press.
Flamm, M. W. (2017). *In the heat of the summer: The New York Riots of 1964 and the war on crime*. Philadelphia: University of Pennsylvania Press.
Hill, S. A. (1999). *African American children: Socialization and development in families*. Thousand Oaks, CA: Sage Publications.
Howard-Hamilton, M. F. (1997). Theory to practice: Applying developmental theories relevant to African American men. *New Directions for Student Services*, vol. 80.
Hunter, A. G. & Davis, J. E. (1992). Constructing gender: An exploration of Afro-American men's conceptualization of manhood. *Gender and Society*, vol. 6.
Hurston, Z. (2018). How it feels to be colored me. ThoughtCo. Retrieved from: thoughtco.com/how-it-feels-to-be-colored-me-by-zora-neale-hurston-1688772.
Leak, J. B. (2005). *Racial myths and masculinity in African American literature*. University Tennessee Press.
Matthews, K. L. (2014). Black boy no more? Violence and the flight from blackness in Richard Wright's *Native Son*. *Modern Fiction Studies*, vol. 60.
Pelzer, D. L. (2016). Creating a new narrative: Reframing Black masculinity for college men. *The Journal of Negro Education*, vol. 85.
Salamone, F. (2006). The depiction of masculinity in classic Nigerian literature. *Journal of the African Literature Association*, vol. 1
Sartre, J. P. (1963). *The wretched of the earth*. By Frantz Fanon. Trans. Constance Farrington. New York: Grove.
Walker, S. M. (2013) Empirical study of the application of double-consciousness among African-American men. *Journal of African American Studies*, vol. 22.
Wright, R. (1993a). *Native Son*. 1940. New York: Harper.
Wright, R. (1993b). *Uncle Tom's Children*. 1937. New York: Harper.

*Chapter Ten*

# The Battle of the New Age Black, Male Hero and Hegemonic/Toxic Masculinity

*An Examination of the Representations of Black Masculinity in* Black Panther

Erika M. Thomas and Malcolm D. Gamble

The 2018 blockbuster Marvel film, *Black Panther*, is a significant cultural text for many reasons. Tompkins (2018) summarized it this way:

> The latest installment of the Marvel Cinematic Universe now stands, quite ceremoniously, as a film of many firsts—the first "black blockbuster," the first Marvel film to feature a black superhero, black director and mostly black cast, the first to make more than $1 billion globally, the first film to get a studio-funded Oscars 2019 campaign, and the list goes on.

According to Tompkins, the film is much more than just another superhero or comic-book movie. The film's box office success is a breakthrough for the Black community. Additionally, the viewing and celebration of *Black Panther* became activism given the cultural background of intensified racial politics fueled by increasingly polarized political parties and a conservative administration. Seeing the film is also a social cause, inspiring and inciting discourse around racial justice due to its marking and countering of the film industry's institutionalized racism and the disproportionate amount of racially inadequate representations in mainstream cinema (Tompkins, 2018). As such, the film's Black cast provides multifaceted and largely positive character roles for challenging Hollywood's limited and normative Black stereotypes.

Given the various credit and praise for *Black Panther*, we argue that it is critical to consider Black representation from an intersectional approach. Black masculinity is widely viewed and marked as a valuable cultural artifact. The film works to construct and influence views of Black masculinity in contemporary contexts. We apply a critical discourse analysis to interrogate (a) the film's framing of race and gender in general, and (b) the way in which the film inspires the audience to rethink traditional, hegemonic characteristics of masculinity specifically. In doing so, we reveal a paradox: angry and violent stereotypes are juxtaposed against positive representations of Black masculinity. Our imaginative critique suggests that *Black Panther* complicates social learning for Black boys, notwithstanding the film's challenge to hegemonic masculinity.

The chapter includes four sections. First, we review the literature on representations. Second, we apply critical discourse analysis to examine common, familiar, and dangerous representations of Black men. Third, we analyze progressive and alternative portrayals of Black masculinity forwarded by the main character, T'Challa. Fourth, we conclude with implications for regressive and progressive Black representations.

## REPRESENTATIONS

Representation is a familiar and reoccurring pursuit in rhetorical, cultural, and media studies. These include intentional and unintentional representations directly related to dominant ideologies. An image, text, or film can reflect a preexisting cultural discourse, shape collective memory, and influence human behavior. Ideologies, working through text, may socialize and shape our attitudes and values toward others and toward ourselves. According to filmmaker and theorist, Parmar (1990), "Images play a crucial role in defining and controlling the political and social power to which both individuals and marginalized groups have access. The deeply ideological nature of imagery determines not only how other people think about us but how we think about ourselves" (p. 116).

Images and representations influence collective identification and reinforce power relations. "The real world of image-making is political . . . politics of domination inform the way the vast majority of images we consume are constructed and marketed" (hooks, 1992a, p. 5). Thus, construction of an image influences society to know or accept an ideological belief, and creates reality of power relations. Imagination and representation help facilitate how an audience will identify with the text.

Representations affirm shared assumptions, while also challenging them. "Cultural products display and participate in ideological conflict . . . they generally reproduce and reinforce dominant ideologies . . . they also present alternatives and participate in the evolution of the dominant ideologies themselves" (Byars, 1991, p. 63). Thus, images and representations may serve to challenge dominant perspectives and assumptions.

## BLACK MEN AND THEIR REPRESENTATIONS IN PUBLIC IMAGINATION

Black masculinity in popular culture has received considerable attention in social scientific studies and critical/cultural analyses which describe the ways that the mainstream American media persistently stereotype and devalue Black bodies on screen and in society (hooks, 1992b; Jackson & Balaji, 2015; Orbe, 1998; Slatton & Spates, 2014; Tyree, Byerly, & Hamilton, 2012). Black masculinity is framed largely as controlling, problematic, and pathologized in the public imagination (Oeur, 2016; Castle Bell & Harris, 2017; Lavelle 2010). For example, Hall (1996) argued that dominant cinematic forms brought Blacks into representation at the expense of fetishization, objectification, and negative figuration.

Tracing the globally hegemonic characteristics of masculinity, Malina and Ratele (2016) note independence, lack of emotion, competitiveness, physical strength, and aggressiveness as cultural trends and the types of behaviors that have become normalized, portrayed, and disseminated. Mediated outlets influence people's sense of reality, by defining or legitimizing certain behaviors, identities, and values.

The dominant cultural framing of Black masculinity is traditionally hypermasculinity. Black men are characterized as hard, physical, muscled, and focused (Brown, 2001). Furthermore, paradigmatic signifiers have long framed Black men as inherently angry, physically threatening, and sexually aggressive (Orbe, 1998). White mainstream media's hypersexual depictions frame Black masculinity as a threat (Gates, 2004). Furthermore, American news sources reinforce these images and, even today, continue to depict Black individuals as dangerous and criminal. Danger, destruction, and incompetence are artificial and intentional discourses irrevocably dispossessed from any sense of ethical, moral, and social responsibility. These have become potent elixirs to stimulate a perpetual hallucination about Black males (Jackson & Balaji, 2015).

Stereotypes teach unconscious gender biases concerning which actions and behaviors are deemed acceptable. Misrepresentations reinforce negative conceptions about marginalized communities. Historically, Black representation was limited to racialized roles in Hollywood movies, which in turn perpetuated stereotypes. Stereotypes essentialized difference (according to unrealistic standards or limited choices), reinforced imbalanced power relations, and contributed to social and symbolic narratives about Black people

(Tyree et. al., 2012). Negative images fed the cultural imagination, normalized problematic expectations, and influenced individuals to view themselves as inadequate. These include unrealistic societal, sexual, and masculine identities for Black men (Slatton & Spates, 2014). Negative perceptions of Blackness inform self-hate. Undoubtedly, children and adults alike are susceptible to subtle and detrimental images of race (Hopson, 2008).

Critics must continue to examine and call attention to (mis)representations in media and popular culture. The interrogation of masculinity in *Black Panther* is vital given the film's cultural significance and popularity. An informed understanding of the trajectory of representations may encourage informed consumption of mediated depictions.

## METHOD

This study applies critical discourse analysis (CDA) to *Black Panther*. Our goal is to illustrate different contrasts of racialized subjects. CDA enables us to study language use, discourse and communication, within their social, cultural and political contexts (van Dijk, 1994). More specifically, the political dimension includes a focus on the power differentials influenced by class, gender, and race. As such, a CDA of race and masculinity may reveal the effect of the film's ideology.

We begin with critical rhetoric to expose and deconstruct discourses of power. In this case, we examine the messages and images that uphold or challenge scripts of hegemonic masculinity. We apply a critique of domination to examine power and the ways in which it is created and maintained. We also apply critique of freedom to move toward liberation (McKerrow, 1989). Our interrogation is meant to determine prevalent ideologies. By producing a description of what is, unfettered by predetermined notion of what should be, we can propose the potentialities against oppressive images and shifting contemporary power relations. By examining gender roles in *Black Panther*, we will reveal how discourse maintains oppressive representations, or calls liberation into being.

## PLOT OF *BLACK PANTHER*

*Black Panther* is based on the American comic book fictional character, created by Stan Lee and Jack Kirby and published by Marvel Comics. The backstory of the superhero stems from the existence of five fictional African tribes and their wars over a land rich with the extraordinary resource, vibranium, the material derived from a meteorite. After digesting a heart-shaped herb transmuted with vibranium, a warrior gained superhuman abilities and united all the tribes except for the tribe known as Jabari.

An abrupt cut to a backstory occurring in 1992 reveals that T'Chaka, the Wakandan king (and original "Black Panther"), accused his brother, N'Jobu, of working with a black-market arms dealer to steal vibranium from Wakanda. The undercover spy, N'Jobu, confirms T'Chaka's suspicions.

The present-day story begins after the death of T'Chaka. His son, T'Challa, becomes the king of Wakanda after defeating a member of the Jabari Tribe in ritual battle. Upon taking power, T'Challa learns that Klaue (the arms dealer) is once again attempting to acquire and deal vibranium weapons. T'Challa, Okoye (the leader of special forces known as the Dora Milaje), and Nakia (a Wakandan spy and T'Challa's love interest) embark on a mission to disrupt the sale of vibranium. The plan is disrupted when CIA agent, Everett K. Ross, is discovered to also want Klaue. T'Challa releases Klaue to Ross's custody, but the plan is thwarted when Klaue's associate, Erik "Killmonger" Stevens, attacks the CIA headquarters to rescue Klaue. Before escaping, T'Challa recognizes Killmonger as a Wakandan. The attack leaves Ross badly injured, T'Challa and the others return to Wakanda in an attempt to save Ross's life.

While T'Challa's sister, Shuri, is caring for Ross, T'Challa unearths the secret that his father killed his own brother, N'Jubo, leaving behind the American son who grew up to become Killmonger. Meanwhile, Killmonger kills Klaue, finds Wakanda, and, after presenting Klaue's dead body, declares his claim to the throne of Wakanda. In the ritualistic battle, Killmonger defeats T'Challa by throwing him over a cliff. Killmonger gains the support of T'Challa's second-in-command, W'Kabi. At Killmonger's command the Wakandan army prepares to extract and disseminate vibranium weapons to oppressed Africans and African Americans throughout the world. However, Nakia, Shuri, T'Challa's mother and Agent Ross flee to seek the help of the Jabari Tribe. They learn that the Jabari Tribe has found T'Challa—he is comatose but alive. When T'Challa's health and abilities are restored, he returns to Wakanda to pursue Killmonger, while Shuri, Nakia, Okoye and the Dora Milaje battle W'Kabi's army until they are victorious. T'Challa stabs Killmonger, and, though T'Challa offers to use their technology to save him, Killmonger chooses death over incarceration. T'Challa regains his rightful title as "Black Panther," establishes an American outreach center, and vows to share Wakanda's resources with the rest of the world.

## ANALYSIS

*Black Panther*'s prominent roles, discourse, and plot development reveal traditional and shifting ideologies surrounding Black masculinity. The film upholds and challenges representations and stereotypes of Black men. Despite breaking the stereotypical mold (e.g., portraying Black characters in positive and heroic roles), *Black Panther* also portrays hegemonic masculinity and, most problematic, the familiar stereotype of the violent, dangerous and angry Black men.

## T'CHAKA AND HEGEMONIC MASCULINITY

Early in the film, we see representations of Black masculinity in the character of T'Chaka. Flashbacks of T'Chaka and N'Jobu are placed throughout the film, and provide traditional characteristics of masculinity and leadership. For example, T'Chaka greets his brother by complimenting him and telling him that he looks "strong." N'Jobu, in turn, acknowledges that he is healthy. Strength remains a cultural marker of masculinity in most cultures (Trujillo, 1991). The exchange reifies positive association of traditional masculine expectations.

The film's characters embrace traditional and masculine approaches to power. Here, power is physical force and control (Trujillo, 1991). For example, N'Jobu bows to his brother and requests permission to speak with the king. In another example, tensions develop when T'Chaka tells N'Jobu that an attack has taken place in Wakanda and a man named Klaue has stolen vibranium and bombed the border. He then reveals that James is really Zuri, a Wakandan spy, who exposed N'Jobu's betrayal and involvement in Klaue's plot. In the scene, T'Chaka displays his position of authority and physical strength by physically intervening and pushing N'Jobu away when N'Jobu angrily and threateningly grabs Zuri by his shirt. T'Chaka demands he will return to Wakanda to be tried for his crimes and aggressively yells, "Stand down!" This is a physical display of strength. Respect comes by way of physicality, power, and status. Visual dominance is reinforced when T'Chaka raises his voice and grabs his brother's arm. In addition to physical strength, T'Chaka displays a lack of compassion toward N'Jobu's concern about other Black people oppressed throughout the world.

T'Chaka prioritizes his decision and Wakanda's protection. Negative stereotypes of masculine leadership downplay displays of emotion. Empathy is sacrificed for a greater good. Masculinity masks weakness, and weakness is coded as femininity (Leal, 2012). In another scene, T'Chaka stabs N'Jobu in the chest with his panther claws in defense of N'Jobu drawing a weapon on Zuri. Later, in a reference to the toxic masculinity, Zuri informs T'Challa that his father murdered his uncle. And, regarding N'Jobu's child with an American woman, Zuri explains the decision to leave him in order to sustain a lie. Consequently, T'Chaka resorts to violence, murder, and abandonment of his nephew in order to maintain power. He defends his actions to T'Challa, during T'Challa's second ancestral visit, informing T'Challa that he chose to omit the truth in favor of his people and his country. However, in doing so, T'Chaka also chose his power over compassion.

T'Chaka's symbolic representation of traditional masculinity is revealed in a scene when T'Challa enters the ancestral plane after ingesting the vibranium heart-shaped herb and succeeding at the ritual battle. T'Challa shows weakness and admits his insecurities as ruler. Upon greeting the spirit of his father, T'Challa acts submissive, kneeling and bowing to T'Chaka. T'Chaka responds unsympathetically and orders him to stand up, reiterating that he is king. T'Challa explains to T'Chaka that he is not prepared to be without him. T'Chaka warns T'Challa that he will "struggle," and advises T'Challa to surround himself with trustworthy people. "You're a good man with a good heart. And, it's hard for a good man to be king." Through this dialogue, T'Chaka continues to represent more traditional and hegemonic masculine qualities and showcase the preferred leadership style. He subtly pushes T'Challa to act strong, proud, and authoritative; these are king-like behaviors. By the end of the scene, he concedes that T'Challa will have a difficult time ruling because he labels T'Challa as "good" as adverse to a king's expected behavior. In most scenes, T'Chaka is portrayed as a loving father. His affection and warmth are given freely to his brother and to his son. Yet these scenes reveal little patience for weakness, compassion, and empathy. In these moments, T'Chaka is dismissing ethics and morality, and reinforcing the stereotype of the socially irresponsible Black male. Though T'Chaka breaks the stereotype of a "bad" father associated with Black men, he also highlights violent and dangerous tendencies toward others, authoritative rule, and an ethically questionable conscience.

## VISIBLE BLACK, MASCULINE BODIES

The film frequently features bodies of Black men. Images of their physicality, muscles, and exhibitions of strength and aggression adhere to traditional notions of masculinity. Hypermasculinity relies heavily on the display and control of the male body, for which muscles, especially biceps and pectorals, function as a synecdoche (Kac-Vergne, 2012).

Three of the Black male leads are characters whose bodies become the source of the viewers' gaze. These characters are defined largely by their bodily performances as they enact violent and aggressive movements that are integral to the plot. First, T'Challa is introduced wearing the "Black Panther" suit, which highlights his physical strength and muscular build. Though the scene moves abruptly, we watch T'Challa rescue a group of women, while he defeats roughly a dozen men. He tosses heavy equipment at his enemies, and is able to kick, punch, and take on gunfire without consequence. During his ritual battles, T'Challa fights shirtless. His muscles are well defined. His body is centered within each battle, including the final fight scene with Killmonger.

Second, physicality is prioritized when M'Baku enters the frame alongside members of his Jabari Tribe. They, too, appear shirtless, chanting, with malicious looks on their faces. Their bodies are marked with war paint and white chalk-like patterns which emphasize the build of their chest, back, arm and shoulder muscles. Members of the tribe are noticeably larger, taller, and more muscular than T'Challa.

Third, Killmonger is domineering in his physical appearance. He is more muscular than T'Challa. Also, Killmonger's body is more intimidating because his abdominals and chest are covered with self-inflicted markings to display the kill-count of people he has killed. In a scene where Killmonger wakes up from the ancestral plane, his muscles are swollen and flexed. The camera pans away slowly, in juxtaposition with his order to burn all heart-shaped herbs. Finally Killmonger's muscular silhouette is at the center of the screen. The king wears a traditional jacket over his bare chest. His muscles and kill-count markings remain exposed to symbolize power and authority.

Corporeality is at work. Camera angles and film speeds emphasize the physicality of Black men. Given the importance in the film, body enhancements and physical training were prominent aspects of playing these characters. Michael B. Jordan (who plays Killmonger) explains, "[The director] wanted him to be muscular and massive, so I treated it like I was training a Marine." Actors were trained in weapons and martial arts to refine the traditional markers of masculinity. Beyond the film, strength, physique, and visual codes were further propagated by magazines such as the *Men's Journal* and *Maxim* (Thorp, 2018; Freeman, 2018).

## KILLMONGER AND THE ANGRY, VIOLENT, HYPERMASCULINE BLACK STEREOTYPE

Hypermasculinity is the socially constructed expectations of male behavior. These qualities are inaccurate, but prevalent in the public imagination. In addition, hypermasculinity is hegemonic masculinity derived from dominant scripts, and idealized in a culture (Trujillo, 1991). Black men are often characterized by hypersexuality, danger, criminality, unreliability, and absence in kinships (Slatton & Spates, 2014). Killmonger embodies and represents hypermasculinity.

Killmonger's character is dangerous as expressed by his own goals and desires. The power of the man and his body is masculinized as physical strength, force, speed, control, toughness, and domination (Trullijo, 1991). Killmonger's personal history is replete with these qualities. For example, Agent Ross informs T'Challa of Eric Stevens's (Killmonger's) past:

Joined the SEALs and went straight to Afghanistan where he wrapped up confirmed kills like it was a video game. Started calling him Killmonger. He joined a JSOC ghost unit. Now these guys are serious. They will drop off the grid so they can commit assassinations and take down governments.

Killmonger's reputation indicates that he is strong, dangerous, and comfortable killing. The description foregrounds hypermasculinity. Killmoger's achievement in the military and his role as a special operative represent the patriarchal and masculine institution. His actions and training are ritualized markers of masculinity. Domination is further reinforced when Killmonger tells T'Challa:

> I lived my entire life waitin' for this moment. I trained, I lied, I killed . . . just to get here. I killed in America, Afghanistan, Iraq. I took life from my own brothers and sisters right here on this continent. And all this death . . . just so I could kill you.

Killmonger necessitates murdering the king, not just overthrowing him.

Killmonger engages in aiding and abetting a known international arms dealer and terrorist in the eyes of Wakandans. Before Killmonger's background in revealed, he is presented as an experienced criminal during the robbery at the museum. Killmonger further proves himself by freeing Klaue. Eventually he kills Klaue to gain access into Wakanda. During his ritual battle with T'Challa, Killmonger exhibits expert fighting skills. When Zuri interferes to sacrifice himself for T'Challa, Killmonger declares he will "take" both and stabs Zuri in the heart, killing him. He mocks T'Challa, and easily overpowers T'Challa's rage. He yells to his audience of Wakandans: "Is this your king? Is this your king? The Black Panther, who's supposed to lead you into the future? Him? He's supposed to protect you? Nah. I'm your king." In that scene, Killmonger both verbally emasculates T'Challa, brutally beats him, and finally throws T'Challa off the cliff.

Unlike T'Challa, Killmonger quickly takes an authoritative approach to ruling. When Killmonger first enters the council of Wakandan leaders, he does not hesitate to reveal his endgame, declaring his desire to rule. Killmonger is angry, domineering, and controlling. His first order is to burn all of the heart-shaped herbs. He dismisses the idea that there will be any other king besides himself. When his demand is challenged by a woman, Killmonger grabs her by the throat, lifts her off the ground and yells, "When I tell you to do something, I mean that shit." He strategizes to overcome the colonizers by enacting their hypermasculine characteristics:

> I know how colonizers think. So we're going to use their own strategy against 'em. We're gonna send vibranium weapons out to our War Dogs. They'll arm oppressed people all over the world so they can finally rise up and kill those in

power. And their children. And anyone else who takes their side. It's time they know the truth about us. We're warriors. The world's gonna start over, and this time, we're on top. . . . You heard your orders. Let's get to it.

For Killmonger, rescuing Black people is not enough. He intends to punish and colonize all other individuals, regardless of allyship or their direct responsibility for the contemporary oppressive ideologies.

Killmonger is associated with stereotypes of misogyny, instability and lacking compassion. Though hypersexuality is not prominent in *Black Panther*, Killmonger is the only character shown acting on sexual desires. After Killmonger and Klaue successfully heist a vibranium weapon from the Museum of Great Britain, Killmonger is shown passionately making out with his girlfriend in their getaway vehicle. Yet, when Klaue takes Killmonger's girlfriend hostage, Killmonger does not hesitate to kill her in order to kill Klaue. Killmonger's lack of regard feeds into misogynist stereotypes that surrounds hypermasculinity norms (Tyree et. al., 2012). Killmonger will destroy anything that makes him vulnerable. He lacks feeling, compassion, and sensitivity, and further reveals his heartless, tough, and aggressive qualities.

Killmonger will sacrifice everything to fulfill his personal goals. He fails to show emotion when he encounters his father on the ancestral plane. N'Jobu asks, "No tears for me?" Killmonger, appearing as a small boy, simply responds nonchalantly, "Everybody dies. It's just life around here." Though a tear eventually streams down his face, it is quickly replaced by an expression of anger and aggression when the visit ends abruptly, and he finds himself back in the Wakandan temple.

Killmonger is revealed to harbor anger as the result of losing his father. Further, Killmonger's abandonment fuels representation of inner-city Black youths as angry and troubled because they are fatherless. Killmonger is the ultimate stereotype of the angry and violent Black man. Killmonger's loss is used as justification to behave ruthlessly. He blames the world for taking everything away from him. The anger defines him like it defines other young Black males.

## *BLACK PANTHER* AND IMAGES OF PROGRESSIVE BLACK MASCULINITY: T'CHALLA AS THE NEW MAN

Despite the problematic representations of hyper or hegemonic masculinity and trite stereotypes of Black men, *Black Panther* challenges assumptions about Black masculinity. The film's conflation of man and king means that *Black Panther* relays traditional masculinity akin to traditional, hierarchical governing, thus hegemonic masculinity is antithetical to successful leadership. While characters like T'Chaka and Killmonger reinforce Black stereotypes, T'Challa also represents the model man and ideal leader. Not coincidentally, his character breaks from commonplace stereotypes, and represents progressive and shifting characteristics. He is the ultimate hero to defeat tradition, and usher in democratic leadership and peaceful conflict resolution.

T'Challa represents a new masculinity. He uses force and strength, yet his physical force is more restrained than the former "Black Panther." T'Challa is different from his father and his cousin. He kills only when necessary, shows compassion and empathy to his enemies, admits vulnerability, takes responsibility, and is guided by humanitarian morals and ethics. He is willing to accept help from others, specifically women. Contrary to normative representations, the new man signals a reflexive masculinity, compared to hegemonic ideas of masculinity (Malinga & Ratele, 2016).

T'Challa's approach to empathy and compassion, and his sensitivity toward others, are illustrated throughout the film. For example, *Black Panther* downplays the necessity of force and violence often expected in strong Black men. In fact, he showed compassion and mercy to challengers. T'Challa exhibits these characteristics in the ritual battle with M'Baku by pleading with him to surrender repeatedly. Though M'Baku declares he would rather die than yield, T'Challa persists: "You have fought with honor! Now yield!" Even after M'Baku grunts and continues to struggle, T'Challa yells, "Your people need you. Yield man!" until M'Baku smacks T'Challa on the leg to signal defeat. T'Challa displays compassion for M'Baku and expresses concern for the Jabari tribe. M'Baku represents stereotypical masculinity. He claims that he would rather die over facing the shame of defeat.

T'Challa consistently chooses forms of justice that avoid acts of violence. When discussing the recent reemergence of Klaue, W'Kabi gives T'Challa an ultimatum asking him to either execute him or bring him to Wakanda. T'Challa responds, "You have my word. I will bring him back." Despite Klaue's terrorist and deadly actions, T'Challa prefers to hold him accountable for his crimes without killing him.

At the end of the film, T'Challa delivers the fatal blow to Killmonger to save Wakanda. Yet, he offers mercy even though Killmonger shows no remorse. After fatally stabbing Killmonger in the heart, T'Challa is sullen. While dying, Killmonger shares memories of his father. T'Challa's eyes begin to fill with tears. T'Challa takes Killmonger to a peak where he can finally see Wakanda, just as N'Jobu had once promised his son. T'Challa suggests to Killmonger that they can still heal him, but Killmonger willingly accepts death over incarceration. When Killmonger dies, T'Challa grieves him. In a final symbol of empathy, he positions Killmonger's arms by crossing them in accordance with the Wakandan symbol.

T'Challa shows humanitarianism and compassion for others. The various conquests indicate that traditional signs of masculinity (e.g. competitiveness, dominance, toughness, and aggression) are not necessary characteristics of a successful leader. In some cases, patience defeats brawn. For example, at the first challenge, M'Baku is more muscular, larger, more dangerous, intimidating, and just as skilled in warfare as T'Challa, yet he does not beat the focused and determined T'Challa. T'Challa's worthiness is confirmed. Furthermore, M'Baku is supported by his army of men, while T'Challa is guarded by the Dora Milaje, an army of women. Although the Dora Milaje adopts an appropriate masculine characteristic, the visual representation of women challenges traditional representations of strength and determination. This is an especially significant cinematic/cultural reversal considering *Black Panther* is a film about a superhero, and we have come to see these characters as hegemonically masculine and capable of saving and rescuing themselves and others single-handedly.

Although T'Challa is the hero of the story, he does not win every battle. He is overthrown by Killmonger in their first challenge. The defeat is unique and consistent with the subtext equating traits of new masculinity. T'Challa is less focused and angry, contributing to his own defeat. T'Challa becomes enraged after Killmonger mocks him, emasculates him, and kills Zuri for revenge. As T'Challa appears to lose the new masculine principles and ideals that separate him from other leaders vying for the throne, he loses his battle.

T'Challa also represents the change from tradition, challenging the principles followed by previous kings. In doing so, he shifts assumptions around gender roles and leadership. This was first shown when T'Challa sees his father on the ancestral plane and admits his insecurities, expressing a child-like vulnerability and stating, "Tell me how to best protect Wakanda. I want to be a great king, Baba. Just like you." While King T'Chaka's character and reputation is valued initially, T'Challa begins to view his own father differently. His father represents stereotypical masculine traits (e.g., violence, political authority, control, dominance, and lack of compassion). Later, when T'Challa sees his father again, after learning about his actions against N'Jobu, T'Challa criticizes his father for abandoning Killmonger:

> You were wrong! All of you were wrong [tears roll down his cheeks]. . . . I cannot rest while he sits on the throne. He is a monster of our own making. I must take the mantle back. I must! I must right these wrongs.

T'Challa expresses his emotion and disagreement with his father's approach and, by the end of the film, indicates that his own leadership will change. These qualities reflect the type of masculinity he embodies.

In T'Challa's first challenge, M'Baku references T'Chaka's children as progressive, emphasizing their interest in technological advancements, and their dismissal of tradition. He asserts that they are insufficient at leading, associating their methods and approaches with weakness, and an inability to "keep his own father safe." In doing so, M'Baku calls T'Chaka's children unfit for leadership. They represent shifts in ideologies as Shuri continues to modernize and update the nation's technological advances. M'Baku also emasculates T'Challa by claiming that T'Challa is to blame his father's death. It is relevant that T'Chaka's death is due to a terrorist attack at the United Nations. Although T'Challa could not have prevented the incident, T'Chaka lost his life engaging in diplomacy with other nations, an act that M'Baku is likely to view as weak.

Finally, T'Challa is the juxtaposition to Killmonger. He does not embrace the same qualities of masculinity and has an antithetical approach to leadership. During his final conversation with Killmonger, T'Challa critiques Killmonger for his approach to ruling and his strategizing for liberating people. He refers to toxic masculinity; engaging in the very colonialization he wants to overturn.

> T'Challa: You want to see us become just like the people you hate so much. Divide and conquer the land as they did!
> Killmonger: Nah, I learn from my enemies. Beat them at they own game.
> T'Challa: You have become them! You will destroy the world, Wakanda included!

T'Challa's approach, consistent with more progressive ideas of masculinity, seeks to end the cycle of oppression and protect both his own country's interests and the rest of the world.

The film also presents a subtle conflation between the role/meaning of a man and the role/meaning of king. Referencing T'Challa's treatment of his brother and abandonment of his nephew, T'Challa asks Nakia: "What kind of king—what kind of man does that?" Nakia replies: "No man is perfect. Not even your father.... You can't let your father's mistakes define who you are. You get to decide what kind of king you are going to be." T'Challa interchanges king and man, implying that a king should have more compassion. The expectation moves beyond a characteristic of a ruler to a quality of a good man. While Nakia points out that no man is perfect, she also implies that T'Challa can break the cycle and change the behavior. In deciding what kind of king he is going to be, he can also determine the qualities of his manhood.

When T'Challa returns to Wakanda to take the throne back from Killmonger, Okoye shows her loyalty to T'Challa. In doing so, the message is sent that a heart "full of hatred" makes a person an inadequate ruler. Thus, we are reminded that Killmonger's qualities are not only inadequate to be a king, but they are also the source that fuels toxic forms of masculinity.

## T'CHALLA AND HIS RELATIONSHIPS WITH OTHERS

According to Palczewski (2005), "The conflict over gender roles is always simultaneously about femininity and masculinity" (p. 379). In other words, the meaning of man cannot change without altering the understanding or expectations of woman. As lead female roles enact traditionally masculine roles (e.g., serving in the military, science and technology, and international relations), viewers also encounter a new masculinity. T'Challa is able to expand the role of Black men by supplementing strength and achievement through his support system, which consists of strong women. Whereas Killmonger has no support, even murdering his only female companion for his own ambitions, T'Challa relies on family and friends, but most importantly, women including his mother, his sister Shuri, his companion and army general Okoye, and his love interest Nakia. *Black Panther* portrays the sociopsychological theory that love, happiness, and a strong support network can positively influence young men when it comes to productively constructing one's masculinity.

In addition to representations that expand meaning and show genders as complimentary, *Black Panther* shows the new man as a progressive leader. He receives assistance from women, works with them, listens to them, and is also openly accepting of and not challenged by their insights. For example, when T'Challa takes Okoye and Nakia on a mission to Korea, W'Kabi offers to go, but T'Challa orders him to stay in Wakanda and guard the border. In the final battle against Killmonger, Nakia, Shuri, and Okoye assist T'Challa. Without the initiative of Shuri and Nakia, the actions to save T'Challa's life and rescue Wakanda would not have occurred.

Additionally, T'Challa is guarded by Okoye and the Dora Milaje, the personal army of the king. When Killmonger becomes king, before T'Challa is discovered to be alive, Nakia seeks the help of Okoye to overthrow Killmonger, referring to Okoye as, "the greatest warrior that Wakanda has." Okoye's reputation as the greatest warrior is upheld when W'Kabi, who is supporting and defending Killmonger, surrenders his entire army when faced with Okoye in battle.

Shuri is arguably one of the most intelligent scientists in Wakanda. When Shuri argues that she is smarter, T'Challa does not question or protest the claim.

> T'Challa: You are teaching me? What do you know?
> Shuri: More than you.

Shuri is constantly working to improve life for her people. She enables most of T'Challa's success through her technological and scientific advancements. At the end of the film, T'Challa informs her that she will take charge of their scientific and technological communication exchange, spearheading the program with other nations.

Finally, when it comes to political advisement, no individual is as persuasive as Nakia. After T'Chaka's death, Nakia returns to Wakanda to support T'Challa in his ritual battle and to pay respects to his father. After winning the throne, T'Challa expresses his desire for Nakia to stay in Wakanda. She expresses her need to serve others and reveals that she cannot feel happy in Wakanda knowing that people are suffering and have nothing. T'Challa asks Nakia how she would solve the current problems. She suggests sharing, offering their technological advancements to other countries and sheltering the refugees in need. T'Challa protests, suggesting that Wakanda is at risk and could lose their way as a result of such actions. Nakia insists, "Wakanda is strong enough to help others and protect ourselves at the same time." T'Challa drops the argument, giving the final say on the matter to Nakia and changes the topic to playful banter. Despite the abrupt end to the conversation, T'Challa takes Nakia's advice seriously. In the next scene, he is distracted and troubled. When border protector W'Kabi asks T'Challa what is wrong, T'Challa explains that Nakia has suggested they provide more aid and assist refugees. W'Kabi, like T'Challa, expresses skepticism at the idea. At the very end of the film, we learn that T'Challa has adopted Nakia's advice. He builds the first Wakandan International Outreach Center and appoints Nakia in charge of it. Finally, he goes to the United Nations, offering Wakanda's assistance to the rest of the world, "to be an example of how we as brothers and sisters on this earth should treat one another." During this final scene, Okoye and Nakia stand on either side of T'Challa slightly behind him. The film visually reminds viewers that behind every strong, moral leader are the support and contributions of women.

## CONCLUSION

This study provided an analysis of *Black Panther*'s representation of Black masculinity. The film is significant because it has been deemed a watershed moment in the cultural history of African-American people (Tompkins, 2018). Simultaneously, *Black Panther* requires careful consideration of its complex portrayal of gender roles.

*Black Panther* makes both regressive and progressive strides in representation. Some of the male characters are based in discriminatory and racist assumptions about Black men asserting the domination of these representations. Yet, the film counters problematic stereotypes, by introducing more complex personality dimensions. To challenge toxic interpretations of hypermasculinity and images of liberation is especially important for Black communities:

> Many civil rights pioneers and other trailblazing forebears have received lavish cinematic treatments. . . . Fictional celluloid champions have included Virgil Tibbs, John Shaft and Foxy Brown. . . . But *Black Panther* matters more, because he is our best chance for people of every color to see a Black hero. That is its own kind of power. (Smith, 2018)

Ultimately, the film is valuable for its visual representations and model characters that have physical and emotional strength and positive, new, liberating interpretations of masculinities.

This discourse analysis revealed a dominant paradox because progressive onscreen heroism depends largely on Black physicality, strength, and force. Social messages and popular imagery limit activist strategies and social movements. It is important to address the film's use of hegemonic masculinity, hypermasculinity, and other familiar tropes associated with Black America. Conversely, *Black Panther*'s liberating subtext shifts assumptions about Black masculinity. There are reasons to celebrate the showcase Blackness on the big screen, especially when viewers feed off these images, and integrate these characteristics into our personalities, ethics, and morals.

## REFERENCES

Brown, J. A. (2001). *Black superheroes, milestone comics, and their fans*. Jackson, MS: University Press of Mississippi.

Byars, J. (1991). *All that Hollywood allows: re-reading gender in 1950s melodrama*. Chapel Hill, NC: The University of North Carolina Press.

Castle Bell, G. & Harris, T. M. (2017). Exploring representations of black masculinity and emasculation on NBC's Parenthood. *Journal of International and Intercultural Communication, 10*(2), 135–52. http://dx.doi.org/10.1080/17513057.2016.1142598

Freeman, T. (Feb. 19, 2018). Here's how Michael B. Jordan got jacked AF for his role in *Black Panther*. *Maxim*. https://www.maxim.com/entertainment/michael-b-jordan-black-panther-workout-2018-2

Gates, P. (2004). Always a partner in crime: Black masculinity in the Hollywood detective film. *Journal of Popular Film & Television, 32*(1). 20–29.

Hall, S. (1996). *New ethnicities from Morely, David and Chen, Kuan-Hsing and Stuart Hall: Critical dialogues in cultural studies*, pp. 441–49. New York: Routledge.

hooks, b. (1992a). *Black looks: Race and representation*. Boston, MA: South End Press.

hooks, b. (1992b). Representing Whiteness in the Black imagination. In L. Grossberg, C. Nelson, and P.A. Treichler's (Eds.) *Cultural Studies*, pp. 338–46, London: Routledge.

Hopson, M. C. (2008). "Now watch me dance": Responding to critical observations, constructions, and performances of race on reality television. *Critical Studies in Media Communication, 25*(4), 441–46.

Jackson, R. L., II & Balaji, M. (2015) Border citizenry and the arbitrary civil protection of Black males. *Cultural Studies Critical Methodologies, 15*(4), 242–47, doi: 10.1177/1532708615578412

Kac-Vergne, M. (2012). Losing visibility? The rise and fall of hypermasculinity in science fiction films. *In Media. 2*, 1–15. http://journals.openedition.org/inmedia/491

Lavelle, K. L. (2010). A Critical discourse analysis of black masculinity in NBA game commentary. *The Howard Journal of Communications, 21*, 294–314. doi:10.1080/10646175.2010.496675

Leal, J. (2012). American cinema and the construction of masculinity in film in the federal republic after 1945. *German Life and Letters*, *65*(1), 59–72. doi: 10.1111/j.1468-0483.2011.01559

Malinga, M., & Ratele, K. (2016). "It's cultivated, grown, packaged and sold with a price tag": Young black men's consumption of media images of love, happiness and constructions of masculinity. *Culture, Society and Masculinities*, *8*(2), 100–17. doi: 10.3149/csm.0802.100

McKerrow, R. (1989). Critical rhetoric: Theory and praxis. *Communication Monographs*, *56*, 91–111.

Oeur, F. (2016). Recognizing dignity: Young Black men growing up in an era of surveillance. *Socius: Sociological Research for a Dynamic World*, *2*, 1–15. doi: 10.1177/2378023116633712

Orbe, M. P. (1998). Constructions of reality on MTV's "the real world": An analysis of the restrictive coding of Black masculinity. *Southern Communication Journal*, *64*(1), 32–47.

Palczewski, C. H. (2005). The male Madonna and the feminine Uncle Sam: Visual arguments, icons, and ideographs in 1909 anti-woman suffrage postcards. *Quarterly Journal of Speech*, *91*, 365–94. doi: 10.1080/00335630500488325

Parmar, P. (1990). Black feminism: The politics of articulation. In J. Rutherford (Ed.), *Identity: Community, Culture, Difference*. (pp. 101–26). London: Lawrence & Wishart.

Slatton, B., & Spates, K. (2014). *Hyper sexual, hyper masculine?: Gender, race and sexuality in the identities of contemporary Black men*. Surrey, UK: Ashgate, 2014.

Smith, J. (2018, February 19). Super powered: *Black Panther* marks a major milestone for culture. *Time*, 41–42.

Thorp, C. (2018). How Michael B. Jordan put on 15 pounds of muscle for '*Black Panther*.' *Men's Journal*. https://www.mensjournal.com/health-fitness/michael-b-jordans-black-panther-workout-was-intense/

Tompkins, J. (2018). Woke Hollywood, all hype the *Black Panther*. *Film Criticism*, *42*(4) doi: http://dx.doi.org/10.3998/fc.13761232.0042.403

Trujillo, N. (1991). Hegemonic masculinity on the mound: Media representations of Nolan Ryan and American sports culture. *Critical Studies in Mass Communication*, *8*, 290–308.

Tyree, T. C., Byerly, C. M., & Hamilton, K. A. (2012). Representations of (new) Black masculinity: A news-making case study. *Journalism*, *13*(4), 467–82. doi.org/10.1177/1464884911421695

van Dijk, T. A. (1994). Editorial: Critical discourse analysis. *Discourse & Society*, *5*(4), 435–36.

*Chapter Eleven*

# "Me Miran Raro"

*Bad Bunny and the Creation of a New Discursive Space in Latin Trap Music*

## Larissa Hernandez

In the music video for "Caro," Bad Bunny's female proxy raps the words "I break the rules and I fix them" in Spanish as she rides atop a blue Ferrari convertible. Bad Bunny, in both his femme and masculine iterations, shimmies and bounces in the colorful and flamboyant attire that he has become known for as he raps and asks the question: "Why can I not be who I am and be happy doing it?" The Latin trap artist's music video accompanying his debut album *X100PRE*, boasts gender-fluidity and inclusivity by playing with the idea of gender binaries and by featuring a cast of LGBTQ, disabled, and other marginalized communities within the video. The song ends with Bad Bunny rapping in Spanish with his characteristic low draw, "They look at me strange, eh, but I'm not stopping for anything."

    In the past five years, Latin trap music has seen increased commercial success, growing as an offshoot from Reggaeton and American Southern hip-hop music. Influenced by its predecessors in Reggaeton and Southern hip-hop, Latin trap music, sometimes shortened to trapeton, possesses the signature undulating boom-ch-boom-ch of reggaeton while maintaining the trademark repetition of hi-hat kicks and 32nd note beats of American trap music. Some of the leading Latin trap artists today include Anuel AA, Farruko, Karol G, and Bad Bunny. And while the seminal point of Latin trap music is debated between the release of Yaga and Mackie's "El Pistolon" in 2007 or the internationalization of Latin trap with De La Ghetto's 2016 video for "La Ocasión" featuring Ozuna, Anuel AA, and Arcangel, the ripple effect of the Latin trap scene has been felt and heard by audiences worldwide. Collaborations between artists like J Balvin and Cardi B or Bad Bunny and Drake have led to an increased presence of Latin trap music on televised award shows and across music streaming platforms, such as Spotify. However, as global as Latin trap music is now becoming, markedly common in the music videos of the genre are the hypersexualized representations of women's bodies, the abundance of money and drugs, and the perpetuation of gender binaries that are present in Latino culture. In his presentation of painted nails, hoop earrings, and an overall unique sense of fashion that challenges gender norms, Bad Bunny is breaking all of the rules that had since been set forth by popular Latin trap artists and realigning them to make room for a different audience and to introduce a new discursive space within Latin trap music.

In the beginning of the music video for "Caro," Bad Bunny, born Benito Antonio Martínez Ocasio, is seen in a white bathrobe receiving a fresh manicure inside a bedroom while a fashion show plays on a small television in the background. From the beginning of this video, audiences see the binary of pink versus blue at play. Martinez is sitting in a baby blue room decorated with pink frames and a pink cross, as well as pink curtains and pink lamps. On the table beside him, where a young woman sits just on the other side painting Martinez's nails, the bottles of nail polish are pink and blue, standing side by side. The audience sees more of this juxtaposition of traditionally binarized colors as the camera cuts back to a fuller view of the room where the pink curtains, pink fur rugs, and other pink knickknacks are more easily seen interspersed among the greater blue of the room. Seeming to suggest fluidity and inclusion, rather than an opposition, the camera transitions from a close-up view of Martinez's face, down to a view of his hands, and finally up to a full view of a woman, Puerto Rican model Jazmyne Joy, with the same shaved hairstyle that Martinez wears, as well as the same white bathrobe. As the camera focuses on Joy's face, Martinez is overheard thanking the person painting his nails as the Bad Bunny-like Joy moves her mouth in sync with Martinez's voice. Throughout the video, Joy dresses, raps, and dances in styles identical to the Latin trap artist. Alongside the juxtaposition of stereotypically opposed colors and the introduction of a female proxy with the full movement and agency of the artist himself, Bad Bunny, through a "rhetoric of difference" (Flores 1996, p. 145), begins the work of carving out a queer space within the greater discourse of Latin trap music.

In her essay, "Creating Discursive Space through a Rhetoric of Difference: Chicana Feminists Craft a Homeland," Lisa A. Flores examines the way Chicana feminist writers have carved out a space in traditional Chicano discourse in which their own experiences as Chicanas and as border-citizens inform this new discursive space. According to Flores, a rhetoric of difference "includes repudiating mainstream discourse and espousing self-and group-created discourse" (145). Marginalized groups mobilize and begin to achieve autonomy through the act of defining themselves and defying the dominant culture, or at least challenging it and pushing up against it to create a new discourse. In a genre that identifies with the hypersexualization and commodification of women, the trafficking of drugs, and the exploitation of riches, "Caro" presents a world of inclusivity where people of different genders, ethnicities, sizes, and even people who are pregnant or have Down Syndrome are made visible. At 01:48:00 into the music video for "Caro," the camera is focused on a scene where these nontraditional models walk down a fashion runway that was playing earlier on the mini television in Martinez's bedroom. Missing the cultural tropes of typical Latin trap videos, Bad Bunny has challenged the genre and separated himself to some degree from the prescribed role of hypermasculine trapero by creating a rhetoric of difference that carves out a discursive space for a new discourse on nonbinary gender identities and inclusivity in Latin trap music. As a leading artist in the industry, Bad Bunny accomplishes this by first rejecting the industry-produced image of the masculine trapero and then using his international platform to give voice to a marginalized community—nontraditional models, the LGBTQ community—and subsequently bridging these identities and these voices to not only the Latin music industry but also to the global market.

In the lyrics to "Caro," Bad Bunny calls for autonomy in the way he chooses to present himself in the Latin trap industry. In the second verse of the song, Martinez raps, "Vive tu vida, yo vivo la mia / Criticar sin dar ejemplo, qué jodí'a mania / Por sólo ser yo y no como se suponía." Martinez asks that he live his life while others live theirs in spite of critics judging him for choosing to be who he is and not the industry-produced image of a trapero. This theme of asking and choosing to present himself as he wishes continues throughout the song and hits a peak as a smooth and slow interlude begins with the question: "Why can't I be like that?" At this point in the song, openly gay Puerto Rican recording artist, Ricky Martin, sings alongside Martinez as they both sing in Spanish: "Why can't I be like that? How am I hurting you? How am I hurting you? I'm only happy." Martin and Martinez also express that they are happy in their presentation of themselves before the final chorus kicks back in with the trademark drum of 808 beats that are characteristic of trap music and Martinez's final declaration of pride in who he is and in his presentation.

Martinez's decision to collaborate with Ricky Martin on a song whose music video challenges gender and industry expectations of trap music is the act of creating a new discursive space in which new conversations can take place regarding gender identity and inclusivity. In her essay, "Fingernails Con Feeling," from the book *Remixing Reggaetón*, Africana studies professor Petra R. Rivera-Rideau discusses reggaetonera Ivy Queen and her support of Puerto Rican LGBTQ communities. Rivera-Rideau states that Ivy Queen's support is an important moment in Puerto Rican LGBTQ discourse because "queer subjectivities have been written out of the hegemonic definitions of Puerto Ricanness [because] dominant discourses of racial democracy rely on constructs of respectability that present nonheterosexual contact as 'deviant'" (2015, 105). Ivy Queen, an artist that served as inspiration in Martinez's taste in music and in his career as Bad Bunny, had decades before Martinez began this discussion of criticizing the expectations of women in an industry that commodified them and that was predominantly operated by heterosexual men. This conversation of challenging gender roles continues and expands under the growing success of artists like Bad Bunny that dare to challenge established cultural tropes that for years have been lucrative and have generated new hit songs.

Here, it is also important to note the nature of the music industry that operates through set contracts that bind artists to certain labels or producers that essentially control the careers of these artists and limit their autonomous output as creators of original music. Bad Bunny, under contract with Hear This Music, a Puerto Rican music label distributed by Sony Music Latin and headed by DJ Luian and Mambo Kings, had his career limited to features and singles for two years before achieving complete artistic autonomy. A part of many hit songs in the first two years of his career, Bad Bunny was able to secure his trajectory to fame but at the cost of waiting to release his own LP until his contract with Hear This Music was completed. When looking at the time line of Bad Bunny's career, audiences can see the incorporation of painted nails and the use of hoop earrings become more common with the more traction that Bad Bunny gained in his career, essentially safeguarding his success in the Latin trap music industry and allowing more space for his expression as an individual. Martinez's autonomy as an artist came gradually until the release of his first album, *X100PRE*, a stylized version of "por siempre." With this album, Martinez secured his autonomy as a musical artist and his creative ideology as Bad Bunny.

The video for "Caro" ends with Martinez appearing again as his male self in the same outfit that Joy wore earlier in the video. Martinez kisses his female proxy in what can be read as a shocking and out-of-the-ordinary display in a Latin trap music video. It can also be read as a melding of Martinez's identities, or a fluidity of gender. And while it can be argued that Bad Bunny as an artist still adheres to the stereotypes that value money, expensive cars, women as commodities, and drugs, he is still creating a new discursive space for the queer community in an area of the world, in an area of the music industry that has traditionally valued a binary heterosexuality. The rhetoric of difference that Bad Bunny, the performer, and that Benito Martínez employ in their presentation is complex and challenges the norms of a lucrative industry that runs on restrictive artist contracts, harmful tropes that promote homophobia, and that exclude some groups in the community, such as LGBTQ members and the people with disabilities.

## REFERENCES

Bunny, Bad. "Caro—Bad Bunny | X 100PRE." YouTube, 23 Dec. 2018. Retrieved from: www.youtube.com/watch?v=7YjgLPINtqo.

Bad Bunny. Lyrics to "Caro." Genius, 2019. Retrieved from: https://genius.com/Bad-bunny-caro-lyrics.

Bad Bunny. *X100PRE*. Rimas Entertainment, 2018. CD.

Flores, L. A. (1996). Creating discursive space through a rhetoric of difference: Chicana feminists craft a homeland. *Quarterly Journal of Speech, vol. 82*, no. 2.

Rivera-Rideau, P. R. (2015). *Remixing reggaetón: The cultural politics of race in Puerto Rico.* North Carolina: Duke University Press.

Spotify Charts. 20 Mar. 2019. Retrieved from: spotifycharts.com/viral/.

*Chapter Twelve*

# Dual Socialization and Black Academic Intellectuals

*A Research Report*

Rutledge Dennis

Black intellectuals have played a pivotal role in advancing organizational and institutional life among Black Americans. That role has been indelibly linked to the group's education, political, and economic experiences, and a role in overtly and covertly agitating for social justice. The concept of the "intellectual" has fewer pejoratives today than it did when Harold Cruse (1967) designated the intellectual as the center piece of the existing cultural, political, and economic deficits in Black communities. Cruse's trenchant critique of intellectuals forced many of us to define and understand the term, not abstractly, but more concretely in its application to various features of group culture, politics, and economics. Parenthetically, E. Franklin Frazier created a similar social, cultural, and intellectual controversy with the study of the Black Bourgeoisie (1997). This controversy also became a part of Du Bois's politics when he sought to alter the social and racial landscape by making the idea of the Talented Tenth (1903) the centerpiece of his movement for social change.

With the exception of autobiographical and biographical sketches of a few widely known individuals, we know very little of the socio-environmental factors and circumstances which shape the lives of Black intellectuals, thus setting them on the path toward the world of, and analysis of, ideas. This is especially true of those born and raised in the South. And here, the concern has to move beyond the sons and daughters of college and university professors and those in media. Indeed, the question may very well rest on the idea that a sociology of intellectuals focused largely, and narrowly, on a few nationally and internationally known intellectuals, may well overlook those engaged in intellectual pursuits on the local and regional level. For this study, I adopted a simple and forthright definition of intellectuals: those who discuss and analyze ideas, issues, and problems on social issues having local, regional, national, and international consequences. These ideas may be presented in books, journals, magazines, and newspapers, or presented in lectures, workshops, or similar venues.

This exploratory study is part of a larger project which entails formulating a Sociology of Black Intellectuals, a theme reflected in previous works. The use of data will aid in better understanding the individual and social dynamics crucial in the making of intellectuals. In addition, that special talents and skills may emerge among dispossessed and disinherited groups is a testament to group strength and resilience, even in the midst of sustained social fractures and tensions. Major aspects of the study entailed questions exploring patterns of family, community, and academic socialization. In addition to "insider" socialization, that is, organizations, institutions, and activities within the minority community, of equal importance were the patterns operative in "outsider" socialization, that is, personal contacts with those of the dominant group, as well as cultural contact via movies, books, television, and national organizations, to which students might belong, but the local racial norms prohibited racial contacts.

This chapter focuses on how individuals engaged in the production of ideas in various formats described the individuals, institutions, and events most influential in their becoming individuals. One part of the study focuses on the self-reflectiveness of individuals as they recount their personal odyssey of navigating the landscape within their own racial-ethnic group; the other entails describing navigating the landscape within the larger dominant group. A few memoirs demarcate the navigations in both landscapes (Gates, 1994). That said, we are attentive to both the social structural forces impinging on individuals, families, and communities in localities where racial exclusion is the norm; we are also attentive to the fact that individuals respond to these structural forces and barriers in different ways, and consciously reflect upon themselves and their world in ways often contrary to the directives suggested or mandated by structural forces.

## STUDYING BLACK INTELLECTUALS

When I wrote my first article on intellectuals in 1980, I challenged and sought to refute the Du Boisian double consciousness thesis with respect to Black intellectuals. By this time, not only had I incorporated Du Bois into my sociological framework on intellectuals, but also the philosopher and cultural sociologist Alain Locke and the novelist and cultural sociologist Ralph Ellison. At the time my definition of an intellectual was simply "one who writes, studies, and creates, loves the play of ideas and understands its importance." Then, and now, I believed that Cruse, and others before him such as E. Franklin Frazier, Du Bois, Allison Davis, and others gave us a narrow and limited view of Black intellectuals. Cruse's study of New York politics and the actors and groups who comprised the backdrop for his views was only a snapshot in time. Cruse and others focused on intellectuals as finished products of their socialization, whereas, I have long been fascinated with the question of who becomes an intellectual and the socialization process which makes this possible.

This study seeks to test three central questions:

1. To what extent have successful professionals disengaged or cut ties from their history, heritage, and culture of birth, and/or chosen to affiliate or assimilate into the larger dominant society?
2. To what extent have respondents demonstrated a "dual marginality" during the socialization process?
3. To what extent have respondents recognized the validity of the Luke Theorem? This Theorem, in Luke 12:48 asserts: "For unto whomever much is given, of him shall be much required; and to whom men have committed much, of him they will ask the more."

Admittedly, this research project and the questions enclosed also seek to examine the extent to which the lives of respondents, especially those born in the segregated South, parallel my own life in terms of how we navigated the mazes of race and class.

## DESCRIPTION OF THE STUDY

Respondents came from two areas: the Washington, D. C. metropolitan area and the Richmond, Virginia, metropolitan area. In Washington, D.C., I focused on the limited and concentrated academicians at George Mason University and universities other than Howard University. At Howard, given its size, I would have had to draw a representative sample. From these two regions, I completed thirty-five interviews. Prospective respondents were sent letters and consent forms, and asked whether they wished to be interviewed or audio-recorded. The interviews generally lasted between 45 and 60 minutes. Some of the interviews were conducted via the telephone, while others were conducted face-to-face in my office or the office of the interviewee.

## DESCRIPTION OF RESPONDENTS

Mini-life histories seek to capture a point in time: The life of the late 1940s and 1950s when the vast majority of Blacks lived in the South. Of the respondents in this study, 68 percent were born in the South, 18 percent in the North, 9 percent in the West, and 9 percent born outside the United States. Also, 54 percent were males. Quite a few respondents were born and raised in rural settings in the South, which offered stark studies in contrast from even medium-sized cities in the South. Such differences made for differences in the curriculum, labs, and exposure to ideas outside of the community. It is significant that 31 percent of respondents were the only children in their families, and of those with siblings 40 percent were the oldest of the children. Much research has been conducted on both the rate of success and degree of success among only children and among the first born. Of their marital status, 54 percent were married, 27 percent divorced, 14 percent single and never married, and 5 percent widows and widowers.

## OCCUPATIONS OF PARENTS

Here we must remember that we are looking back, for most respondents, at the segregated South in the late 1940s, and 1950s. Not only was there a White-Black pay scale, but a male-female pay scale. To understand the differential professionalization of Black males and females and how it differed from those patterns in White communities one had to know how these groups tended to deal with the education of their youth. In White families, if there were choices as to which of the children were sent to college, it was generally the male. In Black families, it would be the female. With this information it is not surprising that among respondents, 27 percent of their mothers were school teachers, while only 9 percent of their fathers held the same occupation. Also, 9 percent of the mothers were nurses, 9 percent were domestic workers, and 27 percent of the mothers were stay-at-home moms. In many large families, mothers were stay-at-home moms. How was this possible? Life was simple in these rural farming areas; many Blacks owned land where they raised vegetables and fruit; had poultry, and may have had a few cattle and hogs. Whatever food they needed could be raised. Plus, the extended family was then more operative, and there was much bartering and trading in those days. Fathers were generally skilled and semi-skilled workers. Thus, according to these respondents, rates of literacy were higher among mothers than fathers.

## PERSONS WHO MOST INSPIRED RESPONDENTS

Here we see the importance of mothers. When Black men were unable to support their families, women acquired education and occupations necessary to pursue economic independence. Moreover, some women experienced multiple marriages, and recalled various reasons why marriages did not survive. I will not call the Black family a matriarchy, but respondents described women among the most inspirational people in their lives. For example, 64 percent said their mothers were their most inspiring persons; 27 percent named their fathers as most inspiring; next came grandparents. Moreover, their lists included teachers, aunts, and church, respectively. I was surprised by the low percentage for the church.

Respondents described how inspirational individuals stood behind them in uncertain times, kept them in their sights, made sure they studied, told them to work hard, get good grades, devote time to reading books, focus on going to college, strive to be the best, and stay away from bad or questionable friends or family members. In addition, when asked about inspirational individuals outside their immediate community, respondents offered the following names:

Ralph Bunche
Pearl Buck
Mary McLeod Bethune
George Washington Carver
Ernest Hemingway
William Faulkner
Jackie Robinson
Joe Louis
C. Wright Mills
Lena Horne
W. E. B. Du Bois
Frank Yerby
Martin Luther King Jr.
Frederick Douglass
Julian Mayfield
Mary Church Terrell

When asked which books inspired them during their teen years, respondents mentioned the following:

The Bible
*The Diary of Anne Frank*
*The Iliad*
Perry Mason books

*Les Miserable*
*Before the Mayflower*
*The Negro Revolt*
*Crisis of the Negro Intellectual*
*Black Power*
*The Old Man and the Sea*
*From Slavery to Freedom*
Essays by James Baldwin
*Black Bourgeoisie*
Mickey Spillane novels
Nancy Drew books
*Calvalcade of Negro Literature*
*The Sociological Imagination*

Here, 64 percent of respondents excelled academically before the age of 12; and 36 percent said they began to excel between 15 and 19 years of old. In elementary and high schools, respondents were active in extracurricular activities such as Honor Society, choir, bands, student government, athletics, debate, and theater.

When asked about their favorite classes, respondents listed the following:

Math
Science
History
Literature
Social Studies
English
Language Classes

When asked to define the role and duties of the Black intellectual, respondents shared these responses:

- Someone who believes in and produces scholarship from the life of the mind. Someone who enjoys the life of the mind and the ideas produced by this process and who believes in sharing the ideas they're writing and thinking about. Intellectuals thrive on ideas, publish ideas, and promote discussions centered around ideas.
- Individuals of vision and ideas who have the ability to reason, perceive, or understand both specific and broad issues affecting the human condition. They seek to share these visions, abilities, perceptions, and understanding with many different audiences through a variety of forms.

When asked about issues concerning African American life today, common sentiments included the following:

- Economic dislocation and marginality, and the civil rights community has failed to deal with the problems. Unfortunately, as Blacks become more prosperous they, like Whites, fail to see how to deal with the problems of Blacks. For many on the national level, they give us political theater, not substance. We have no Adam Clayton Powell or A. Phillip Randolph, and Blacks are no longer looking within themselves to rely upon themselves to save Blacks. Many of us expect Whites to save us. They can't and won't.
- In education we've lost our way from valuing education as we did before and right after the Brown Decision. We haven't done a good job in helping this generation to understand the value of education for us. We've allowed them to think that education should be acquired just to get a degree or a job. We have not stressed the value of education to our young people as being a source of ideas, a source of problem solving and as a source of critical thinking. We've failed our young people because we've slipped into a materialist mode of life where we emphasize things. Well, our young people bought into the lifestyle but not the work, and they didn't buy the agenda we thought we were offering them, that of service, dedication, and helping our community. They've been seduced by the money and because of the money they're doing and saying very destructive things about our people and our community, and think it's acceptable. Capitalism has seduced us as much as it has the larger White society, and we're also going for the money.

When asked about issues of concern about the larger society and culture, respondents shared the following:

- White supremacy and nationalism are still the driving forces in the nation. Race is still a factor to be dealt with, and we haven't really honestly dealt with it.

Is the U.S. racial problem solvable?

- Yes, according to 59% of respondents
- No, according to 40% of respondents

If yes, why?

- Progress has been made, and is being made. We're all getting along better than before.
- We're solving a part of the racial problem only because we have a Browning of the country and we have what is now "Ambiguous Ethnicity." We do not know quite often who's who, now that we've got so many people in-between. Racial attitudes are changing because the color scheme of the

nation is now so different from what it was in the past, and people simply adjust to this change.

Are you currently involved in a religious community, fraternity, sorority, or social club?

- Yes, according to 82% of respondents
- No, according to 8% of respondents

Which organizations?

- Churches, according to 32% of respondents
- Fraternities and Sororities, according to 49% of respondents
- Community Boards, according to 14% of respondents

While growing up was your community segregated?

- Yes, according to 90% of respondents
- No, according to 10% of respondents

Did segregation hurt or help your intellectual development?

- Hurt, according to 32% of respondents
- Help, according to 32% of respondents
- Not sure, according to 36% of respondents

How did segregation help or hurt?

- Segregation is oppressive. [It determined] who got the jobs and who could feed their families. You can't imagine how it hurt me while I was growing up, to see and hear my grandfather calling a ten-year-old White boy, mister; I went to school and had to cut the wood to heat our classroom. Our schools had outdoor toilets. From 6th to 12th grade, never had a new textbook.
- I lived on the border between Black and White neighborhoods and saw both sides, the contradictions and pretense; how Black and White friends had to pretend they weren't friends or both sides would be angry with them.
- When I grew up, all Blacks lived on one side and Whites on the other side. It was a matter of segregation within an integrated setting, or integration within a segregated setting. The experience of living close to Whites taught me many lessons. One was that contrary to what Whites were telling Blacks about how dumb we were and how smart Whites were, and

for this reason we were undeserving of consideration. I saw and lived among so many dumb White kids who simply got by because they were White.
- I survived in the South growing up because the negative messages Whites sent us never entered my mental space. My family, teachers, neighbors, and mentors sent positive messages to us, and these were the messages we believed. We really didn't pay much attention to what Whites were saying, and my family and relatives told me to simply ignore and avoid Whites as much as I could, which is what I did, especially the ones with negative messages.
- I lived in segregated housing but attended an integrated school. That experience taught me that there were good and bad Whites, just as there were good and bad Blacks. Above all, being in school with Whites taught me that there were no master races or groups. Racial ideology may tell you one thing, but when you interact with people and see for yourself that they have strengths and weaknesses like all humans, you see them in a different light.

The subtext to this study is the culture of resistance. These brief life histories speak to how children learn to ignore negative ideology and to accept the positive values. Black intellectuals have had to, as Ralph Ellison said, create and live their lives on the horns of the White man's dilemma. This is why one respondent said that Blacks, especially those living in the South, had to be communal and social Darwinists.

In the future I want to expand this study on a national scale. My objectives will include explicating patterns in Northern and Western regions. In addition, I will explore whether gender differences are central to who, and how one, becomes an intellectual. A national study will also reveal the degree to which age is a factor in socialization patterns of intellectuals of the pre-1960s eras and those in the post-1960s.

## CONCLUSION

In conclusion, respondents overwhelmingly and implicitly understand the tenets of the Luke Theorem. They see Black (public) intellectualism and involvement as a way to give back to their respective communities. Many respondents described growing up under dual marginal positions, if only in their imagination. Due to segregation, they could not associate with White teens. They were also prevented from enjoying the same type of young adulthood enjoyed by White teens. They were restricted by age and race, hence, they are dual marginals. This dual existence in their imagination, as C. Wright Mills described it, is a potent force (1959).

It is evident that the overwhelming percentage of respondents have maintained contacts with their churches, fraternal, and social groups, though they work and live among the majority culture. In many cases, they maintain dual memberships in a variety of institutions and organizations. The sense of duality has prompted the need to reimagine Black existence in public spaces. Indeed, his dual existence in their imagination continues to be a potent force.

## REFERENCES

Cruse, H. (1967). *The crisis of the Negro intellectual: A historical analysis of the failure of Black leadership*. New York: The New York Review of Books.
Du Bois, W. E. B. (1903/2019). *The souls of Black folk*. New York: GD Media.
Frazier, E. F. (1997). *Black Bourgeoisie: The book that brought the shock of self-revelation to middle class Blacks in America*. New York: Free Press.
Gates, H. L., Jr. (1994). *Colored people: A memoir*. New York: Vintage Books.
Mills, C. W. (1959). *The sociological imagination*. Oxford: Oxford University Press.

# Afterword

## *The Beautiful Ones Were Born Some Time Ago*

## Mark Anthony Neal

After a sixty-year career, Soul singer William Bell had every reason to be surprised by his first Grammy Award nominations. He was, after all, 77-years old, still putting in a Soul Man's work, decades after some of his more well-known peers—Sam Cooke, Otis Redding, Isaac Hayes—had long passed on to a Soul Heaven. Though his single "Three of Me" would lose in the category of traditional R&B, Bell's album *This is Where I Live*, would win the Grammy in the category of Best Americana Album in 2017.

When Bell sings, "Last night I had a dream / And there were three of me / There was the man I was / The man I am and the man I want to be" he does so from a vantage, rarely witnessed in the mainstream from Black men past their prime. The data tells us that many Black men will not live long enough to talk about the men who they were, and if they do live that long—battered, bruised, dismissed—few are willing to hear who they are. That Mr. Bell can imagine who he wants to be, seems a luxury.

And Mr. Bell does so with a level of defiance, one might say, laying down roots in the country that bred him and, like so many African-Americans, a country that also broke his heart. *This is Where I Live* is the title of an album that was literally recognized for its Americaness—Americana, a category born out of the folk music tradition that reminds us of Bob Dylan, Johnny Cash, and Woody Guthrie, and in which Bonnie Raitt, Emmylou Harris, and Rosanne Cash were recent winners. Mr. Bell sings of the "Three of Me" and where they live, and he is speaking as a weathered and worn Black Man, who is not in contradiction of the idea of the American experience, but as a bellwether, of sorts, for the condition(s) of masculinity in America.

Mr. Bell sings at a moment when American masculinity seems to be literally unravelling right before our eyes; the intrepid and insipid late night tweeting of President Donald Trump, merely the lowest hanging fruit. As "breaking news" alerts arrive in a volume that feels something akin to the pandemic that we are all living through, the nation wondered aloud about the secret lives of a generation of largely White male gatekeepers in the film industry, the legislature, the newsroom, and the dressing room, who used their privilege, power, and penises—yes overused terms—to punish, threaten, coerce, and reward women and some men, whose livelihoods and lives, in some cases, were entrusted to these men.

These totems of falling and failing power stand in juxtaposition to yet another group of American men: unemployed, underemployed, opioid-addicted, alcohol-addicted, angry, racist, depressed, and failing in health, who helped elect Donald Trump president largely in response to the very conditions that men of Mr. Trump's ilk helped create. This unraveling of American Masculinity has exposed the long ill effects of a patriarchy unchecked; a legitimate reckoning for the women, children, and less powerful and privileged men, who have borne the brunt of that patriarchy. To be sure these men—a cauldron of misogyny, racism, xenophobia, anti-intellectualism—are no victims, and are in some cases victimizers, but they are fathers, sons, husbands, partners, brothers, uncles, friends; They too are portraits of a masculinity fastly immolating and they too matter in the battle for the spirit and survival of a nation.

We are a nation that embraces promise and possibility; it is perhaps why, even in the midst of a divisiveness that became so publicly pronounced with the election of a Black man as president, and the subsequent election of what could only be described as his antithesis—in every way imaginable—we, as in Black Americans, mourned so hard for Trayvon Martin, Sandra Bland, and Tamir Rice. While indeed it was with the deaths of Michael Brown and Freddie Gray that Black Lives Matter set it off, that was as much about the rage associated with seeing these deaths with our own eyes and handheld devices—and our vision subsequently being both denied and delegitimized; Brown and Gray were not the pristine victims that our moral groundings previously required to move forward politically—a presumed innocence in a culture that always renders suspicious our humanity.

The same can be said for the adult Black males—the grown-ass men—who also succumbed to anti-Black police violence. In Terence Crutcher (aged 40), Eric Garner (aged 43), Alton Sterling (aged 37), Keith Lamont Scott (aged 43), and Walter Scott (aged 50) are men who were not innocent, at least in the ways that we assign such innocence to the young, but Black men that were flawed, frayed, and who had weathered—ways that don't always make us comfortable—the challenges of being grown, Black, and male in a society that has long dismissed them.

Their strategies of survival—for themselves and their families—which ran the gamut of hustling on the margins of illegality (though they were not criminals), self-medicating on recreational drugs of choice, balancing the responsibilities of fatherhood in the face of State dictated child support laws where the choice of impoverishment and incarceration, is really no choice—to name just a few—are harbingers to the very crisis that American masculinity currently confronts. If we are to take seriously the stories of out-of-work, and out of healthcare, out-of-futures, middle-aged, American men, who as the ground is removed from them find Black men already adapting to the free fall, then perhaps it is the examples of those dead Black men—the canaries in the coal mine—that hold solutions for the future of the American male.

# Index

Abdi, Shukri, 86
academia, Black intellectuals in, 163–172
academic performance: Black intellectuals and, 168; versus masculine stereotypes, 104; mentoring and, 108; Snowdy on, 94, 98
activism, 3; Black intellectuals and, 163; *Black Panther* and, 139; Fortune and, 117; Illinois labor issues, 113–126
administrators, and mentoring programs, 110
admission process, bribery and, 55
adolescence, extended, Mama's boys and, 15–16
Adult Attachment Scale (AAS), 25
adult attachment theory, 5
advice on relationships, 44, 46, 71
affection, inhibited, 14; assessment of, 24; attachment and, 26; *Black Panther* on, 144, 148. *See also* emotionality; empathy
affirmative action, 55
Afro-American Citizens' Protective League, 123
age: of Black children, estimates of, 82, 95; of first sex, 34, 37
agency: and Black male sexuality, 34, 48; Mama's Boys and, 10, 11; women and, 46
aggression, 141; Black masculinity and, 69–70; *Black Panther* on, 144; Freud on, 131; *Native Son* on, 134; White masculinity and, 133
AIDS incidence, and Black males, 104
Alexander, C., 7
Alexander, Marissa, 80–81
Allen, K., 47
Altgeld, John, 121, 123
American Railway Union (ARU), 118–120
America's Promise/The Alliance for Youth, 107
Amir, Menachem, 34
Amos, Jacob, 113–114, 115
André 3000, 67–72
Anuel AA, 157
anxious/ambivalent attachment, 13
anxious/avoidant attachment, 13; and masculine behavior, 27
approval, Mama's boys and, 16–17
Arbery, Ahmaud, 76
Arcangel, 157
Arnesen, Eric, 125–126
athletes: Kaepernick, 53–64; Snowdy on, 93; stereotype of, ix, 105
Atlanta, Georgia, 68, 91, 115–116
attachment: assessment of, 25; and Mama's boys, 5–28; theory on, 5, 13–14; types of, 13
authenticity, Snowdy on, 100
autoethnography, 76–78

Bad Bunny, 157–160

Bailey, De'Von, 76
Baldwin, James, 130, 136, 168
Baltimore Collegiate School for Boys (BCSB), 91–100; outcomes, 100–101
"Baltimore Uprising", 91, 101n1
Balvin, J, 158
Barnett, Ferdinand L., 123
b-boys, 68, 72
Bederman, Gail, 114
behaviors, masculine, 141; attachment styles and, 5, 13–14, 26–27; factors affecting, 104; Mama's boys and, 24
Bell, Derrick, 55
Bell, Sean, 76, 82
Bell, William, 173–174
beneficiary role, Mama's boys and, 22–23
Bethune, Mary McLeod, 167
Big Boi, 68
Big Brothers Big Sisters of America, 106, 109
Bigger (in *Native Son*), 129, 131–137
Biles, Simone, 60
Billson, J. M., 12, 104
Birmingham church bombing, 81
Black codes, 82
Black intellectuals, 163–172; role and duties of, 168; study of, 164–165; and Washington, 116
Black Lives Matter, 77, 174
Black masculinities: in *Black Panther*, 139–154; Brown on, 104; and education, 53–64; emergence of, 11; and Illinois labor activism, 113–126; images of, 141–142; literature on, xv; Mama's boys and, 5–28; mentoring programs and, 103–110; in *Native Son*, 129–137; Outkast and, 67–72; psyche and, 132–133; reimagination of, xiii–xv, 1–3, 37, 50, 173–175; research on, ix–x; Snowdy on, 91–100; term, 2
*Black Panther* (film), 139–154; plot of, 142–143
Bland, Sandra, 77
bodies, Black: *Black Panther* and, 145–146; and gender roles, 11; images and, 141; media and, 81, 82
Booker, Muhlaysia, 77
boundary setting, Mama's boys and, 10
Boyd, Rekia, 77

boys, Black: education of, 91–100; first sex partners of, 33–50; mentoring programs and, 103–110; *Native Son* on, 134; and the talk, 75–87; term, 7
brand awareness/loyalty, 62
bribery, and college admission, 55
Brody, G. H., 47
Brown, Michael, 76
Brownmiller, Susan, 34
*Brown v. Board of Education*, 56
Bryant, Roy, 81–82
Buck, Pearl, 167
Bunche, Ralph, 167
Byars, J., 140–141

Cardi B, 158
caregivers, Mama's boys as, 21–22
"Caro" (Bad Bunny; video), 157–160
Carver, George Washington, 167
Castile, Philando, 77
castle doctrine, 81
cause-related marketing (CRM), 60, 61
Cha-Jua, Sundiata K., 116
charm, Mama's boys and, 22
Chauvin, Michael, x
Chicana feminism, 158
child mortality, and Black males, 104
Clark, Stephon, 2
class: and early sexual experience, 34; and gender discourse, 114
Cleveland, Grover, 121
Coates, Ta-Nehisi, 130, 132, 135
collaborative critical autoethnography, 76–78
colonialism: *Black Panther* on, 147–148; and gender discoruse, 114, 137
commitment issues, Mama's boys and, 8
communication: Mama's boys and, 21; mother-son, Snowdy on, 95; on sex, 40–44, 48
community support, and mentoring, 103–110
conflict management, the talk and, 79
conspicuous consumption, 62–63
consumerism: Black, context of, 61–63; levels of, 62–63
Conyers, John, Jr., x
cool pose, 104–105; hip hop and, 68; in literature, 129; Snowdy on, 93

coronavirus pandemic, 174
corporate investment, 53, 59; and Black consumerism, 61–63; and cause-related marketing, 60, 61; Nike and, 56–58, 60–61
Cosby, Bill, x
Cousteau, Jacques, 70
critical autoethnography, 76–78; on the talk, 75–87
critical consciousness, mentoring programs and, 109
critical discourse analysis (CDA), 140, 142
critical race theory, 55; and education, 55–56
Cruse, Harold, 163, 165
Crutcher, Terence, 174
cultural responsiveness, mentoring programs and, 109
Cureton, Steven, xv
Curtis, Lynn, 34–35

data collection, 15
Davis, Allison, 165
Davis, Jordan, 81
Debs, Eugene, 118–119
De La Ghetto, 157
desegregation, 54, 56
Devos, Betsy, 59
Diallo, Amadou, 82
dialogue: recommendations for, 86–87; steps for, 86
disabilities, people with, Bad Bunny and, 157, 159
Dogg, Nate, 68
Dogg, Snoop, 68
domination: *Black Panther* on, 144, 147; critique of, 142
Dora Milaje, 143, 150
double consciousness: and Black intellectuals, 164–165; Hurston on, 136; in *Native Son*, 129–137
Douglas, S., 10
Douglass, Frederick, 116, 167
Drake, 158
Dre, Dr., 67
driving while black (DWB), 79
dual socialization, and Black intellectuals, 163–172

Du Bois, W. E. B., 1, 116, 119, 163, 165, 167; on double consciousness, 129–137, 164–165
Dunn, Michael, 81

Eagle Academy for Young Men, 99
economic issues: Black intellectuals on, 169; Illinois labor activism, 113–126; investment in public education, 53–64; Washington on, 115–116
education: Black intellectuals on, 169; and dialogue, recommendations for, 86; and employment, 63; funding issues in, 54; history in U.S., 55; investment in, 53–64; Snowdy on, 91–100. *See also* sex education
education debt, 54
education deficit, 54
Ellison, Ralph, 164–165, 171
emasculation: *Black Panther* on, 147; Mama's boys and, 28; Snowdy on, 94–95
emotionality, restrictive, 14, 104, 141; assessment of, 24; attachment and, 25–26; *Black Panther* on, 144, 148; *Native Son* on, 133; Snowdy on, 93. *See also* affection; empathy
empathy: *Black Panther* on, 149, 150. *See also* affection; emotionality
employment: categories, race and, 121–122, 166; education and, 63; and strikebreaking, 121–125
Essence CARES. *See* National CARES Mentoring Movement
ethnicity, ambiguous, 169

Fab Five Freddy, 68
Falcon, Ebenezer, 54
family structures, and Black intellectuals, 166
Fanon, Frantz, 129–131, 133, 134, 136
Farruko, 157
fashion: Outkast and, 67–72; and protest, 83
fathers: *Black Panther* on, 144–145, 150; and Mama's boys, 8, 19, 22; Moynihan Report on, 9; *Native Son* on, 132; Snowdy on, 95
Faulk, Marshall, x

Faulkner, William, 167
fear, Black masculinities and, 132
feminism: and Black male sexuality, 34–35; Chicana, 158; and new momism, 10
Ferracuti, F., 34
50 Cent, 98
films: *Black Panther*, 139–154; industry, racism in, 139; and Mama's boys, 9; and *Native Son*, 135
first love, Mama's boys and, 19–20
first sex: age of, 34, 37; attraction and, 40–41; dates as partner for, 35; friend as partner for, 33–50; as mutual exploration, 38–40; peer pressure and, 42–47
Fletcher, K., 46
Flint, Michigan, water crisis, 61
Flores, Lisa A., 158
Florida stand-your-ground law, 78, 80, 81
Floyd, George, x, 77
Forcey, L., 96
Fortune, T. Thomas, 116–118
Franklin, Terrance, 2
fraternities: Black intellectuals and, 170; and mentoring programs, 107, 109
Frazier, E. Franklin, 163
Freeman, Alan, 55
Freeman, Morgan, x
Freud, Sigmund, 5, 8, 19, 131
friends with benefits (FWB): as first sex partner, 33–50; negative associations of, 36; research on, 36–37; term, 36

Gaines, Korryn, 77
gangsters, 69; stereotype of, ix, 105
Garner, Eric, 76, 174
Gause, C. P., 105
gender: Bad Bunny and, 157–160; *Black Panther* on, 152–153; colonialism and, 137; linguistic singularity of, xiv; and occupation, 166; Victorian discourse on, 113–115
gender roles: conflict in, 13; reimagining, 50
Geragos, Mark, 60
Giordano, P. C., 35–36
Goodie Mob, 70
graduation rates, for Black males, 103

Grant, Oscar, 82
Gray, Freddie, 91, 101n1
Guide Right Program, 109
Guillen, Vanessa, 86
Gurian, M., 19

Hall, S., 141
Hamilton, Mary, 130
hardness: and Black masculinity, 11–12; Brown on, 104
Harris, F. III, 104
Harvard Mentoring Project, 106
Harvard University, 60
Hazan, C., 13
Hear This Music, 160
hegemonic masculinity: in *Black Panther*, 139–154; definitions of, 133; *Native Son* on, 131; T'Chaka and, 144–145; unraveling of, 174
Heinze, J., 61
help, accepting, *Black Panther* on, 149, 152
Hemingway, Ernest, 167
Henry, Patrick, 131
hip hop, 67–72, 157
historically Black colleges and universities (HBCUs), 91, 165
history: of education in U.S., 55; of Illinois labor activism, 113–126; of mentoring programs, 106–107; and the talk, 80–82, 87
Hitchcock, Alfred, 9
Holmes, Karen, 35
homophobia: Mama's Boys and, 13; music industry and, 160; Snowdy on, 96–98
hoodies, 83
hooks, bell, 11, 35, 140
Horne, Lena, 167
Howard, William Lee, 33–34
Howard University, 165
Hurston, Zora Neale, 136
hypermasculinity: and Black bodies, 145; *Black Panther* on, 146–148; stereotypes of, 33, 37, 105, 141

Ice Cube, 67–68
identification, and mentoring, 108
ideologies, 140–141
Illinois labor activism, 113–126

images, 140–141; of Black bodies, 145–146; of Black masculinity, 141–142
imagination, 1; and representation of Black men, 141–142. *See also* reimagination
immigrants, versus African American laborers, 120–124
Inclusion of Other in the Self scale (IOS), 24
inclusivity, Bad Bunny and, 157–160
indignation meetings, 123–124
industrial work, labor activism and, 113–126
inquisitiveness, and Black masculinity, 70–71
insider socialization, 164
inspiration, Black intellectuals and, 167–171
integration, 54. *See also* segregation
intellectual: term and definitions, 163, 164, 165. *See also* Black intellectuals
intentionality: and dialogue, 86–87; Snowdy on, 92, 97–98
interest convergence, 56–57; effects of, 56; reverse, 53, 57–59
interpretive description, 38
intersectionality, and *Black Panther*, 140
investment in urban public education, 53–64; issues with, 54; recommendations for, 63–64
invisible burden, *Native Son* on, 129–131
Ivy Queen, 159–160

Jackson, Michael, x
Jean, Botham Shem, 76
Jeantel, Rachel, 84–85
Jefferson, Atatiana, 77
Jim Crow laws: elements of, 115; and Illinois labor activism, 113–126
Johnson, Levena, 86
Jones, John "Indignation", 123
Jones, M., 92
Jordan, Michael B., 146
Joy, Jazmyne, 158

Kaepernick, Colin, 56–59; effect of, 60–61
Kager, India, 77
Kappa Alpha Psi, 109
Kardiner, Abram, 34

Karol G, 157
Kelly, R., x
Killmonger (in *Black Panther*), 143, 146–148, 149, 151
Kimmel, M. S., 11
King, Martin Luther, Jr., 1, 56, 80, 167
Kirby, Jack, 142
Kirkham, S. R., 38
knowledge consumption, and Black masculinity, 70–71
Kogan, K., 47
Ku Klux Klan, 82
Kunjufu, J., 93

labor: Illinois activism, 113–126; and reimagination, xiv; teacher strikes, 59; unions, and race issues, 113
Latin trap music, 157–160
leadership, *Black Panther* on, 145, 148–151
Leak, Jeffrey B., 130
Lee, Stan, 142
Levinson, D. J., 11
Levy, D., 9
LGBTQ community, Bad Bunny and, 157–160
Life Span Development Model, 11
linguistic relativity, xiv
literature: Black intellectuals and, 167–168; Black masculinities in *Native Son*, 129–137
lived experience, Black: autoethnography and, 76; literature and, 130; ontology of, 1; and theories on sexuality, 50; versus White privilege, 85
lobbyists, educational, 53–64; and advocacy for African American and Latino children, 57, 63–64; and dominant assumptions, 58; and outcomes, 57–58, 63; race and, 56; recommendations for, 63–64
Locke, Alain, 1, 164
Lombardi, K. S., 8, 9, 10
Longmore, M. A., 35–36
lost essence, Coates on, 130
Louis, Joe, 167
Love, P., 9
Lucke, S., 61
Luian, DJ, 160

Luke Theorem, 165, 171
Luniz, 68
Lydston, George Frank, 33

Mackie, 157
Maher, Bill, 85
Mama's boys, 5–28; benefits of, 10, 17–19; context of, 7–8; definition of, 6; negative assumptions regarding, 6, 8, 9; phrase, 6, 7, 18, 28; roles of, 5, 20–23; self-perceptions of, 26; themes in study, 5, 15–20
Manning, W., 35–36
Marathon Kids, 61
marginality, dual, Black intellectuals and, 165
marital status, and Black intellectuals, 166
Martin, Ricky, 159
Martin, Trayvon, x, 75, 87, 106, 174; circumstances of death, 77–78; media and, 82, 83; reactions to death, 80
Martínez Ocasio, Benito Antonio. *See* Bad Bunny
masculinities: attachment styles and, 13–14; term, 2, 6; Victorian discourse on, 113–115. *See also* Black masculinities; hegemonic masculinity
Mathews, J., 48
Matthews, Kadeshia, 135
Mayfield, Julian, 167
McClain, Elijah, 86
McCray, Ariane, 2
McKenna, Natasha, x
McNabb, Donovan, x
McWhorter, John, 100
media: and Black deaths from violence, 81–82; and construction of race, 75, 83; and images of masculinity, 141–142; and labor activism, 121, 124–125; and mentoring programs, 107; and *Native Son*, 135; Snowdy on, 93; and stereotypes, 92, 105; and Zimmerman trial, 78, 85
mentoring programs, 103–110; best practices for, 108–110; definition of, 108; history of, 106–107; objectives of, 106; qualifications for, 110
mercy, *Black Panther* on, 149
Messner, M. A., 11

methodology: critical autoethnography, 76–78; critical discourse analysis, 140, 142; on first sex partners, 37–38; on Mama's boys, 14–15, 23–24
#MeToo movement, x
Michaels, M., 10
Michele, Sister, 132
Middle College at North Carolina A&T State University, 99
Milam, J. W., 81–82
Mills, C. Wright, 167, 171
misogyny, *Black Panther* on, 148
momism, 9; definition of, 8; new, 10
Montgomery Bus Boycott, 56
Mora, Selma, 85
Morehouse College, 91
mothers: Black intellectuals and, 167; and gender of offspring, 6; and Mama's boys, 5–28; *Native Son* on, 132, 134; Snowdy on, 94–96; vilification of, 9
mourning, 131
Moynihan Report, 9–10
Muhammad, Wesley, xv
music: Bell and, 173–174; hip hop, 67–72; industry, issues in, 160; Latin trap, 157–160; *Native Son* on, 133–134; and stereotypes, 93, 105
Mutua, Anthony, xv
My Brother's Keeper, 106

Nakia (in *Black Panther*), 143, 151–153
National Afro-American League, 116
National CARES Mentoring Movement, 106–107
National Defense and Education Act (NDEA), 54
National Football League (NFL), 57, 60
*Native Son* (Wright), 129–137
Nelson, Judge, 84
Night Riders, 82
Nike, 53, 56–57, 58, 60–61; and Black community, context of, 60–61
N'Jobu (in *Black Panther*), 143, 144, 148
nonviolence, *Black Panther* on, 149
Norwood, Stephen H., 117
Notorious B.I.G., 69

Obama, Barack, 80, 93, 106
Oedipus complex, 8, 131

O'Flynn-Magee, K., 38
Okoye (in *Black Panther*), 143, 151, 152
O'Mara, attorney, 84
100 Black Men of America, Inc., 109
oppression: and gender roles, 11–12; history and, 80–82; the talk and, 75–87. *See also* strategies
options, as success, Snowdy on, 98–99
organizations, Black intellectuals and, 170, 172
Othello, 129–130
othering: Fanon on, 130–131; in *Native Son*, 129
outcomes, educational: BCSB and, 100–101; Black males and, 104
Outkast, 67–72; *ATliens*, 68–69
outsider socialization, 164
Ovesey, Lionel, 34
Ozuna, 157

Palczewski, C. H., 152
Pannell, Jack, Jr., 91, 98
paralytic complex, 135–136
parental relationships: mentoring programs and, 109; occupations, and Black intellectuals, 166. *See also* fathers; Mama's boys; mothers
parenting-in-connection model, 11
Parmar, P., 140
peer pressure, and first sex, 42–47
physicality, *Black Panther* and, 145–146
*Plessy v. Ferguson*, 115
Pocock, A. M., 47
police violence against Black people, x, 174; statistics on, 77; the talk and, 75–87
Pollack, W., 10
posturing: impact of, 94; Snowdy on, 93
Powell, William Clayton, 54
power, critical autoethnography and, 76
pride, mentoring programs and, 105, 109
property rights, 56; stand-your-ground laws and, 81
psyche, Black, 132–133; and paralytic complex, 135–136
public, 1; and Black masculinity studies, xiii–xiv
Pullman strike, 118–120

race: construction of, media and, 75, 83; Debs on, 118–119; and education funding, 53; and employment categories, 121–122, 166; nature of, 79–80; and Zimmerman trial, 84–85
racial profiling, term, Zimmerman trial and, 84
racism, x; critical race theory and, 55; film industry and, 139; nature of, 79–80; and Zimmerman trial, 84–85. *See also* strategies
railway strikes, 118–120
Randolph, A. Philip, 1
Randolph, S., 96
rappers: Snowdy on, 93; stereotype of, 105
redistricting, precautions with, 64
Reed, Eric, 60
Reggaeton, 157
reimagination of Black masculinities, xiii–xv, 1–3, 173–175; *Black Panther* and, 139–154; of gender roles, 50; of Mama's boys, 5–28
relationships, romantic: advice on, 44, 46, 71; *Black Panther* on, 153; Mama's boys and, 19, 23; role models and, 71–72
religion: Black intellectuals and, 167; *Native Son* on, 133–134
representations, 140–141; term, 140
research directions: on Black intellectuals, 171; on first sex partners, 47, 48; on Mama's boys, 27; on sex education, 48
resiliency, 105; Black intellectuals and, 164
resistance: Black intellectuals and, 171; Fortune and, 117; to labor exclusion, 115–117
respect: *Black Panther* on, 144; and first sex, 41; Mama's boys and, 18; and mentoring programs, 109
responsibility: intentional dialogue and, 86; Mama's boys and, 6, 10; mentoring programs and, 109; stereotypes and, xv
reverse interest convergence, 57, 58–59; nature of, 53; tenets of, 57–58
Rice, Tamir, 77
Richardson, Riche, xv
The Rising, 107
Rivera, Geraldo, 83

Rivera-Rideau, Petra R., 159
Robinson, Jackie, 167
role models: André 3000 and, 67–72; Black intellectuals and, 167–171; Brown on, 105; mentoring and, 105; and success, Snowdy on, 99
Roosevelt, Theodore, 114
Rose, Antwon, 2
Roth, Philip, 9
rural environments, and Black intellectuals, 166
Rush, Bobby, 83
Rustin, 1

safe sex, 39, 40, 42, 44, 45, 48
safe space: and first sex, 44; mentoring and, 109
Santos, C. E., 10
Sartre, Jean-Paul, 134
#SayHerName, 77
scabs. *See* strikebreaking
school discipline, 103–104, 109
Schott Report, 103
Scott, Keith Lamont, 174
Scott, Walter, 174
secure attachment, 13
segregation, 115; Black intellectuals and, 170–171
self-care spending, 62
self-esteem, and academic performance, 108
self-reliance/control, exaggerated, 14; assessment of, 24; attachment and, 26
separation model, Mama's boys and, 8
sex education: lack of, 34, 46; research directions for, 48
Sexton, Jared, xv
sexual abuse, Black males and, 47–48
sexuality: first partner choice and, 33–50; Latin trap music and, 158; and stereotypes, ix, 33–35, 37, 47, 48, 141
sexual orientation: and first sex partner, 37; Mama's Boys and, 12–13; Snowdy on, 96–98
Shabazz, Rashad, xv
Shakespeare, William, 70–71, 129–130
Shakur, Tupac, 68–71
Shaver, P. R., 13
Shuri (in *Black Panther*), 143, 150–153

Simmons, Russell, x
single mothers, 94; Moynihan Report on, 9
slavery: and Black male sexuality, 33; and Mama's boys, 7
Smiley, Tavis, x
Smith, J., 154
Smith, Yvette, 77
Snowdy, John Hawkins, 91–100
socialization, types of, 164
softness: André 3000 and, 69; *Black Panther* on, 150–151; Mama's boys and, 12–13; Snowdy on, 93
sororities, Black intellectuals and, 170
South: Black intellectuals and, 163, 166; Fortune on, 117; Outkast and, 69; Washington and, 115
Soyinka, Wole, 137
special education, and Black males, 103–104
spirituality, *Native Son* on, 133–134
staff, and mentoring programs, 110
*Stagecoach* (film), 135
stand-your-ground laws, 78, 80, 81
Staples, Brent, 2
Staples, Robert, ix
status materialism, 62–63
stereotypes of Black masculinity, ix, xiv–xv; and academic performance, 108–109; André 3000 and, 69; *Black Panther* on, 148–151; Brown on, 105; and children, 75; critics of *Native Son* on, 130; images and, 141–142; and labor issues, 115, 116; media and, 83; *Native Son* on, 134; opposition to, 12; and scholarship, 48, 49; and sexuality, ix, 33–35, 37, 47, 48, 141; Snowdy on, 92; and victim blaming, 83
Sterling, Alton, 174
Stevens, L. B., 119–120
Stinney, George, Jr., 77
Stone, Brayla, 86
Stone, Grace Zaring, 9
strategies, coping/survival, 175; Black masculinities and, 12; double consciousness and, 129–130; mentoring programs and, 109; *Native Son* on, 132, 134; sexual conquest as, 47; the talk as, 75, 79; transmission of, 105

strikebreaking: Black male workers and, 117–121, 125; as new normal, 121–125; trends in, 122
style: Bad Bunny and, 157–160; Brown on, 104; Outkast and, 67–72
success dedication, 14, 94; and antisocial behaviors, 26; assessment of, 24; attachment and, 25; Snowdy on, 98–99
suicide rates, for Black males, 104
suspension rates, for Black males, 103
sustainability, 61

the talk, 75–87; history and, 80–82, 87; recommendations for, 86–87; setting stage for, 79–80; uses of, 75
Tanner, John, 124–125
Tarver, Darius, 2
Taylor, Breonna, 77
Taylor, Susan L., 107
T'Chaka (in *Black Panther*), 143, 144–145, 151
T'Challa (in *Black Panther*), 143, 145–146, 148–153
teacher strikes, 59
technology: *Black Panther* on, 150–151; and mentoring, 110
Terrell, Mary Church, 167
thematic analysis, 15; on Mama's boys, 15–20
Thorne, S., 38
Till, Emmett, 81, 82
Till, Mamie, 81
Tompkins, J., 139
toxic masculinity. *See* hegemonic masculinity
*Trader Horn* (film), 135
training, and mentoring programs, 110
Trump, Donald, ix, 174
trust, mentoring programs and, 109

unemployment, and strikebreaking, 121–125
urban environment: and Black masculinity, 12; *Black Panther* on, 148; and public education funding, 53–64
Urban Prep Academies, 99

validation, Mama's boys and, 16–17
Van Den Oeuvre, R., 9, 10

Vereen, Ben, x
vicarious consumption, 62–63
victim blaming, 83; and unemployment, 121
violence: Baldwin on, 136; *Black Panther* on, 146–148; Fortune and, 117; labor activism and, 120–123; in literature, 130; mentoring and, 106; *Native Son* on, 131, 132, 134; and sexuality, 34; the talk and, 75–87. *See also* police violence
vulnerability, *Black Panther* on, 149, 152

Walker, Sheena Myong, 130
Warren G, 68
warriors: *Black Panther* on, 139–154; stereotype of, 105
Washington, Booker T., 115–116, 121
Washington, George, 119
Wells, Ida B., 116, 125
West, attorney, 84
Whatley, Warren, 121
White masculinity: definitions of, 133; and labor issues, 113–115, 120–124; *Native Son* on, 131, 136; unraveling of, 174
White privilege, and Zimmerman trial, 85
White supremacy, 82; Black intellectuals on, 169; history of, 120; and violence, 131
Williams, Joyce, 35
Williams, Serena, 60
Williams, Tennessee, 9
Willis, Morgan Mann, xv
Wolfgang, M., 34
women and girls, Black: *Black Panther* on, 148, 149, 150, 152–153; and first sex, 33–50; and mentoring, 105; police violence and, 77; and sexual agency, 46; and stand-your-ground laws, 80–81
Wright, Richard, 129–137
Wylie, Phillip, 9

X, Malcolm, 1

Yaga, 157
Yerby, Frank, 167
Yu, T., 47

Zimmerman, George, 75, 78, 83, 84–85

# About the Contributors

**Gina Castle Bell** is assistant professor at Saint John's University located in Queens, in New York City. She earned her PhD from George Mason University in May 2012. Her MA degree work focused on interpersonal communication with a specialization in active listening and romantic relationship communication, which she earned from the University of Central Florida, in December 2008. Areas of expertise include: co-cultural communication practices, interracial communication, intercultural communication, and research methods and methodology. Castle Bell examines how racism is facilitated through language. She is particularly interested in interracial communication challenges between Black and White community members in North American contexts. Dr. Castle Bell can be contacted over email at: g.r.castle.phd@gmail.com.

**Kenneth Brown** is a manager of specialized instruction for the District of Columbia Public Schools. He provides leadership to the school's special education department in the areas of instruction and compliance. An established, performance driven professional with proven experience overseeing the development of programs, lesson planning and implementation, special education, advising, and budget management, Dr. Brown works to ensure that all school supports and services are leveraged to purposefully serve the social-emotional and academic needs of students with individual education programs (IEPs). Charged with leading high-quality specialized instruction and programming for students with disabilities, Dr. Brown ensures compliance with all aspects of federal laws, state regulations, and DCPS policies and procedures regarding special education.

**Sakile K. Camara**, PhD, is professor and chair of the Department of Communication Studies at California State University, Northridge. She completed her doctorate degree at The Ohio State University and her research focuses on the inextricable relationship between communication, culture, and power. She has published several articles and books. She is also a serial entrepreneur, who has designed several software solutions including Bravofolio, iTraine, SOC builder, AMEE, and Farmers Xchange.

**Richard Craig** is associate professor of communication at George Mason University. Dr. Craig received his PhD in mass communication/media studies from Howard University. His research centers on mass media political economy, and the production, distribution, and consumption of media content. His goal is to use research to influence the development of policy to enhance opportunities for media production and distribution by marginalized cultures.

**Tommy J. Curry** is professor of philosophy and personal chair of Africana philosophy and Black male studies at the University of Edinburgh. His research interests are nineteenth-century ethnology, critical race theory, and Black male studies. He is the author of *The Man-Not: Race, Class, Genre, and the Dilemmas of Black Manhood* (2017), which won the 2018 American Book Award, and *Another White Man's Burden: Josiah Royce's Quest for a Philosophy of Racial Empire* (2018), which recently won the Josiah Royce Prize for American Idealist Thought. He has also re-published the forgotten philosophical works of William Ferris as *The Philosophical Treatise of William H. Ferris: Selected Readings from the African Abroad or, His Evolution in Western Civilization* (Rowman & Littlefield, 2016). In 2019 he became the editor of the first book series dedicated to the study of Black males entitled *Black Male Studies: A Series Exploring the Paradoxes of Racially Subjugated Males*. Dr. Curry's research has been recognized by *Diverse* as placing him among the Top 15 Emerging Scholars in the United States in 2018, and his public intellectual work earned him the Society for the Advancement of American Philosophy's Alain Locke Award in 2017. He is a past recipient of the USC Shoah Foundation and A.I. and Manet Schepps Foundation Teaching Fellowship (2017), the Ray A. Rothrock Fellowship at Texas A&M University (13–16), and the past president of Philosophy Born of Struggle, one of the oldest Black philosophy organizations in the United States.

**Isaih Dale** is a doctoral student and a recipient of a Presidential Fellowship at the University of Notre Dame. His research includes Black masculinity and racialized spaces in twentieth-century Black texts. Also, Isaih is interested in W. E. B. Du Bois's theory of double consciousness, Black solidarity, and violence in Black texts.

**Rutledge Dennis** earned a PhD at Washington State University after having completed a dissertation titled "The Sociology of W. E. B. Du Bois." Dr. Dennis was the first coordinator of the African American Studies Program at Virginia Commonwealth University. He is currently professor of sociology and anthropology at George Mason University. He is the recipient of The Joseph S. Himes Award given by The Association of Black Sociologists, and the Du Bois, Johnson, Frazier Award given by The American Sociological Association. In addition, he is the recipient of the Sigma Rho Sigma Research Award, and holds membership in Alpha Kappa Mu Honor Society and Sigma Xi Research Society.

**Malcolm D. Gamble** completed his MA in communication studies at California State University, Fullerton, in 2020 and his undergraduate degree in communication studies at Concordia University in 2016. His research interests include the instruction of public speaking and oral interpretation and their impact on diverse students from multicultural backgrounds and communities.

**Aaron J. Griffen** is a chief operating officer at Prosperity Educators, LLC. Dr. Griffen's expertise includes diversity, equity, and inclusion. He is a consultant, author, and speaker in the areas of urban education, policy, and analysis. Dr. Griffen's research seeks to identify, discuss, and address equity issues impacting students, schools, and staff members. This includes facilitating sessions to build skills for others to lead equity trainings and discussions.

**Larissa Hernandez** is a writer born in Eagle Pass, Texas, and raised near the mountain ranges of southeastern Arizona. Larissa writes creative nonfiction that reflects her experience as a borderlands transplant, a mother, and a classic car enthusiast. Her scholarship includes third space theory and reggaeton as a new discursive space within music. She holds an MA degree in literature, creative writing, and social justice from Our Lady of the Lake University. She has served as a staff editor for *Eleven Rivers Review* at Palo Alto College, *The Thing Itself* at Our Lady of the Lake University, and she has displayed her written work at art exhibits around San Antonio. She is currently a creative writing editor at *The Journal of Latina Critical Feminism*. Larissa currently lives in San Antonio, Texas, with her son, dog, and pet rooster.

**Mark C. Hopson** is director of African and African American Studies at George Mason University. Also, he is associate professor in the Department of Communication. He teaches undergraduate and graduate classes in intercultural communication, African American studies, the rhetoric of social movements, and organizational communication. Research and publications include critical intercultural communication, the rhetoric of race and racism, and studies in Black masculinities. Dr. Hopson offers workshops in equity and organizational development; Changing Lives through Literature; and the communication of violence prevention.

**Ronald L. Jackson II** is past president of the National Communication Association and a professor of communication, culture, and media, and former dean of the McMicken College of Arts and Sciences at the University of Cincinnati. Jackson is the author of *Scripting the Black Masculine Body: Identity, Discourse and Racial Politics in Popular Media*. Additional works include the coauthored book *African American Communication: Exploring Identity and Culture*.

**Carmen M. Lee** (PhD, University of California, Santa Barbara) is clinical associate professor of communication at the Annenberg School for Communication and Journalism. Her research focuses on factors that contribute to the establishment and maintenance of interpersonal and intergroup (intercultural/interethnic) relationships. She also conducts research on media portrayals of marginalized group members. Dr. Lee has published journal articles and book chapters on intercultural and interpersonal relationships. Her publications appear in journals such as *Human Communication Research, International Journal of Intercultural Relationships, Howard Journal of Communications, Communication Research Reports*, and edited books such as *Handbook of International and Intercultural Communication* and *The Dark Side of Interpersonal Communication*. She has received multiple "top paper" awards for her research from the Western States Communication Association, National Communication Association, and International Communication Association.

**Marquese McFerguson** is assistant professor of intercultural communication at Florida Atlantic University. His research examines Black masculinity through the lens of hip-hop and American popular culture. McFerguson situates his research within performance studies using spoken word poetry and auto/ethnography, and media cultural studies using Black feminist informed Black masculine theory. He is a 2018 recipient of the John T. Warren Top Paper Award sponsored by the NCA Ethnography Division. Research interests include hip-hop, Black masculinity, and auto/ethnography.

**Kimberly Moffitt** (PhD, Howard University) is director and professor in the language, literacy, and culture PhD program, and affiliate professor in the Department of Africana Studies at University of Maryland Baltimore

County. Her research focuses on mediated representations of marginalized groups and the politicized nature of Black hair and the body. She has published five coedited volumes, including *Gladiators in Suits: Race, Gender, and the Politics of Representation in Scandal* (2019) and *Blackberries and Redbones: Critical Articulations of Black Hair and Body Politics in Africana Communities* (2010) and published in academic journals and edited volumes. Her current research projects explore representations of the Black body in Disney television programming and the effects of colorism. She often provides commentary on political and pop culture phenomena on local public radio programs/podcasts. She is the cocreator of the blackhairsyllabus.com project and recently launched the color treatment Podcast, along with Dr. JeffriAnne Wilder, to discuss the effects of colorism within Africana communities. She is the founding parent of a public charter school, Baltimore Collegiate School for Boys, which opened its doors in 2015.

**Mark Anthony Neal** is chair of the department of African and African American studies and the founding director of the Center for Arts, Digital Culture and Entrepreneurship (CADCE) at Duke University. He offers courses on Black masculinity, popular culture, and digital humanities, including signature courses on Michael Jackson and the Black performance tradition, and the history of hip-hop, which he co-teaches with Grammy Award winning producer 9th Wonder (Patrick Douthit). Dr. Neal is the author of several books including *What the Music Said: Black Popular Music and Black Public Culture* (1999), *Soul Babies: Black Popular Culture and the Post-Soul Aesthetic* (2002) and *Looking for Leroy: Illegible Black Masculinities* (2013).

**Mika'il Petin** is assistant vice president of student success at Motlow State Community College. He previously served as associate dean of student success, director of the Office of Diversity, Equity, and Inclusion, and assistant professor at Illinois College; and associate director of African and African American Studies at George Mason University. His doctorate is in cultural studies with general research interests in cultural theory, critical race theory, visual culture, film and media studies, and gender studies. Dr. Petin focuses on aesthetic structures of race and ethnicity in the United States, emerging Black masculinities, and Muslims in U.S. popular culture.

**Derrick Robinson**, PhD, is assistant professor of educational leadership at University of Memphis. He received his BA from Morehouse College, an MBA from Johns Hopkins University, and a Masters of Educational Leadership from Wingate University. In 2016, he earned a PhD in curriculum and instruction with a focus on urban education from the University of North Carolina at Charlotte. Dr. Robinson has fifteen years of K–12 teaching and seven years of K–12 leadership experience in urban schools from Prince George's County, Maryland; Washington D.C.; and Charlotte, North Carolina. Dr. Robinson's research examines the contextual nature of school climate and culture, leadership effectiveness, and teacher effectiveness.

**Erika M. Thomas**, PhD, is associate professor in the Department of Human Communication Studies at California State University, Fullerton. She earned her doctorate from Wayne State University in 2011. She teaches and researches in the area of rhetorical theory and criticism and examines gender and LGBTQ mediated representations in popular culture through critical/cultural theories to examine. Her work has most recently been included in *Beyond Princess Culture: Gender and Children's Marketing* (2019) and in the journals *Women and Language* (2018) and *Relevant Rhetoric* (2017).

**Ebony A. Utley**, PhD, is a professorpreneur. As a professor of communication studies at California State University, Long Beach, she researches, publishes, and teaches interpersonal communication. Her expertise has been featured on The Oprah Winfrey Network and other national and international radio, print, and online outlets. As an entrepreneur, she curates experiences and develops technology products for social impact. Her contributions include raising awareness about the dark side of technology, improving romantic relationship communication, supporting women recovering from infidelity, preventing domestic violence through entrepreneurship, and healing via ebony.yoga. Her two worlds collide as the associate director for the Institute for Innovation and Entrepreneurship at California State University, Long Beach. Recent publications include: *He Cheated, She Cheated, We Cheated: Women Speak about Infidelity* (2019); and with T. Curry, "She Touched Me: Five Snapshots of Adult Sexual Violations of African American Boys" (2018), *Kennedy Institute of Ethics Journal 28*:2.

**Alonzo M. Ward** is assistant professor of African American and U.S. history at Illinois College. His research interests include Black activism during the late nineteenth and early twentieth centuries, and the history of Black labor throughout the midwest in conjunction with the labor movement of the late nineteenth century. Ward is the recipient of the Harry J. Dunbaugh Distinguished Professor Award for 2020—considered the greatest honor bestowed upon an Illinois College faculty member.

His current book project *Relegated to the Bottom: Illinois African American Workers and Their Struggle against Systematic Oppression during the Early Jim Crow Era* is a multifaceted examination of African Americans in Illinois prior to the mass migration of the twentieth century.

www.ingramcontent.com/pod-product-compliance
Lightning Source LLC
Chambersburg PA
CBHW050906300426
44111CB00010B/1396